ITALY

THE FATAL GIFT

ITALY
THE FATAL GIFT

WILLIAM MURRAY

DODD, MEAD & COMPANY   New York

A substantial portion of the text
appeared originally in The New Yorker,
in slightly different form.
"Uncoupling, Italian-Style" appeared originally
in Cosmopolitan.
"The Best Available Engineer and Expert"
appeared originally in Italia.

1 2 3 4 5 6 7 8 9 10

Library of Congress Cataloging in Publication Data

Murray, William, 1926-
    The fatal gift.
    1. Italy—Civilization—1945-   —Addresses, essays,
lectures. 2. Murray, William, 1926-   . 3. Americans
—Italy—Biography. I. Title
DG451.M87   945.092   81-19588
ISBN 0-396-08049-9   AACR2

This book is dedicated to my children—Natalia, Julia, and Bill, Jr.—in the hope they will become, like some of the people in this book, "real heroes of our age."

CONTENTS

"Italia! O Italia! thou who hast
The fatal gift of beauty."

—LORD BYRON

PRELUDE

I n the spring of 1981, as I was once again preparing to leave for Rome, an old friend of mine asked me why I didn't seem nervous about going. He had been reading in the press and hearing on television about terrorist shootings, bombings and kidnappings, as well as such other afflictions of daily life in Italy as occasionally violent street demonstrations, recurrent strikes, and the continuing breakdown of public services and institutions. "How can you even think about going there?" he asked. "I'd be scared. After all, the whole thing could come tumbling down any minute, couldn't it?"

I was surprised by his question. Afraid to go to Italy? Because I might be kidnapped or shot or caught in a riot? And what did he mean by "come tumbling down"? A revolution, a military coup, chaos and anarchy? What was the man talking about? I must have betrayed my astonishment, because he went on to explain that he himself would not go anywhere these days that didn't guarantee him at least a minimum of law and order. From what he had read about and heard, Italy had become a dangerous place to visit, especially for Americans. "They hate us over there," he said. "I'd rather go to Russia or China than to Italy."

I laughed at him. In the Los Angeles area, where we both live, the crime rate is one of the highest in the world. He and his wife have been mugged once and burglarized twice. My oldest daughter and her boyfriend have been held up at gunpoint; my younger daughter is nervous about going home alone after dark because of a neighborhood rapist; and on a recent Labor Day midafternoon, with several thousand people in the vicinity of our beach house, two teenaged thugs broke into our apartment right under the startled eyes of our next-door neighbors. Every day someone we know in this great country of ours has at least a brush with violence of one kind of another, and I'm never without the feeling anymore that I could be killed or maimed at any moment for no reason at all. I pointed all this out to my friend and went on to observe that law and order had reached such a state of perfection at home that not only did he and I now own guns, but the whole country was being turned into an armed camp.

The conversation did serve, however, to make me think about this aspect of life in Italy as a whole. Over the past three decades, I have been in various parts of the country during times of stress— in Rome during the great Communist open-air demonstrations of the late forties; in the so-called Red Belt of Emilia during the days after the attempted assassination of the Communist leader Palmiro Togliatti; in Sicily during the hunt for the bandit Giuliano; in Milan during the labor unrest and street marches of the early seventies; in the back alleys of the worst slums in Naples; in Rome for the Moro killing and many other acts of terrorist violence; everywhere as a spectator and observer at political rallies and demonstrations of various kinds that often deteriorated into confrontations, provocations, acts of petty thuggery, occasionally real violence. Why, then, had my friend's remarks surprised me? Just because there was a great deal of violence in America, why should I be any more tolerant of it or less frightened by it abroad?

I still haven't come up with an entirely satisfactory explanation, even to myself. I used to feel safer in Italy, and in most of Europe, than in my own country. Until very recently, I was convinced I was in no danger of being blown down in the streets of Rome one day because some psychopath had been able to get his hands on a gun and shoot me simply because I happened to be standing near whichever celebrity he had identified in his sick head as the source of all evil. Italy closed up its lunatic asylums a couple of years ago and sent the inmates home to their relatives, but no one has since begun potting people from the top of the Leaning Tower of Pisa or torturing young women to death in the back of a Fiat camper. The irrational, gratuitous act of violence was still, I thought, an American specialty. Then, even as I was writing these words, a young gunman fired three shots into the abdomen of Pope John Paul II and, in doing so, also gunned down two absolutely irrelevant bystanders, one of them an elderly American woman who just happened to lean into the path of a bullet.

Nevertheless, no matter what else may happen, I do know that the distorted, irrational face of violence, so prevalent elsewhere these days, is not the true face of Italy, whatever may be reported in the media. (The pathetic young terrorist who shot the Pope was, after all, a Turk, not an Italian.) If it were, I could not come back to it so lightheartedly year after year. Despite everything that has happened, I never think about violence at all in Italy, in fact, except to wonder at it when it does occasionally manifest itself. The picture I retain when I'm away from the Peninsula is more like the one Federico Fellini once conjured up when he interviewed himself a few years ago on the subject of Rome. I, too, see a muddy, brown terrain; an ample, broken sky as vivid as an operatic backdrop; an overfed, ruddy face like Alberto Sordi's or Aldo Fabrizi's. I envision a beautiful, comforting scene—scarred, strewn with rubbish, exhausted by past excesses—but always astonishing, unique, unforgettable. How could anyone who knew it well not long to return to it?

This book is an account of many such returns and extended visits. It is also the chronicle of a love affair with a whole country—Italy—and especially with the city of Rome. It begins in the spring of 1947, with my arrival there as an aspiring opera singer, and it continues to flourish year after year. Like all long love affairs, it has had its low points, its disillusionments and sorrows, but it refuses to subside permanently. In fact, I cannot now imagine a year going by without my setting foot at some point in this other country of mine, one blessed as well as cursed throughout her long and tumultuous history by Lord Byron's aptly phrased "fatal gift of beauty"—the lure that throughout the centuries has enticed not only lovers but invading armies, marauders of every sort, and the oppressive foreign-dominated governments that for a thousand years made of her a plaything, an object of exploitation and misuse. Italy is still paying today, more than a century after the Risorgimento, for this rape, though she continues to reward all of us who love her not only with her beauty but with the unfailing hospitality and generosity of spirit of her people.

When I began to think about this book and work on it, it seemed to fall naturally into two distinct sections. Part One contains the best, I think, of the writing that came out of my roughly four and a half years, from 1947 to 1952, as a music student and part-time journalist, mostly in Rome. (One piece, "Voices," an account of day-to-day life in a Roman piazza was actually written later, but is partly based on an earlier time there.) My view of the world then was intensely subjective; I wrote about myself, my family, my friends, and my early adventures in love, life, liberty, and the pursuit of happiness through the streets, piazzas, and *palazzi* of Rome. I was young, full of myself and my own desires and ambitions. Clearly, I was indifferent to intimations of mortality and I thought the world revolved around me.

Part Two contains what I dearly hope is the most enduring and still pertinent of the reportage I've done from Italy, mostly for *The New Yorker*, since 1962. I wrote from and about not only Rome this time but Milan, Naples, and the Tuscan countryside. I wrote about events, past and present, and tried my best to interpret them without editorializing. Most of all, I wrote about people—terrorists, policemen, actors, politicians, bureaucrats, opera singers, peasants, businessmen, journalists, artists, grifters, criminals, students, priests, and even simple law-abiding citizens. The latter, in my opinion, are the "real heroes of our age."

PART ONE

CHAPTER ONE

L'AMERICANO

O n a fine spring morning about a year and a half after the end of the Second World War, I found myself, to my amazement, weeping on one of the top decks of the *Saturnia,* an aging Italian liner that was about to sail from New York for Naples. For some time, I had been placidly standing up there, gazing down at the stern of the ship, where my fellow passengers in tourist class were crowded against the rails waving goodbye to the friends and relatives they were leaving behind. Quite a few of those making the voyage were evidently going back to Italy for the first time in a great many years, and they were excited and emotional. The air was full of large white handkerchiefs and brightly colored scarves, fluttering in the breeze off the river or being pressed to tear-stained cheeks, and voices of grief bridged the thin strip of scummy green water that separated us from the pier and our land.

But why was I crying? I wasn't one of these people; I had nothing in common with those old men and women shouting at each other in Neapolitan and Sicilian dialects, or with the younger ones, the gaudily dressed Italo-Americans on their way over to have a first look at "the old country." Although I am half Italian and had spent the first eight years of my life in Italy, I had got used to thinking of myself as an Anglo-Saxon. I was going back to Italy only because I had what I thought was a fine lyric tenor voice and I couldn't afford to pay ten dollars an hour to train it, which was what singing teachers were getting in New York in those days. I had been told that Italy was very cheap; my mother had given me a thousand dollars to supplement the monthly benefits I was entitled to under the G.I. Bill and I was going to Rome to become, if not a Caruso, at least a John McCormack. My motives were entirely practical and selfish. But as I stood above the other weepers and wept my own peculiar tears, I realized dimly that it wasn't merely empathy I was feeling. It was entirely possible that I was crying because I had been shut off from that purely Italian world on the deck below me, and because I had never wanted or tried to understand it. Suddenly, I was ashamed of the thought that I was in some way weeping for myself, and, as the old ship honked and drifted out into the tidal current, I dried my eyes and hurried below.

The *Saturnia* had been a hospital ship during the last years of the war and it hadn't yet been completely reconverted to the passenger trade. The ship was full, and most of the passengers slept in tiered bunks, forty or fifty to a cabin area. Children ran up and down the corridors and played games between the beds. Luckily, I had been put into a cabin for eight, in a smaller space up under the bow. I had only glimpsed my cabinmates earlier, when I had stopped in just long enough to sling a bag onto an upper berth. Now, on re-entering the room, I was glad to find it empty. I went into the washroom and splashed cold water on my face, and then came back to the cabin and peered out of an open porthole. We were well out into the river by this time and the shoreline was slipping away. I stood there and watched the ferries and lighters and the sun glinting off the windows of skyscrapers and office buildings. New York is a fine sight from a distance, I thought—a view not without glory. When I finally turned away, an old man was sitting on the bunk underneath mine, looking at me with mild curiosity.

"We are out to sea yet?" he asked.

"No," I said. "Come and look."

The old man shook his head. "Why should I?" he said. "I will come and look when there is nothing to see anymore."

I introduced myself, and without getting up the old man shook my hand. He was in his late seventies, I guessed, but he looked in wonderful health. His cheeks were pink and the flesh of his face, though deeply wrinkled, was firm. His eyes were alert, and his hands were large and strong, with stubby fingers and hard-looking nails. He was short; as he sat up very straight on the bed, the top of his head was well below the springs of my bunk. He was dressed in a dark, heavy suit with a vest, and his black shoes gleamed below the edge of his trouser cuffs. His shirt was slightly worn at the collar and his bright-red tie was tied in a huge knot directly beneath a rather prominent Adam's apple. A few wisps of long gray hair stuck out from under a dark-blue beret that hugged the top of his skull.

"You have been crying," the old man said, releasing my hand.

"No, I haven't," I answered. "What makes you think so?"

"Your eyes are red."

I looked away from him, embarrassed.

"You are not crying, I hope, because we are leaving the United States of America," the old man said. "I have been here for forty-seven years and it does not make me cry to leave it. Do you smoke?" He produced a wrinkled pack of cigarettes from his pocket.

"No, thanks," I said, glad to change the subject. "I gave it up. I'm a singer. I mean, I'm studying."

"Ah, a singer," the old man said and nodded, his face disappearing temporarily behind a cloud of smoke. "What kind of singer?"

"It's hard to tell just now. I think I'm a *tenore leggero*, but my voice might get heavier when I get older and I could become a *lirico spinto* eventually," I answered pompously.

The old man nooded again. "You are not Italian?" he asked.

"I'm half Italian. My mother was born in Rome."

"Ah, in Rome," the old man said. "That is why you are going to Italy to study."

"One of the reasons."

"I have never been to Rome," the old man said. "It must be very beautiful. I am from the Abruzzi. You know where is the Abruzzi?"

"Yes."

"The Abruzzi is the most beautiful part of Italy," the old man said, "but it is very poor. That is why I left it to come to America. In America there is work. I worked, *caro mio*. But now I am going home. I am going home to spend the rest of my life in the Abruzzi. I have a brother there."

Sitting in the cabin, on our way out to sea, the old man smoked one cigarette after another and told me the story of his life. He had married in America, but his wife was dead, and his children, Americans to the bone, had all married and gone off to live elsewhere, in towns and cities with strange names where the old man had never been and had never had any desire to go. He thought he would miss his grandchildren, but he felt that they would soon forget him and that his own children, wrapped up in their own lives, were glad to see him go because his advanced age was threatening to make him a worry to them. He hadn't seen the older brother he had left behind in the Abruzzi since they were both young men, but they had written each other faithfully and their love was the only thing, I gathered, that seemed real to him anymore. The brother, too, was alone now, and the old men were planning to become dust together, in their own good time, in their own house and on their own soil.

I was grateful for the old man's conversation, mainly because he took my mind off myself. I didn't know why he was telling me his life history, but I sensed that he was deeply troubled by this departure. Later, after he had finished telling me about his mountain village in the Abruzzi, he took a flat gold watch out of his vest pocket and looked angrily at it. "Where are we now?" he asked.

I walked over to the porthole. "We're past the Narrows, I think," I said. "Let's go up on deck."

"No," the old man said. "I will go up when we are really away from here." He sank back against his pillow and stretched out on the bed. "I will go later, after we eat."

"You didn't like America, I gather."

"I liked to work," the old man said. "There was work."

"What did you do?"

"I did several things," he said. "I shined shoes, I cut hair, I worked in a restaurant. I did this and that. I saved my money. I had a store, too. And I sold it. And I saved the money from the selling of the store." He gazed calmly up at the springs of the bunk above him. "My brother couldn't believe all the things I did, and sometimes I also wondered. But there was always work, even in bad times, for one who looked. You didn't know about such things, *caro mio*. You did not know the Abruzzi. Your people were *signori*. Not rich, maybe, but *signori*. I can tell."

"My father lost his money in the Depression," I said, "but I don't remember ever being hard up."

"No," the old man said. "When you came downtown to Mulberry Street, you came as a *turista*. Is that not so?"

I admitted that was so.

"In Italy, when your people came to the Abruzzi they came as *turisti*," the old man said. "In America, at least there is work."

I saw a great deal of the old man during the trip over. We ate at the same table, and after meals we would usually take a turn around the deck together. Often I would pass him in one of the lounges and we would never fail to nod politely to each other. He seemed to have no interests, and I never saw him pick up a book or even a magazine. Though the other occupants of our cabin— two waiters, three students, and a priest—were a talkative lot, the old man remained aloof from all discussions. He took no part in any of the planned activities on board, preferring to sit off by himself, usually in a corner, his hands flat against his thighs, the stubby fingers resting on his knees, his eyes roving disinterestedly about the room. Whenever the forced gaiety of shipboard companionship threatened to include him, or the noise of the young at play battered at the edges of his self-containment, he would rise and move away to some more peaceful area. Hardly anyone spoke to him, and I seemed to be his only friend, though I couldn't imagine why he had singled me out.

He frequently seemed tense and preoccupied, and I soon guessed it was because he was carrying all the money that he had saved in his forty-seven years of hard work. I was sure he wore a money belt, but I never actually found out. The old man never removed a single article of clothing in my presence. He would lie down fully dressed on his bunk and sleep on his back under a single blanket. The points of his worn black shoes stuck out from underneath the blanket, and sometimes, when I peeked down at him, I'd see his small brown eyes staring straight up at me, unwinkingly intense. In the mornings, he got up very early and padded noiselessly to the bathroom, where he locked himself in for twenty minutes and washed, emerging as before, with every article of clothing, including the beret, in its proper place. Late one evening, when I suggested that he might be more comfortable if he removed his jacket before going to bed, he snorted and then whipped his gold watch out of his pocket, dangling it in the air before me like a pendulum. "You see this watch, huh? You remember this watch, huh?" he said, his eyes glittering with rage. "I buy this watch two days before I leave America. It is a present I make to myself after so many years. That jeweller, he finds out I am leaving. Like a fool, in my happiness I tell him I am leaving. So you know what? That watch, she stops the second day after we leave! What you think of that, huh? That's what I call honest, huh? That jeweller is a crook, like everyone is a crook! That's what I know, *caro mio!* The world is full of gallant gentlemen!"

No one could understand my friendship for the old man, and I wasn't too sure about it myself at first. It was as if we shared a secret, but neither of us knew what that secret was. Of course, he did help me with my Italian; I spent a great deal of time wrestling with the language. I had grown up in America listening to my mother and my grandmother speak Italian around the house and feeling perfectly secure in the aura of my once perfect knowledge of it, but now, dumped into a world of casual everyday conversation, I discovered I didn't really speak it at all. I stumbled over words and groped blindly for them with a tongue grown suddenly huge and clumsy, and could only produce, through stiff lips, the half-paralyzed, comical mumblings of any raw tourist. My chief embarrassment was an inability to address anyone except in the intimacy of the second person singular—the *tu* that is always reserved for family and friends of more than one day's standing. The old man helped me make the transition to *voi* (though I was to discover later that this form is considered vulgar and that the third person singular, *lei,* is much more suitable), and he patiently corrected my worst blunders. After too many of these, I would sneak away by myself and pace the top deck of the ship, ducking around lifeboats as I doggedly plowed through pronoun declensions and conjugated verbs at the top of my lungs above the wind off the sea. I was a chastened American Demosthenes, grinding words like pebbles on my tongue and shamed by my own ignorance. But the old man never made fun of me, and I was grateful to him.

The whole trip, in fact, was full of humiliations. I was one of seven tenors on board and the only one, it turned out, who couldn't sing a note. I know that I'll never forget the expression on the face of the corpulent opera enthusiast in the main lounge, a fishmonger from Queens, who could play entire scores from memory on the upright piano and who forced me one afternoon to embark on an aria from *Tosca*. When I cracked the first high note, he blanched, stopped playing, and left the room, shaking his head. No one asked me to sing after that and in the evenings I had to sit and listen to the other tenors sing at informal musicales. One of them was a celebrity, Giovanni Martinelli, a white-maned lion from the golden age of the Met. He didn't sing much, either, but he was always present; he sat off to one side, making snide remarks about the younger men, who would stand braced against the rolling of the ship, bouncing high notes off the ceiling. "What dogs, what dogs!" I heard the lion confide to an acquaintance one night as the younger men came and went, full-throatedly seeking applause. Still, the lion's remarks were not much comfort to me, the worst dog of all, and it was at that moment the old man, sitting stolidly beside me, tugged gently at my sleeve. "He is right, they *are* all dogs," he whispered. "They sing before they have learned how. Let us go up for some air or they will make me vomit."

Quite apart from the old man's unfailing support, there was a quality in him I responded to—something fierce, something grimly constant under the surface stolidity, the indifference, the calm. Also, he was my first real link with an old world I had shut out in the years of growing up in America. I tried to imagine him as a young man, getting off the boat around 1900, clutching a worn suitcase full of clothes that had probably begun to smell from the cheeses and sausages his relatives in the Abruzzi had lovingly packed away for him. I could see him standing on the pier while the customs authorities coldly and efficiently stripped him of his cheeses and his sausages. The noises and gray colors of the strange city into which he was about to disappear must have been hard and menacing, and the visions and sounds of his village in the Abruzzi already terribly distant to him in the light of this new reality. And in the forty-seven years since that day, he had been preparing for his death, working like a mole under the concrete city, while his relatives in the Abruzzi died off one by one, and his children, speaking only the new language of the hostile concrete world, grew up around him and then went their own ways. I wondered what his meeting with his brother would be like and whether the two old men would recognize in each other the faces of their youth. I remembered reading a newspaper story some years before about an old peasant going back to his village and being met there by the wife he had left behind half a century before. "Hello, my husband, I knew you would come home," the wife had said. "As you can see, I have waited for you."

In the dining room, the old man and I sat across from one of the other men in our cabin. His name was Marco and he was in his forties. He had a lean, hungry, furrowed face, with black eyes and a mouth that twisted slightly at the corners, whether smiling or not, as if it had never tasted anything to its liking. He was an intellectual, originally from the Veneto, and he had a tongue that was quick to ridicule and censure. He had spent fifteen years in America, had become a citizen, and had served in the Army during the war. Since then, he had been lucratively employed as a headwaiter in a well-known East Side bistro, and he told us that he had been able to save a lot of money in a very short time, owing mostly to the amount of undeclared income in tips he had regularly stashed away. Nevertheless, he seemed to have enjoyed none of his experiences and to have liked nothing about the country in which he had taken refuge. However, I soon realized that his cynicism embraced the whole world, not merely his adopted land, and that he flavored his bitterness with a sharp wit. I spent a good deal of time laughing at his gossipy stories and I took nothing he said very seriously. I did notice that he and the old man rarely spoke to each other, but this didn't strike me as odd, because the old man hardly spoke to anyone.

At lunch one day, Marco, who had been toying with his food, suddenly looked up from his plate and smiled maliciously at the old man. "Well, it won't be long now, eh?" he said. "Three days and we'll be in Naples. What do you think of that?"

The old man did not answer. He didn't seem to realize that Marco had aimed the question at him, and he continued imperturbably to eat, keeping his chin an inch or so over his plate and cramming forkfuls of pasta into his mouth.

"I think it's great," I said. "I'm getting pretty excited, in fact."

Marco ignored me and continued to stare at the old man. "And you? How do you feel, eh?" he said.

The old man looked up at him, "How should I feel?"

"Forty-seven years is a long time," Marco said. "What do you know of Italy since then, since the war?"

"What should I know?" the old man asked. "What is there to know?"

"You think it's going to be like it was, eh? No changes. Just the same." Marco leaned back in his chair and crossed his arms, then he winked at me. "Look at him," he said. "He has no idea."

The old man merely grunted and returned to his food.

"Well, of course there must have been changes," I said. "And then, there was the war."

Marco laughed. "Tell that to *him*," he said, indicating the old man. "Have you tried to tell that to him?"

"I'm sure he—"

"But of course he doesn't realize it," Marco continued. "You know how he sees his precious village in the Abruzzi? I'll tell you. It is a little paradise perched on a mountaintop. Below, there is a beautiful green valley full of sheep grazing and flowers and girls picking the flowers. Gentle winds blow down the streets of his village. The people of the village are all young and smiling and handsome. There is good wine to drink and a lot to eat. No radio, no automobiles, no noise. In the evenings, the men gather at the café in the piazza and there is much good serious talk. Oh, it is a splendid life and a splendid village he lives in, all right!"

I glanced at the old man, but he simply went on eating, betraying not a flicker of emotion. "I think he knows about his village," I said. "He has a brother there and they've been writing to each other."

"Oh, sure," Marco said. "They all have a brother they write to. Or a cousin or a wife or an uncle—someone who writes them back and tells them how it is. They know, all right. You know what they're saying now in his village? That the rich American is coming home. That's how they call him now back in his village—'l'americano.' He'll get a big welcome, he will. The whole town will turn out, palms up. You know that big trunk I have in the cabin? It's full of sugar and chocolate and nylons. But with me, buddy, it's a two-way traffic. I bring in the goods and the old folks fork out the lire. With him, it'll be different. He'll give a little here and a little there. Soon he'll be what he was forty-seven years ago— broke. *L'americano!* You know what he'll find? A dusty little town full of old people and children in rags and a lot of poor, all begging for something. If there *is* a town."

"What do you mean?"

"If the war didn't blow it away." Marco laughed again. "Look at him! A year from now, he'll be sitting in the piazza of his town wondering where his money went, and he'll be full of hate for everything Italian. I've seen it before, many times. I've seen it in my own town, and we're not as miserable as they are in the Abruzzi. And that was before the war, when Mussolini had everything running on time and there was work for some. Imagine it now! He'll become more American than Uncle Sam, and all he'll do is talk about how it was back in the States. But by that time nobody's listening, see, because the dollars are all gone."

"Knock it off, Marco," I said, annoyed.

"Let him talk," the old man said quietly. "He likes to talk."

Marco again leaned forward over the table toward the old man. "Your Italy," he said, "that Italy you dream about and talk about—it's gone. You know where it exists? Back on Mulberry Street, old man—that's where. The Italy of fifty years ago, that's where it is. Back on Mulberry Street, not where you think it is."

"I am anxious to see my brother," the old man said. "I do not dream of paradise."

"Your brother? Forty-seven years of work to go home and see your brother? What did you get out of the States, eh?" Marco said. "I at least made money, but what did you get?"

The old man shrugged. "Get? I got what I could."

"And all you ever thought about was the day you'd go home."

"I don't know," the old man said, putting his hands flat against the table and pushing himself to his feet. "I don't know, but I tell you this, Marco—I don't spit in the plate where I eat."

After the old man had gone, I asked Marco why he had been so hard on him.

"I can't stand these old peasants," Marco said. "They never learn; it's always the same for them. Wait till you travel some in Italy. Every town you go into, especially in the south and in Sicily, you'll find these old men. They'll come up to you and introduce themselves and they'll be wearing the last of their American clothes. They'll say, 'Hey, you from the States?,' and then they'll tell you about how it was for them in Brooklyn or the Bronx or Elmira or someplace. You'll see."

When I went back to our cabin after lunch, the old man was lying on the bed. His eyes were closed and I thought he was asleep, but suddenly he said, "That Marco, he thinks my life it means nothing, that it is all foolish, all waste. But what has he done with his life? Nothing. He brings back chocolate and sugar to sell, that's all this means to him. Many Italians are like that, and I know many people in the States like Marco. There is no monopoly on them. They make use of people like me. So what? The world is full of gallant gentlemen like Marco, *caro mio.* I don't pay attention to them. They are dirt."

The last time I saw the old man was on the pier in Naples. I had lost track of him the morning of our arrival, partly because I was wild with excitement and too busy with my own concerns. I had been among the last to get off the ship, owing to a missing suitcase, and I had just finished going through customs and was on my way to a taxi when I spotted him. He was sitting in the middle of the pier on the edge of his trunk, his hands resting on the handle of an ancient black umbrella, the expression on his face as stolid as ever. I went over to him to say goodbye and wish him luck.

We shook hands. "What are you waiting for?" I asked. "Can I help?"

"No," the old man said. "I am waiting for my brother." He reached into his pocket, took out the gold watch, and handed it to me. "Here," he said. "I wish to give this to you, even if it doesn't go. I bought it from a gallant gentleman."

"You could have it fixed," I said.

"What for?" the old man answered. "Now there is time enough."

CHAPTER TWO

CITIZENS

I n the fall of 1933, my mother brought me back from Europe because she had decided that, having been born an American, I ought to be raised as one. Although I remember that the idea of it excited me when I was first told about it, I wasn't prepared for it. With the exception of a long happy year on Capri and a couple of terms in a Swiss boarding school, I had spent most of my first eight years in Rome and I thought of myself as Italian. It was only natural. Though she had become an American citizen after her marriage to my father, my mother was herself a Roman, and the faces of my earliest memories, the voices that filled my days, were those of her two sisters and their families. When we arrived in New York and settled into a small hotel on Washington Square, I spoke only Italian and French. In a couple of old family albums my mother still has there are a lot of photographs of me during that last summer abroad and I know exactly how I looked then. I was a skinny, prim little boy who wore shiny black shoes, white ankle socks, short pants, and tight-fitting, elegantly tailored jackets with wide collars and big buttons. I had a dark, round face and a towering mass of curls, and in any gathering of little bourgeois Roman boys on their way to church or school I would have been absolutely indistinguishable. Who could have anticipated that within three months of my arrival I would deny my Italian heritage completely and think of myself only as an American?

Certainly not my father, who came to see us the day after our return and was visibly shaken by my appearance. The feeling was mutual; I had no idea who the man was. He and my mother had separated not long after I was born and I didn't remember ever having lived with him. The crash of 1929 had temporarily ruined him and made it impossible for him either to visit us in Italy or send for me, and my mother had not talked to me about him. When he entered the room that morning, trailing a miniature dachshund on a leash, our eyes met in disbelief. To me he was a very old (he must have been in his early forties at the time), bald, plump man with a ridiculously small, nervous dog. What he thought of me I was to find out almost at once.

After a forced and very awkward embrace, I backed away to stare at him from a distance and he turned to my mother, addressing her in imperfect but serviceable French. "Does he speak any English?" he asked.

My mother smiled and shook her head. "He knows 'yes,' 'no,' and 'ham-and-eggs,'" she said.

"That's all?"

"He will learn," my mother said. "Children learn these things very quickly." She turned to me. "Get your coat, Billino," she said in Italian. "*Papà* is taking you out to lunch."

Out in the street, my father, who had not said a word to me all the way down in the elevator, took me firmly by the hand and led me directly into a nearby barbershop. I was hoisted into a chair, a sheet was tied around my neck and the barber attacked my head with a gleaming pair of clippers. Twenty minutes later, the masses of curls my mother had nurtured through my childhood lay scattered in bunches on the floor around me. The crew cut I walked out of the shop with made me feel naked, but for some strange reason it helped ease the tension between my father and me. At lunch we began awkwardly to talk to each other.

The haircut was the first dramatic step in my conversion and it has remained rooted in my memory ever since, primarily because, when my father brought me back to the hotel that afternoon, my mother and he had a short but savage altercation in English over it, during which she actually shed tears. I was amazed by the sight of them (my mother is not the sort of woman who is frivolous with her public emotions) and I was also quite aware, despite the language barrier, of what the argument was about. But by that time I was enormously impressed with my father and firmly on his side. After all, wasn't I an American? Wasn't that why we had come back to New York? Didn't she want me to look like everybody else? I couldn't understand what all the fuss was about and, after my father had gone, I tried to please my mother by reciting all the new American words and phrases he had taught me during lunch. She listened, but with a lack of enthusiasm that seemed incredible to me and was oddly irritating.

Buck Rogers was my second American discovery. A boy named Paul Rosenthal, who befriended me at the progressive day school I was immediately enrolled in, introduced him to me. My reading until then had been limited to the familiar worlds of Pinocchio, the traditional fairy tale, the standard Greek and Roman legends. Buck Rogers was a dazzler—the glamorous hero of the here-and-now, the dispenser of justice with a ray gun, the explorer of the future—and I couldn't get enough of him. Paul, who spoke excellent French, translated for me and loaned me the books my new hero starred in. I was swept breathlessly into the intoxicating sub-culture of the comic strip and the bubble-gum card. For a week or so Buck Rogers reigned supreme, but soon he was merely one star in a galaxy of Flash Gordons, Mandrakes, and Lone Rangers. The childish passions may seem trivial and amusing to adults, but they are overwhelming just the same. I can date my complete identification with my schoolmates from the day I was first able to flip G-Men cards in the bathroom as well as everybody else. By the end of my first two or three weeks in school I could speak a fluent if slightly peculiar English, full of the slang and jargon of the new literary world I inhabited; by the middle of the winter term I was, in fact as well as fancy, a child of the Upper East Side, as normal-looking in my new habitat as I had been in my old.

There was nothing difficult or painful in this metamorphosis. I was shielded by the obliviousness of the very young and inspired, too, by a truly awesome desire to conform, which, I suppose, is considered even more natural in children than adults. However, the speed and totality of my conversion shook my mother, who had not been able to imagine it. She had counted, I'm sure, on a long, slow transition period during which I would master the language and be introduced to strange customs, treated all the while with understanding and gentleness. I would doubtless eventually blend gracefully into the American scene, but I would also retain all that was most desirable in my Italian upbringing, especially my impeccable manners and my carefully cultivated taste in food. When, in a matter of days, I began to come home with filthy hands, rolled-up comic books, half-chewed pieces of gum behind my ears, and an appetite for hamburgers and Tootsie Rolls, she was appalled. Nor could she understand the language I spoke, thick with street profanities and the hot classroom sayings of the day, all expressed in an accent she identified with gangland life in Chicago. The first laugh I had at her expense came on the day she denounced me for talking like a "hudlum." I was quite suddenly aware that I had made it, that I had slipped into another world where she couldn't possibly be superior to me or instructive in any way. I had become an American, in a manner neither she nor any of my other English-speaking Italian relatives could.

I wasn't ashamed of my European background. Not exactly. For one thing, I discovered quite early in the game that being able to speak a couple of foreign languages gave me a certain standing with my classmates. I knew some Italian popular songs and I sang them with great success at public gatherings such as school assemblies. My friends used to show me off to strangers by asking me to "say something in Italian" and would bask in my reflected glory when I obliged. I used to boast that I had *lived in*, not just visited, various foreign countries. (The actual number varied from three to seven, depending on how hard-pressed I was to make an impression.) Also, French was an obligatory subject and I was always the star of the class. Such were the small but comforting benefits I never failed to exploit during my school years.

There were only a few minor perils to be coped with. I became aware, of course, that the average native-born American tends to look down on most of his fellow citizens for one reason or another. The large immigrant groups that cluster in the slum sections of large cities are inevitably regarded with fear and contempt, if not outright hatred, and it didn't take me long to find out that lower Manhattan teemed with Italians. The general impression seemed to be that these people were all small, dark, ignorant, untrustworthy, and dirty; that they ate spaghetti and something called *pastafazool* smothered in garlic; that they laughed and cried easily, and made fine gangsters or musicians. Though I was sent to the more fashionable liberal-minded private schools, ones with respectably large Jewish quotas and a symbolic Negro or two, I very soon became used to such words as "dago" or "wop."

Still, I wasn't deeply affected by it. For one thing, thanks to my father, I could hide behind a safely Scotch-Irish nomenclature. I didn't even have to reveal I had Italian blood, if I didn't want to, though the going seldom got that rough. I was tall and skinny for my age, and I have hazel eyes, so I didn't fit the physical cliché at all. I could allude vaguely, and I often did, to an aristocratic background, because the other thing I soon discovered about the American concept of Italians is that the lower classes can be sharply distinguished from the upper: a fat man sitting on a stoop in Mulberry Street is a wop; the suave, smiling fellow you see in the movie is some kind of prince or count and, though he's not to be trusted, he's clean enough to invite into your home. I clung to a few salient facts of my Italian heritage and knew how to impart them under pressure. People often asked me how I could be part Italian with a name like mine and I would explain. It wasn't difficult to elaborate, once I had the opening. "One branch of my mother's family is called Danesi, which means 'Danes,'" I would say, allowing the impression to get across that some of my ancestors had swept into the Peninsula with the safely Nordic hordes on their way to the sack of Rome. "The other branch is the Traversari," I'd continue casually. "They were the patron family of Ravenna, you know." Only a Klansman could have pierced that defense, and I felt so impregnable behind it that during my prep-school years I cheerfully allowed my classmates to refer to me as "the Irish wop," or sometimes just "Woppo."

Between school and camp, I never got back to Italy at all in the years before the war, nor did I have any desire to. Italy really meant little to me, tangibly or spiritually. I was so wholeheartedly committed to being an American that I wouldn't speak Italian at home, even though the predominant language of the house became Italian after my maternal grandmother came to live with us in the late thirties. I spoke only English, interspersed with an occasional phrase of Italian, and conversations around our apartment sometimes baffled monolingual visitors. "*Che hai fatto* in school *oggi?*" my mother might ask. "Well, I turned in my French theme, *ma non era* the best I could do. *Non ho avuto tempo*, what with all that *storia* of the Trojan War to read," I might answer. It got so we spoke to each other this way quite naturally and thought nothing of it. It wasn't until a good deal later, when I began to think of myself in relation to Italy again, that I looked back on this language as something uniquely, hilariously ours.

My grandmother was no Latin chauvinist—in fact, she was a tremendous admirer of the classical American ideals of equality and democracy—but she had her own opinions about the humbler, less abstract virtues of the good life. She believed in well-cooked food, sunshine, and good manners, and she abhorred waste. In all of these respects she found her native land vastly superior to her newly adopted one and she wasn't reluctant to say so. For my part, I couldn't bear to hear the United States compared unfavorably to Italy in any way and clashes were frequent. "Oh, come on, Mammina Ester," I can hear myself saying, "if it were so damn good over there, why, hell, no one would want to leave, would they?" I wasn't conscious of being arrogant; I simply couldn't believe anything Italian could compare with its American equivalent.

I had my family at a serious disadvantage. My grandmother, a journalist and magazine editor, had left Italy partly out of disgust with Fascism, a feeling entirely shared by my mother. The growing arrogance of the regime, culminating in the invasion of Ethiopia and the participation of Fascist troops in the Spanish Civil War on the side of Franco, embittered them. We were descended, I discovered, from a long line of passionately committed democrats. My grandmother was especially contemptuous of a sixteenth-century Traversari who had risen in the church to the rank of Cardinal and had compounded his treachery by leaving his estates to the Vatican at his death. Like most Italians, Mammina Ester and my mother considered themselves reasonably good Catholics, but, like many Romans, they had little use for the political apparatus of the church and the clergy in general. "We are a family of *mangiapreti*, priest-eaters," my mother once said to me. "That does not mean we aren't Catholic or do not go to church." I once tried, many years later, to explain this subtlety to an American Catholic friend of mine, using as an example a story I had heard about the Roman Curia referring to a well-known American Cardinal as "Shirley Temple," but I got nowhere.

When Italian troops began murdering helpless natives and various representatives of the church openly endorsed the crime, Mammina Ester and my mother were louder in their criticism and indignation than I was. They became passionate New Deal liberals, fervent and outspoken admirers of the American democratic process, and they agreed wholeheartedly with Thomas Jefferson in regarding the United States as "the world's best hope." All this made it difficult for them to resist the weight of my total, unqualified endorsement of the American scene.

Despite my grandmother's small nostalgias, my mother's frequent complaints that distances were so enormous, and their reliance on chatty family letters from Rome, I didn't imagine that this might actually be costing them something, that the minor symptoms might have come bobbing comically to the surface from some real depth of pain. I was sixteen and the war had broken out before I had my first glimpse of the truth. My mother had invited a friend of hers out to our summer cottage on Fire Island for the weekend. (My grandmother, who loathed insects, dogs, cats and all other unreliable forms of life, had remained in the city, as usual.) The friend was one of those clean, crisp, confident lady executives who, in American legend, are supposed to be infallible arbiters of taste in everything from sex to metaphysics. Somehow, during dinner one night, the conversation got around to people's accents and to the grammatical mistakes the foreign-born are likely to make when grappling with the baffling intricacies of the American language. I recalled my grandmother's inability to distinguish between the various *ough* pronunciations, and I told of her asking me one day just what sort of a soldier a "duffboy" was. Then I laughingly pointed out to my mother that she herself sometimes pronounced *c* in the soft Italian style as *ch*, as in a reference she had once made to the Ohio metropolis of "Chinchinnati." The friend roared with laughter. I reminded my mother of her fondness for misusing certain interrogative phrases, as in "It's a beautiful day, doesn't it?" or "I love New York, aren't you?" More laughter. "It doesn't matter," my mother said quietly. "The important thing is to feel American."

"Of course, darling," the friend said, "but you can't ever really *be* American. You have to be born here to be one. That's only natural, isn't it? Bill, for instance, is American, while, really, you'll always be Italian, won't you?"

"No," my mother said, "I'm as American as you are."

"Of course you aren't," I said. "How can you be? It's another way of thinking entirely. For one thing, the way you treat servants. To you a servant is a servant, while to an American a servant is an employee. You still think like an Italian, you'll always think like one."

My mother got up and left the room; I heard a door close. The friend and I looked at each other in alarm, and I rushed out of the room to find her. She was behind the bathroom door, crying soundlessly to herself. I didn't know what to do or say, so I simply put a hand on her shoulder. "It's very hard, Bill," my mother said. "It's very hard not belonging anywhere. The distances are hard and the people are hard." She walked past me and went out of the house. After a few minutes, I followed her out and joined her at the end of the boardwalk, on top of the dunes overlooking the sea. I was unable to speak because I was ashamed; I was having my first experience of adult suffering.

I mark that week as a turning point in my attitude toward Italy. Nothing changed very much as far as my basic feelings were concerned, but at least I had become aware of people in my life with emotions and longings quite different from my own. Politically, of course, it wasn't hard to make a distinction between Fascism and Italy, but, though Italy's position in the war did not affect me directly in the least, I was able at last to understand how deeply it did affect Mammina Ester and my mother. Also, I began to realize that I had certain odd, tenuous memories of my own that linked me, however lightly, to this country I had denied so completely.

For instance, I remembered a park in Rome of sloping green fields and huge pine trees, with a dirt track around which I used to pedal a small automobile; there was a booth in which puppets hit each other with sticks; a soft, shadowed clearing where I would go with my nurse to find pine cones and dig the tasty nuts out with my fingers. I had clear, unlinked images of Capri: of rocks jutting out from the sea and cool, dark caves; of hot, pebbly beaches crowded with children and bronzed swimmers; of small, twisting, cobblestoned streets down which I would walk in the company of a black cat named Milù; of Teresina, a wonderful, warm woman with leathery skin and a smell of earth about her, who used to shuffle through our rooms on rags in order to keep the floors polished and who used to slip me candy and raisins at forbidden times; of Carmine, a tall, dashing fisherman who used to take me with him in his boat and sometimes allowed me to stroke his mustache; of being caught stealing grapes with my aunt in a vineyard high on the slope of some hill, and the angry sound of the old peasant's voice chasing us off his land; of a white dog I grew fond of and lost; of long walks down sun-filled steps to a piazza crowded with round tables at which people sat, drinking, laughing, talking. Familiar memories these, common to all childhoods, but because I knew that they belonged to another world, not merely another time, they seemed exotic to me and strangely comforting. After some disaster at school, I'd use these distant memories to go to sleep on and they represented a refuge to me, something uniquely mine, to be shared with no one I knew.

Then, in 1943, as Italy's situation in the war became more and more desperate, my family's concern increased, and their contempt for Mussolini's "black apes" turned vituperative and bitter. Both my mother and Mammina Ester were broadcasting shortwave to Italy for the Office of War Information, and they lived for the fall of the Fascist government. They were, of course, terribly worried for our relatives in Rome, but their involvement went beyond the merely personal.

On the night Marshal Badoglio declared an armistice and took Italy temporarily out of the war, Mammina Ester, my mother, and I climbed into a cab and drove down to Mulberry Street, through the heart of Little Italy. I don't know what we had expected, probably nothing as exciting as dancing in the streets, but certainly some manifestation of relief and enthusiasm. But we found nothing out of the ordinary. It was a warm summer evening and kids played in the streets, the older people sat and watched from stoops and open windows, the sounds of radio music and traffic filled the night. We finally stopped in front of a barbershop. The door was open and five or six men were lounging about, smoking and talking quietly. My mother gripped my arm. "There, there!" she said. "Go in and ask them what they think."

"They probably don't think anything," I said. "Maybe they don't know."

"Of course they do," my mother insisted. "Go in and ask them."

Reluctantly, I got out of the cab and went into the shop. No one looked at me. "You've heard," I said. "Italy is out of the war."

One of the men turned to me. "You a reporter, sonny?" he asked.

"No," I said. "I'm half Italian. I thought you might want to hear the news."

"We heard it," the man said. "So what?"

"My kid's been in the army three years," one of the other men said without even glancing at me. "I hope it gets over with soon, that's all."

I felt then that I was being horribly false in some way and that I was being condemned by these men for that falseness. What in God's name *was* I doing on Mulberry Street in the middle of the evening, playing quite suddenly a role I had never before allowed myself to play? These men and I had nothing in common beyond the fact that we did not want to be Italian, especially in that time and place. I went back to the cab and climbed quickly in beside my mother and Mammina Ester.

"Well?" my mother asked.

"They've heard," I said. "And I suppose they're happy about it."

My mother knew I was lying and she did not press me for details. I didn't want to look at her or at Mammina Ester, so I sat and stared resolutely out the window. We hadn't gone more than a few blocks when the implications of the encounter in the barbershop suddenly became clear to me. It was as if a great window had opened, and I could see and understand a few things I had never grasped before. I turned to look at these two extraordinary women beside me and I realized I had a secret I could share with them. I think I must have laughed aloud because I remember my mother's startled expression as I seized her hand. Outsiders all, we drove back uptown in silence.

CHAPTER THREE

THE HOPE OF
YOUNG ITALY

W hen my boat arrived in Naples that spring of 1947,
a young man named Ruggero Anselmi was on the
pier to meet me. He was a distant cousin of mine,
one of the few relatives I had there, but still I was
surprised. I had had no direct contact with any of my Italian relatives since childhood, but I imagined that my mother's letters to
her sisters in Rome must have alerted the whole family to my
impending arrival. I knew that Ruggero was about my age and
that we had been friends as little boys during a summer on Capri,
but, by my adopted Anglo-Saxon standards, this remote past gave
us no claim on one another. I was, therefore, all the more touched
when he introduced himself by throwing his arms about me and
kissing me on both cheeks, after which we stood facing each other
at arm's length for some time, grinning foolishly. "How did you
recognize me?" I asked. "I wouldn't have known you."

"Your mother sent me a photograph," he said, beaming. "She
didn't tell you?"

"No."

"Never mind," Ruggero said. "I would have known you anyway. You remember the year you all lived on Capri? I was there
with you often. I would have known you, Billino."

"Call me Bill."

"Ah, yes, Bill. The nickname, no?"

"The diminutive."

"Ah, *il diminutivo!*"

"Yes."

"It is not right to say Billino, like on Capri?"

"I'm a little too old for it."

"Ah, of course. How is your Italian?"

"Not as good as your English."

"My English is terrible. With you I will practice."

"Let's speak Italian," I said. "I need the practice more than you."

Ruggero laughed. "Fine. *Allora parliamo italiano!*" And he pinched me affectionately on the cheek. "*Benvenuto! Benvenuto a casa nostra!*"

He was a short, chunky, good-looking young man with thick blond hair and he spoke Italian in a way I had never heard before, rolling his r's nasally up from the back of his throat like a Frenchman. It was a pronunciation, I found out later, that in Italy is identified with the moneyed upper class from the north, but I never did learn where Ruggero acquired it. His father was a civil servant in Rome and his mother came from the southern nobility, the petty gentry of some small Calabrian town.

"Are you living in Naples?" I asked.

"Yes, I'm a journalist here," he said. "But all about that later. Now let us get out of this lunatic asylum."

Ruggero set about clearing me through customs. He did it briskly and efficiently, swinging all the weight he could by waving his press card in people's faces. I parted with a few thousand lire in judicious tips and nothing was opened. Within an hour we were free and clear. On our way to a taxi, Ruggero took my arm. "How much time do we have?" he asked.

I told him that I wanted to be in Rome that evening and that I had planned to take a bus in the early afternoon. "That will give us at least a couple of hours," he said. "You must see something of Naples first. You can't understand Italy without knowing Naples. We will start with a little drive around the city, then perhaps an *espresso* in the Gallery before you go. All right? You must see the Gallery. It is the heart of Naples."

We deposited my bags at the American Express office and I bought a ticket on a three o'clock bus for Rome. Standing on the sidewalk and waiting for another taxi, we were assailed by a horde of beggars, flower salesmen, peddlers of fountain pens and curios, all the sad, small grifters of that particular Neapolitan beat. Among them were children—wizened, ageless children with the inscrutable faces of the very old. I wondered what they were selling, but Ruggero would not let me find out. Waving for a taxi with one hand, he shooed away the horde with the other, disposing of their wants with the icy disdain of an untipped headwaiter. When a taxi arrived and we had settled safely inside it, I asked him what all those people were selling. "They merely wish to part you from some of your dollars," he said. "You must never buy anything on the streets of Naples. Nothing genuine is sold there. Not even shellfish. If you buy a clam on the streets of Naples, you are buying typhoid fever. That is the way of everything here. Better to *give* them the money."

"How did you get rid of them? That *was* dialect you were speaking, wasn't it?"

"Yes," Ruggero said, smiling. "I told them you were a policeman."

"A policeman?"

"Certainly. They can't stand policemen, not even American ones."

We spent the next two hours touring the city. It was not the sort of tour that would have met the approval of the American Express; we did not visit any churches, museums, or famous landmarks. Ruggero, I discovered, was intent on impressing me with the city's squalor, and we soon abandoned the cab to stroll on foot through the narrow, stinking alleys of the poor. "I wish you to see how things are here," he explained. "I wish you to know why I am a socialist. So you will not be shocked."

"Why should I be shocked?" I asked.

"Because I know that in America it is not permitted to be a socialist," he said, looking grave.

I told him that it was, indeed, permitted. "The Socialist Party in America is an old and very respected one," I said. "Haven't you ever heard of Norman Thomas?"

Ruggero shook his head but did not pursue the discussion. I suddenly had the uncomfortable feeling that he didn't believe me; it was as if my being an American, newly arrived in Europe, made it impossible for me really to understand or judge. I wasn't quite reliable. As I glimpsed his stern, unsmiling face trudging along beside me, I knew that whatever I told him now about America would be weighed against what he had already read. I suspected that, like some other young European intellectuals I had met since the war, Ruggero had fashioned himself a dogma about my country and that he would reject whatever I said that didn't happen to conform to it. I decided to keep quiet.

In any case, Ruggero was only partly successful in his indoctrination of me, because, though I was certainly appalled by the dirt and the sheer physical discomfort in which the poor of Naples lived, often a dozen to a room with a single soiled bed behind an open doorway leading directly into the street, I was much more struck by the gaiety around me. The faces of the poor in these alleys seemed neither pinched nor sullen to me, and I found myself comparing the sun-filled clamor of these *vicoletti*, with their swarms of running, shouting children, to the sombre, iron-bound horror of a row of New York tenements in winter, with the poor banished out of sight behind crumbling brick walls and fire escapes.

I confided this thought to Ruggero and he answered me with facts and figures on the prevalence of tuberculosis. He told me about caves along the waterfront where people teemed bestially in darkness. He pointed as we passed to the scabby sores on children's faces and limbs. I saw all this and dutifully nodded, because his arguments seemed statistically unanswerable. But something in me continued to deny them. I despaired of ever being able to explain to Ruggero what the atmosphere of poverty could be like in my country, where there was less reason for it. "You've had a war," was all I could say at this point.

"A war? Yes, a war, that's true," Ruggero said. "But it was no better than this before the war. The war of Naples, *caro* Bill, has been going on for centuries. If you Americans will help us, we are going to build a new Italy, to put an end to this war."

"Aren't we helping?"

"Yes," Ruggero admitted, "but not enough. It's not enough to give things to people."

"It's a start, isn't it?"

"You must give us hope for the future," Ruggero said. "That's what America has always meant to Italians—the future."

I couldn't really quarrel with any of this, but somehow it didn't touch me as it should have. The sentiments Ruggero expressed were noble, but they didn't seem to belong to him. It was as if he were wearing them, had molded himself into some kind of iron suit. Inside the suit was Ruggero, the real Ruggero, screaming with pain at how badly he fitted the suit, but reluctant to take it off for fear of his own nakedness. Through the fabric of his dogmatic observations, for instance, ran a tiny thread of irony. When he spoke of "the people," it was usually with a touch of contemptuous humor, as if he knew and suspected that I knew it was a game we were both playing; "the people" was an abstraction, a mere phrase, and it had nothing to do with *people* in their infinite variety. I thought of Ruggero coping with the porters, the cab drivers, the petty customs officials on the dock, the crowd of beggars in front of American Express, and I sensed no genuine humanitarianism there, only a kind of good-natured worldliness rooted in ancient class customs. So I did not challenge his statistics or question his generalizations. We continued to plod earnestly through the alleys of the poor until at last Ruggero indicated it was time to go and have lunch.

We ate quickly in a small, undistinguished trattoria, then Ruggero hurried me into the Gallery where we sat at a tiny table and ordered *espressi*. "You will see everything from here," he said, indicating with a sweep of his arm the four main corridors of the Gallery lined with shops and cafés. "People promenade here at this time. You will see everyone."

All of Naples did, in fact, seem to be moving leisurely past our table. The corridors of the Gallery were full, the tables around us were full, and over our heads the rays of the midday sun struck down at us through yawning arches from which bombs had stripped the protecting glass. Ruggero pointed out celebrities, characters, colleagues, as well as several large groups of people, representatives of various professions, who gathered here at this time of day. His socialist duties evidently behind him, Ruggero proved unexpectedly to be a convivial gossip, and I remembered that he was a journalist. I asked him what paper he worked for and the smile faded from his face. "Let's not talk about it," he said. "It's of no importance."

"I'd like to know."

He shrugged. "It's a Fascist sheet," he said, and gave the name of one of the more conservative Neapolitan dailies.

"Why do you work for them?"

"They pay me," he said. "There are no really socialist papers in Naples. There is a Communist paper, but it pays very badly. I have to eat."

I was suddenly unsympathetic, but I contented myself with nodding politely.

"Are there socialist papers in America?" Ruggero asked.

"I guess so," I said. "I don't really know."

"They probably do not pay enough to live on," Ruggero said. "Anyway, I do not write politics, only about sports, so it makes no difference, really, what I think." He frowned, then leaned forward across the table, gazing at me very seriously. "And you? What are you doing to advance socialism in America?"

"Nothing," I said, regretting now that I had steered Ruggero back into his favorite subject. "I'm not a socialist. I guess I'm more of an anarchist, if you must know."

Ruggero shook his head. "That won't do at all," he said. "It's silly."

"Look, Ruggero," I said, "I really don't know what I think at this point. I've only been here a couple of hours and I still can't believe I'm here. Frankly, I couldn't care less about socialism one way or the other. I came back to Italy to become a singer."

"No one is exempt from political responsibilities," Ruggero said. "Especially the artist. The artist must be committed." He paused and drummed his fingers lightly on the table. I had the feeling he was groping for something specific to say, something simple that would illuminate his position to me. "Do you know what I would do if I visited America?" he said, after a minute or two. "I would come to New York and stay only in Harlem. Do you understand?"

"I think so," I said, "but I'm not sure you'd like it."

"I would *love* it!" Ruggero exclaimed. "That is the *real* New York! The Negroes—and the Indians, of course—are the *real* Americans!" A short, embarrassed silence succeeded this outburst. I had no idea at this point what I could possibly say to Ruggero, so I merely sat there and let my gaze wander idly about. Ruggero drained his coffee cup and set it down on the saucer with a sharp, decisive little click. "I knew that being an American you could not possibly be a socialist or understand what a socialist is," he said, shaking his head. "You are a *menefreghista*."

"What's that?" I asked.

"A *menefreghista* means literally someone who does not give a damn," Ruggero explained. "They say all the time, '*Me ne frego,* I don't give a damn.'"

"Oh."

"A *menefreghista* is a man who lies sleeping in his cabin on board ship when that ship strikes an iceberg and begins to sink," Ruggero said. "So people come and they pound on the door of the man's cabin and they wake him up to tell him that the ship is sinking. *'Me ne frego,'* the man replies. 'The ship is not mine.' Now do you understand about *menefreghismo?*"

"Yes," I said, continuing to survey the comings and goings around us. "Please tell me about all those fat men over there and what they are talking about."

Ruggero turned to look at the group I had singled out. There were ten or twelve middle-aged men, all fat, all dressed in loud pin-striped suits, and they had been arguing heatedly with each other for twenty minutes. "Ah," Ruggero said, smiling in spite of himself, "they are impresarios of vaudeville. They meet here every day at this time to hire people and to discuss the season. They are not socialists."

"No, I didn't think so," I said.

"They are buyers of flesh," Ruggero said. "They peddle and sell flesh. That is not socialism. Why don't you want to talk politics, Bill?"

"Ruggero, I'll talk politics all you like, but some other time, all right? It's my first day in Italy. Don't you understand?"

He nodded, but doubtfully. "One should not be sentimental about facing conditions," he said, then temporarily relented. "But of course, *caro* Bill," he added, putting a hand on my shoulder. "I am being a bad host. Why should you care about socialism your very first day? You will care, I know you will, one day, when you see how things are here."

I promised faithfully to care.

"*Caro* Bill," Ruggero said, "I will be coming to Rome soon. By that time you will be settled, you will have seen, you will have learned, and we will talk again."

"Yes," I said.

"It is too bad you have to leave Naples so soon. There is much to see here."

"I wish I could stay," I said, "but I'll come back, I'm sure."

"You like Naples, then?"

"What I've seen."

"Even the misery? Even the horrors?"

I nodded guiltily.

Ruggero looked suddenly wretched, as if I had confirmed a truth he had suspected all along. "It's hopeless here," he said. "Socialism will never work in the south of Italy."

I was about to ask why not, but held my tongue. I could have spared myself the effort.

"The people here are hopeless, because they are sheep and they will never reform," he continued. "We will have to build the new Italy in the north and force the south to come along." He waved an arm about, including in the gesture the entire crowd thronging the Gallery. "All, every one of those people would benefit from the new society and every one of them at the next election will go and vote for the King. Or whoever will give them fireworks and a plate of free spaghetti. You don't believe me? Come on, I'll show you what the Neapolitan mentality is like."

Ruggero paid for the coffees, took my arm and led me out of the Gallery, down a short side street and out into a rubble-strewn piazza devastated by bombs. In the middle of the little square stood a small, battered metal booth sheltering a single public urinal. At this time of day, with the entire city in the streets, a line of customers curved irregularly away from the entrance. "There he is, there he is!" Ruggero said excitedly, as we gazed at the single file of impassive male faces awaiting admittance. "Watch the old man in the middle of the line, the one with the old brown jacket that has a patch in the sleeve! Watch him!"

The man Ruggero referred to was short and thin, with sunken cheeks and wispy gray hair. Though obviously very poor, it was also evident that he had made every effort to tidy himself up: his suit was baggy but clean, his shirt was buttoned, he wore a tie, and a cane hung elegantly from one wrist. He stood quietly in line, expressionless, dignified, moving slowly, calmly toward the entrance.

"Who is he?" I whispered to Ruggero.

"Wait! Watch!" Ruggero answered fiercely.

As the little man approached the entrance to the booth, Ruggero began to fidget excitedly. Then, as the little man paused in the entrance and looked back toward the end of the line, Ruggero gripped my arm. "Watch!" he said again. As if on cue, the little man said something to one of the others. A brief discussion ensued, then the man who had been next to last in line stepped out and changed places with him. As the two men passed each other, I saw the little man pocket something swiftly.

"What happened?" I asked.

"Don't you understand?" Ruggero wailed. "He sold his place to that other one! Sold it for twenty lire!"

I laughed. "What's so awful about that? Wasn't it you who said earlier that a man has to eat?"

"But don't you see?" Ruggero said. "Not one of the others protested! How is one to bring social justice to such people? Every day I stop by here and watch this scene, and every day I wait for one person to protest. No one ever does. It is hopeless!"

"In America that little man might have been a millionaire by now," I said. "I suppose that's what you mean by social justice."

"Oh, you Americans," Ruggero said. "You will never understand anything. But you wait. We are going to do something about it, I and others like me. You wait and watch. We are the hope of young Italy!"

It was nearly three years before Ruggero and I met again. During that period I had occasion to go back to Naples several times, and Ruggero, for all I knew, might have been to Rome often since that first meeting, but neither of us had taken the trouble to call or do anything, in fact, to cement the renewal of our childhood friendship. I had often wondered rather casually what Ruggero was up to, what form of public struggle his commitment to social justice might have taken since, but I had been so engrossed in my new life and my own selfish pursuits that I had never seriously considered finding out. Also, I felt sure that I had proved more than a little disappointing to Ruggero, that my lack of interest in the plight of the Neapolitan poor that first day in Italy had only confirmed his idea about the callousness and indifference of all Americans to the urgencies of the class struggle. Anyway, despite his promise to look me up, he had made no attempt to get in touch with me and I assumed that I had been judged, found wanting and discarded.

I finally bumped into him again very late one night on the Via Sistina in Rome. I was on my way home from a party when Ruggero appeared on the sidewalk in front of me with a group of smart-looking, rather flashily dressed young Italians. They had evidently just emerged from a small night club that featured an American folk singer and had recently become very fashionable with the faster set of Roman high society, and they were taking leave of each other in an atmosphere of considerable hilarity. I hadn't recognized Ruggero and I had been about to skirt the group on my way down the street, when the distinctive sound of his voice, high-pitched and rumbling on its nasal French r's, made me stop and turn. He was telling a long, involved joke that was then making the rounds and, in the laughter that greeted his punch line, I suddenly realized who he was. "Ruggero!" I said. "How are you? Remember me?" His face looked blank and he seemed to be trying to focus on me from some considerable distance. "Bill. Your cousin Bill."

His face broke into a smile and he grabbed my hand, pumping it up and down vigorously. "*Caro* Bill," he said. "*Che piacere!* How has it been with you? So often I have meant to come and see you, but with one thing and another...." He gaily shrugged and, still holding on to my hand as if afraid I might disappear again, he quickly introduced me to his friends. "*Mio cugino americano Bill,*" he said, not bothering to include my surname, as if the mere fact of my being an exotic somehow exempted me from the customary interplay of formalities. "My American cousin Bill is living and studying here in Rome," he elaborated, then presented his companions: "The Prince and Princess Massimelli, the Doctor Pontini, the Engineer Moro, the Duke and Duchess Noli, the Marquis Caroni...."

I shook hands all around, the men bowing slightly from the waist, the women extending their hands languidly and allowing them to rest against my palm like wounded birds. I was struck by how much alike these people were. The men's suits were dark and close-fitting, made of some cloth that looked sculptured, unpressable; the collars of their shirts were starched, and expensive raw-silk ties gleamed in the darkness against their white shirtfronts; below the immaculate cuffs of their trousers, the tiny, sharp points of their shoes skimmed the sidewalk. The women wore long evening dresses that showed off their fine shoulders and bosoms; earrings, necklaces, bracelets glittered in the dim light and clinked softly as they moved. All the faces were tanned and their features appeared to have been painted on by a skillful miniaturist. I could not have said who was who five minutes after I had completed the circle of outstretched hands.

Ruggero now indicated the dark, slim young woman standing beside him and said, "And this is Paula, my wife."

Another cool bird settled in my hand and a small, round, smiling face bobbed at me above the shimmer of pearls. "How do you do," she said in careful, precise English. "I am so happy to know you."

I looked at Ruggero. "Congratulations. I didn't know you were married."

"Ah, *caro* Bill," he said, laughing and flinging his arms out wide, "so much has happened, so much. Paula and I, we got married nearly two years ago, in Naples. But we are living in Rome now." He produced his wallet and began leafing through the papers inside it. "You must come and see us."

"We should be most honored to entertain you," his wife said. "Ruggero has spoken to me of you."

"I'd like to come very much."

Ruggero found the card he was looking for and handed it to me. "*Ecco,*" he said. "Now you must telephone me. Everything is on the card." He blinked at me a little doubtfully. "You are happy here in Rome?"

"Very," I said. "But what are you doing, Ruggero? Are you still in journalism?"

"Ah, no, not exactly," he said. "That was an impossible situation."

"I remember. I'm glad you've found something more congenial."

"Congenial? Ah, yes, of course." He nodded his head rapidly several times, then laughed again and clapped me on the shoulder. "Telephone me," he said. "We will discuss it all in good time. OK? Telephone me either at the office or at home, where Paula can make all the arrangements. OK, Bill? Good. Then we will see you soon." And before I could ask him anything else, he again shook my hand vigorously and was off toward a parked automobile, with Paula skipping along beside him.

After I had parted from his friends and turned the corner of the street on my way home, I glanced idly at Ruggero's card. His name, two addresses, and four telephone numbers were printed on it in elaborate, curlicued italics. "The Honorable Cavalier Ruggero Anselmi," I read in Italian, "Investment Counseling."

About a week later, Ruggero invited me to dinner. He lived on a slope of the Aventine, an old and still elegant quarter of the city, in a square, two-story villa surrounded by a garden and a high stone wall lined by jagged pieces of broken glass. When I rang the bell at the gate, a police dog came loping down the path and crouched menacingly on the other side of the bars, ears flat against its head and snarling. A manservant in a white jacket soon appeared, seized the dog by its collar and let me in. *"Buona sera,"* he said, indicating that I should proceed quickly to the house. As I passed, I could hear him clucking soothing admonitions to the dog: *"Stai buono, cuccia! Giù! Calma!"*

Ruggero was at the door to meet me and swept me expansively inside. I commented that he seemed to be living in a fortress and he nodded, smiling. "This used to be a very good section," he said, "but now people from the Testaccio, the slums by the river, have been coming over at night to break into the villas. We all have dogs here and some of us have guns. Fortunately, nothing has ever happened to us, but several of our neighbors have been robbed."

We went up the stairs and into a large, cool, dark room with French windows and a marble floor. From almost any place in the room you could look out over the tops of trees down rows of other villas and gardens to the broad, naked expanse of the Circus Maximus. Expensive Persian rugs were scattered at our feet and the furniture consisted of a massive couch, a desk, a grand piano, several high-backed armchairs, and a number of low tables crowded with rococo ornaments and inlaid pieces of china—the furnishings of an undistinguished, comfortable mid-Victorian drawing room. On the piano were framed photographs of my hosts in formal pose and the walls were festooned with large canvases depicting romanticized, imaginary landscapes on which little girls dressed in lacy white frills and boys attired in knee-socks, short pants, tight jackets, and caps gamboled endlessly. "My wife's family gave us these," Ruggero explained, waving at the walls. "Do you know the period? Neapolitan school of the nineteenth century. Fantastic, no?" He sank into an armchair. "Sit down, sit down, *caro* Bill," he said. "Paula will join us soon and I have ordered drinks. Do you smoke? Try mine. American cigarettes. I buy them from an old woman who comes by here once a week and keeps the packages stuffed into her bosom, which is very large and safe from the police. When you first smoke them they are warm and have a most distinctive flavor, but I cannot stand Italian cigarettes, the tobacco is so bad, and these that I buy from the old woman are genuine, smuggled in through Switzerland. Now tell me all about you and what you have been doing."

I began to bring Ruggero up to date on my activities in Rome and he nodded vigorously as I talked, but I had the feeling he wasn't really listening at all, that he was abstracted into some private world of his own. My account was soon interrupted, never to be resumed, by the arrival of the servant I had met in the garden with glasses, ice cubes, and a bottle of Scotch. "Over here, Filippo," Ruggero said. "That's your American whisky, Johnny Walker, excellent. I buy it for twenty-six hundred lire a bottle from the *portiere* of a very good hotel who is a friend of mine and can sell it more cheaply than the stores. You like Scotch? Good. You can see that I have plenty of ice, as I know that Americans are fond of ice in their drinks. Water? Soda? There, how is that? Good, eh? Italians make terrible whisky, you know. It makes the head hurt for days and poisons the entire system. I never drink it."

The conversation lagged for a few minutes, during which Ruggero fidgeted endlessly, rising from his seat several times to reach for ashtrays, snuff out cigarettes, light new ones, search for matches, and shout for Filippo to hurry with the *hors d'oeuvres.* When he seemed ready to perch again for a while, I asked him about his marriage. "Ah, that is very interesting," he said. "You know that Paula is from a very old Neapolitan family. Her grandfather was a senator, right after the first war and before Mussolini, and her father is very distinguished, very highly connected here in Rome. He is very close to the Christian Democrats and most influential. He knows everyone, which, of course, is very helpful in business. He is in the building business—apartments, offices, things like that—and has firms in Naples, Rome, and Milan. He is an extremely nice man, very delicately mannered, very considerate. And, of course, very generous. You must meet him."

"So you met Paula in Naples," I said.

"Paula? Ah, yes, in Naples. At a party. Then we discovered that we had gone to the same school together—*liceo,* high school I think you call it—though she was, of course, two or three years behind me. And then I began to see her quite often here and there, you know." Ruggero paused briefly to refill our drinks. "And then I was introduced to the family," he continued. "It was difficult at first, you know, because they are a very old family and rather old-fashioned. Chaperones and all that kind of thing. And, of course, they were not happy with my career. Journalism is not really very respectable, you know. Not for people like that. And so it was not so easy in the beginning."

"How about your politics?" I said. "They can't have been pleased to hear you were a socialist."

Ruggero laughed. "No, indeed, they would not have been at all happy," he said, "but, of course, I did not tell them."

"Why not?"

"It was not conceivable to them that a young man from my background, with my education and family position, could be a revolutionary," Ruggero said. "It simply never occurred to them, so I saw no need to tell them."

"And are you still a revolutionary?"

"Ah, yes, of course, in a way," Ruggero said. "But you see, it is not easy in Italy, as you know. The world cannot be made over in a day. I did not realize this and so many other things when we last talked." He got up and began to walk aimlessly about the room. I suddenly had the odd impression that, though he was talking to me, the real dialogue was inaudible. He would pause occasionally to stare blankly into space, as if intent on some new point in a debate raging just out of earshot. "*Caro* Bill, Italy is a most difficult country," he said. "You Americans will never understand the Italian character. Perhaps, to make a joke, it would be a better place without Italians in it." He chuckled, shrugged, and continued to pace. "What was the future for me? Years of bad, dishonest, underpaid journalism, mere hack work, and for what? Not even for an ideal. And then, you know, I used to attend meetings, rallies, all that kind of thing, and listen to those people talk. It was hopeless, they accomplished nothing. Truly, Bill, I could see no way out, no future anywhere. Then, when I married Paula, I found this new career and I like it. And Paula's father has been very generous. He gave us this villa, you know, and helped in my business, oh, in many ways. Like business everywhere, it is not easy to get started without help, you know. I have no regrets, *caro* Bill. Paula and I like to live well and we will have children soon and we will let everything else take care of itself, though, of course, I do not regret one moment of all that time in Naples. You might say that I will always have a platform ticket to socialism, but that when the train pulls away, *caro* Bill, I will still be on the platform, waving."

After Paula, looking very elegant in a low-cut black cocktail dress, joined us, we finished our drinks and went into the dining room. With the appearance of his wife, Ruggero became calmer and stopped fidgeting, though he did continue to smoke all through the meal. We did not discuss politics again and the conversation became forced. Paula asked me a number of polite formal questions about how I was enjoying my time in Rome and followed up my answers with more equally desultory questions about life in New York. She would nod thoughtfully after everything I said, purse her lips, and say, "Very interesting, very interesting." Once, when I happened to mention a liking for jazz, she varied her reply by stating that she found American music very interesting, too, but also very noisy. I admitted that it was noisy and Paula apologized by adding that America must unquestionably be a most picturesque country and that one day she hoped to visit it, though she was sure she would not enjoy living there. Over dessert, Ruggero told me about a long trip they had taken on their honeymoon to the Greek islands, and at every mention of the place they had seen or stayed at Paula would nod and say, "Yes, it was most beautiful, most beautiful." I couldn't decide whether she was fanatically determined to give nothing of herself away or whether she was merely stupid. In any case, she had a soporific effect on Ruggero, who, by the end of the meal, was stifling yawns.

I left soon after coffee, and Ruggero walked me to the gate. "*Caro* Bill," he said, shaking my hand, "it was very nice to see you. You must come back again often and talk about America. I know that Paula likes you very much. You must telephone me, eh?" I promised to telephone, we said good night and parted with relief.

I never saw Ruggero again. About a year later, I was visiting another of my Italian relatives, an elderly female cousin who occasionally used to have me up for tea and liked to gossip about the family. I had barely sat down when she shook her head, clucked severely, and said, "Isn't it terrible about poor Ruggero!"

"Is he ill?"

The old lady leaned forward in her chair. "You mean you have not heard? Ruggero killed himself last week." She hastily crossed herself and blew her nose into the handkerchief she always kept tucked into her sleeve for such emergencies. "What a terrible thing! And we did not even know he had a gun! Paula knew, because she said he had bought one to protect the house from burglars. He locked himself into his room and put the pistol into his mouth. No one was home at the time and it was Filippo who found him. Paula, thank God, never saw him."

"But why did he do it?"

"He had been cheating on the stockmarket. That is, he had

taken money from people—many of the family had given him money to invest, I myself lost nearly a million lire—he had taken the money and gambled in the casinos with it. At San Remo, I think. He lost and lost and then he must have imagined there was nothing else for him to do, though he could always have turned to Paula's family, you know. They are very rich. Something could have been arranged." The old lady sniffed her disapproval and handed me a cup of tea. "Luckily, Paula's father, that good man, had enough influence to keep the affair out of the newspapers. Poor Paula! What a scandal! But I never will understand why he felt he had to do this terrible thing. I suppose it was because he had a peculiar conscience. You know he was once a Communist, don't you? In Naples, before he married Paula. He must have been totally corrupted, poor boy. I liked him—he was so full of charm—but I never did understand him."

CHAPTER FOUR

A DAY AMONG
THE IMMORTALS

ammina Ester first met Gabriele d'Annunzio, the Italian poet, novelist, playwright, and professional super-patriot, in the fall of 1921, when he summoned her from Rome to the Cargnacco, the villa on Lake Garda where he had been living in clamorous seclusion since the end of the Fiume adventure. The poet had cemented his position as a national hero in 1919 by leading a few hundred volunteers, the famous *arditi* of the Legion of Fiume, to occupy the town, then being disputed between Italy and Yugoslavia at the peace conferences, and he had ruled there for fifteen months as a Renaissance prince, successfully defying all of Europe and embarrassing his government by printing his own currency, flying his own flag, and issuing thundering proclamations. When at last he was chased out of Fiume by regular Italian troops, he took possession of the villa and declared, "I have come to enclose my sadness and my silence in this ancient rustic house, not so much to humiliate myself as to put to a more difficult test my powers of creation and transfiguration."

My grandfather Giulio had been dead for some years, and Ester, my grandmother, had been supporting herself and her three daughters—my mother and her sisters—by freelance journalism and editing. After the war, she had become involved in an organization dedicated to "safeguarding the glorious traditions of Italian popular art" and had written d'Annunzio, one of the founders, to ask him if there was any way she could make herself useful. His answer had been the invitation, really a command, to visit him, and my grandmother packed a suitcase and took a train north.

Even to her, it must have seemed a daring thing to do, because d'Annunzio enjoyed a vast and well-documented reputation as an unscrupulous charmer, but Ester was probably not really nervous about the visit. Her character was rooted in the period of Italian history known as the Risorgimento. It was still the age of beards, and if my grandmother had been a man she would certainly have sported one; she gazed out on the modern world with the stern, unflinching eyes of Giuseppe Verdi, Garibaldi, and King Victor Emmanuel II, the splendidly whiskered heroes of the new Italy. She was already a notorious figure in her own way. Italian women were not supposed to support themselves and engage in careers, and there had been a public outcry when Ester visited the Austrian front as a war correspondent in 1917, the first Italian woman ever to do such a thing. "What was I supposed to do? Not go and see d'Annunzio?" Ester wrote me years later. "Yet I must admit that everything I had ever heard about him—his loves, his eccentricities, that scandalous publicity—disgusted me a little. But he was then at the height of his literary fame and he was the kind of man I had never dreamed I could meet, though I had devoured with passion all his many books and poems. And you must remember that his true glory was to restore to us in Italy a consciousness of our heritage. As you know, I myself was a Traversari, one of the oldest and most respected family names in Italy. Of *course* I would accept his invitation!"

The story of Ester's meeting with d'Annunzio was told to me in a series of letters we exchanged in 1947, shortly after I had moved to Rome. Ester was then still living in New York, and I had begun to write letters home, complaining about everything Italian. Like so many Italo-Americans on their first visit to the old country, I started, soon after my arrival in Italy, to criticize and compare, generally unfavorably. I ignored most of my relatives, found fault with every Italian I met, and saw Fascism rampant everywhere. One of my aunts had lent me a copy of d'Annunzio's masterpiece, *La Figlia di Jorio,* a tragedy of peasant life in the Abruzzi, and I denounced it as a fraud, full of pomposities and archaic turns of phrase. I even identified the poet's flowery rhetoric and public posturing with the rise of Fascist Italy.

It was at this point, I think, that Ester lost patience with me. "You know nothing about Gabriele d'Annunzio," she wrote me, "and yet you condemn an entire generation, as well as all the members of our family, because of him. D'Annunzio was an extraordinary man and not a true Fascist at all. Did you know that he used to call them 'the black apes'? They copied everything from him: the black shirt, the eagle, the insignia of death, everything. Perhaps d'Annunzio approved of the original idea—he was excessively patriotic—but never of the actual regime itself. In 1925, when Mussolini went to visit him at his villa on Lake Garda, d'Annunzio took him for a ride in his speedboat. He aimed the craft straight at a little passenger steamer that was making its regular crossing of the lake and turned the engine up to full speed, shouting 'To the attack!' He turned away only at the last second, and poor Mussolini nearly fainted with fright; he lost his balance and fell over backward. The poet lost all respect for him after that. No, you must not lump d'Annunzio together with the Fascists. He was a *brave* man. Do you remember that photograph I have on my desk of the three Army pilots standing by that old open airplane? One of them is d'Annunzio, and that picture was taken in August of 1918, at about the time the poet flew over Vienna dropping propaganda leaflets instead of bombs. Such a civilized thing to do! You must always remember, *caro nipote,* that a man like d'Annunzio may have influenced a generation of posturers, but he himself was his own greatest creation."

D'Annunzio sent his automobile, a bright-red touring car decorated with patriotic emblems and flying the yellow, wine-red, and blue flag of Fiume, to pick Ester up at her hotel in Brescia. On the chassis was engraved the poet's favorite motto, *"Andare in brocca,"* which means, roughly, "Aim straight for the mark!" But Ester had little time to note all these details or to enjoy the panoramic drive from the town along the winding, hilly roads above the lake, because the driver, an ex-Legionary of Fiume, who had introduced himself laconically to her as "Virgil," had evidently taken the motto to heart, and he whisked her off on the narrow roads leading to the villa at sixty miles an hour.

On her arrival at the Cargnacco, Ester was told that the poet was meditating in the garden but would soon join her. A maid ushered her into a large, elegant sitting room on the ground floor and left her alone. The room, Ester remembers, had a warm, intimate atmosphere, despite the furniture, which struck her as Brobdingnagian—a vast table, towering straight-backed armchairs, an endless sofa, an enormous black chest. But there were shelves full of books, and delicate Oriental rugs, and windows that gazed down over the gentle slope of a garden to the bright-blue waters of the lake below. It was a musician's room, Ester thought, and she recalled that Cosima Wagner and her first husband, the pianist Hans von Bülow, had once lived there. Ester couldn't help wondering what it cost to run such an elaborate establishment, although it was public knowledge that d'Annunzio had recently become a rich man, for the Italian government had agreed to pay him a huge yearly subsidy in return for his authorization of an official state edition of his complete works—a splendid arrangement for a proud writer with wildly expensive tastes. Only a few years before, he had been forced to flee his creditors in Italy and take up residence in France; he had stayed there until 1915, when he returned to invite Italy into the war on the Allied side.

Ester did not hear the poet enter the sitting room; she happened to turn around, and there he was. He bowed over her hand and proffered a small bouquet of rosebuds. "Welcome, Donna Ester," he said. "You will find much to admire here, because everything in this house is rooted in my thought, is an aspect of my spirit, an expression of my devotion. Let us chat and then we will have lunch. I usually eat alone at midday, but on special occasions I make exceptions."

"I don't remember what *I* said to *him*," Ester wrote me. "I was too moved by the sight of this man who, at fifty-eight, had actually become a legend to two generations of Italians." She was struck by the pallor of his face, which was accentuated by his baldness. He had lost the sight of his right eye in an airplane accident, and wore a patch, but his left eye was large and clear, and was fixed on her with unsettling intensity. His mouth was broad and full, framed by a somewhat scraggly mustache and beard, and his nose was long and straight. Though short, he was an elegant, athletic-looking figure. His hands, too, were quite extraordinary. He himself had once described them admiringly as "free and pliable, quick and strong, well made and supple." His voice was deep and musical, a singer's voice, in which, in spite of the polished cadences of his acquired Tuscan accent, Ester detected echoes of the Abruzzi, where he was born.

They were joined at lunch by two other ladies. "One was a Madame d'Espagne," Ester recalled, "a very rich lady, no longer young, who lived alone in a nearby villa, where she consoled her nerves, doubtless strained from the dangerous effects of having too much." The other was Luisa Baccara, a young Venetian concert pianist who had followed d'Annunzio to Fiume. She was a straight, slim, elegant woman, with rather severe features. Ester knew all about her, because the year before, in Fiume, d'Annunzio had written his "Portrait of Luisa Baccara," an impressionistic hymn to her beauty and talent. "Never before has the physical structure of an accomplished artist corresponded so vividly to the qualities of his art," he wrote. "She is as much in harmony with her vast grand piano as a violinist with his more subtle instrument. The black and lucid mass, with all its bedded strings, is as much a part of her as the remarkable tresses that flow above her brow like waves of melody. Just as the smooth wood reflects the play of her strong hands, so does the entire sonority of the mass shape itself into a semblance of her pathetic beauty. And music becomes something to be enjoyed by one's eyes as well as one's hearing."

Lunch was announced by the ringing of a gong and the appearance of a tall, emaciated butler. "My ex-gondolier," d'Annunzio said, smiling affectionately at the servant. "He has the soul of Dante, so that is what we call him. My driver is Virgil. I surround myself with genius."

The lunch was, to say the least, dreamlike. Although the project that had brought Ester to the Cargnacco was discussed at some length and d'Annunzio promised to write letters of introduction for her to the directors of various museums, he soon embarked on a monologue about himself and his career. He told how, at the age of nineteen, he had come from his home in Pescara to Rome, where he thrust himself at once into the artistic life of the city and began to submit his poems to all the best-known literary reviews. "I was not afraid of the language, this noblest of the world's tongues—of using words, even of inventing them," he said. "So of course I was hated by all the professors. It was only when Giovanni Pascoli, the famous poet of simple, intimate things and of small emotions, praised my work that the professors woke up. By then, of course, I did not need them. In any case, I never suffered or starved. The editor who published my first books could not pay me what I was worth, so he opened charge accounts for me with a florist and a confectioner. No one ever starves who is well loved, and I became the poet of bouquets and bonbons. What better way to pay an artist? Did not the early painters turn out pictures for a sack of beans or a pair of fat capons? Ah, marvellous times!"

After a heavy dessert of *marrons glacés*, the poet suddenly rose to his feet. "We are approaching the seventh centenary of the death of St. Francis of Assisi," he intoned. "We must visit the sacristy." He led the way out of the dining room, and his guests followed him through the ground-floor rooms of the villa until they came to a passage that terminated in a huge red velvet curtain. "Out of respect, you must lower your voices," the poet said, and dramatically pulled the curtain aside. Enveloped in an odor of incense and benzoin, they entered a long, rectangular darkened room. Tapers burned on a hearth in one corner and a small oil lamp flickered in another. A lectern supported an open missal; other religious objects—books, emblems, chalices, statuettes— were scattered over shelves and tables. A pew rested against one wall, and from somewhere came the sound of a fountain playing. "Sister Water and Brother Fire," the poet said, quoting from one of the Canticles of St. Francis. He indicated a painting of a woman that hung above the pew. "Donna Luisa—my mother," he said reverently. "I keep the lamp lit here in her memory."

The other ladies now excused themselves, and d'Annunzio swept Ester out on a tour of the garden, which they entered along a path, bordered by tall hedges, that passed under an arch supporting a statue of a headless Venus. The foliage was dense and luxuriant, and Ester felt almost suffocated by the heavy brilliance of the surroundings. Great masses of flowers grew on all sides, crushed together in their beds. "I do not allow my flowers to be picked," d'Annunzio explained, waving his arms expansively. "Your roses and the other flowers you saw in the house came from the markets in Brescia."

The path led to an open space around a large beech, where there stood a statue of St. Francis, open-armed, as if blessing the world. Rocks had been piled around his feet. "The stones of the Grappa, the Sabotino, the Pasubio," d'Annunzio said. "Those Alpine peaks above the trenches where our troops fought so hard and so well from 1915 on." From the side of the hill above the lake, Ester stared out over a sea of roses, azaleas, violets, gardenias, and other blossoms. Wild flowers sparkled in the shadows of cypresses and cedars, under thickets of laurel and tufts of oleanders that flowed down to the edge of a dark, mossy-looking orchard by the shore. Ester saw what looked like the mast of a ship rising above the tops of the trees, but before she could comment on it d'Annunzio took her arm and led her into a more heavily wooded section of the garden.

Trees shut off their view of the lake, and soon they came to a stream that meandered through the shadows. It was crossed by several small wooden bridges that bore fantastic names. The Bridge of the Iron Heads was decorated with cannon shells; the Bridge of Hares sported carved wooden statues of hares. "And that one," the poet said, leading Ester to a bridge guarded at each end by enormous pairs of horns, "that one is the Bridge of Desires. The horns will guard you from the evil eye, and the coin you must throw into the brook here will grant you your wish."

They followed the stream down, past a row of guest cottages and a votive chapel dedicated to the Archangel Gabriel. Here the path broadened into an avenue lined by cypresses, olives, and oaks that led directly to a clearing in which there stood the gigantic prow of a modern warship, complete with cannons and foremast. Ester looked up at it in astonishment.

"The cruiser *Puglia*," the poet said reverently. "Embedded here forever in my land and heart." They stared at the prow, which was flanked on each side by tall cypresses. "When the ship was decommissioned a few months ago," d'Annunzio said, "I requested her from the Ministry of the Navy, and this prow, the entire forward section of the ship, was brought here in twenty separate pieces to be reassembled. I wished to have a ship in order to commemorate my raid of 1918 in the Bay of Buccari. Thirty of us took three torpedo boats into the harbor, guarded by shore batteries and a steel net, where we thought the Austrians had a battleship. There were no battleships, but we sank a smaller ship and left three sealed bottles bobbing in the water with this message: 'Armed with steel and fire, the sailors of Italy have come, laughing at all barriers and nets, ever ready to dare the undared, to disturb the prudence of the Austrian fleet within its most comfortable refuge.'"

D'Annunzio paused and then pointed up at the silent guns. "You see? They are silent now, but they are still alive. When I wish to reopen my dialogues with the future, I will give the order to fire. The thunder of my guns will echo across the water and throughout the world!"

Again taking Ester's arm, he pointed off toward a hilltop in the garden. "And up there," he said, "in that open space—that is where I shall entomb my immortals, my heroes and friends, and where I, too, will one day lie!" (The poet is, in fact, buried on the premises.)

When they got back to the villa, d'Annunzio led Ester to a guest room on the second floor. "Now you must rest," he said, ushering her inside. "We will meet again at dinner."

She protested feebly that she had nothing suitable to wear and would have to return to the hotel to change.

"Oh, that's not necessary," the poet said, indicating a large wardrobe in one corner of the room. "Luisa will pick something out for you." He turned to Luisa Baccara, who had followed them up the stairs. "Luisa, you will take care of everything, please." And he vanished.

Luisa Baccara strolled across the room and opened the wardrobe. Inside were at least a dozen of the most beautiful silk evening gowns Ester had ever seen. "From Palmer, in Milan," Luisa said, naming the most celebrated dressmaker of the day. Ester picked out a dress in pale blue, and Luisa Baccara set it aside for her, then excused herself.

"I was exhausted," Ester recalled, "like a child who had missed his nap and spent the day eating candy. I went over to the bed and lay down. My bedside table was piled high with books of the sort the French call *livres de chevet*—collections of confessions, thoughts, maxims, the diaries of great authors, the sort of volume one opens at random and reads with pleasure. But all I could think about was sleep. I was about to close my eyes when, on a smaller end table near the books, I noticed a tiny package bound in the tricolored ribbon of Fiume. Underneath it was a card addressed to me. I sat up and opened it. Inside the box was a lovely brooch. It was in the form of a phoenix, with lacily woven golden wings encrusted with tiny garnets and a body of small matched pearls; the neck and beak of the phoenix were of gold-and-blue enamel. It was beautiful workmanship, and inside the band were inscribed the words, 'Mastro Paragon Coppella.' I knew that this was the name d'Annunzio used in one of his many roles, that of master artisan—he was famous for his jewelry—and I naturally assumed that he himself had designed and executed this exquisite gift for me. It is the one you have often seen me wear. I immediately put it on, of course, and I never did get to sleep."

D'Annunzio appeared for dinner in a Franciscan tunic of heavy brown silk, bound at the waist by a long knotted cord. "In honor of St. Francis," he explained, leading Ester and Luisa into the dining room. "I am a tertiary in the lay order of this splendid saint." When the servants entered, he addressed them as if he were a benevolent father superior. In addition to Brother Dante, who presided over the meal, Ester made the acquaintance of Sister Bee, Sister of the Andirons, and Sister Spider, while the unseen cook was referred to as Sister Sauce. The monastic motif did not affect the quality of the food, which was superb and was accompanied by several bottles of Château Lafite. The meal culminated in an elaborate dessert consisting mostly of two pyramids of whipped cream topped by maraschino cherries. "Ah, the Breasts of St. Agatha," d'Annunzio announced. "Hers was a most extraordinary martyrdom!"

During dinner, d'Annunzio talked of his plans for converting the Cargnacco into a national victory memorial, "Il Vittoriale degli Italiani"—a plan that was later carried out. He talked so fast and so brilliantly that Ester began to feel quite giddy with the occasion. Though she had never approved of the poet's many, much-publicized love affairs, she could now understand why all those ladies had hurled themselves into his arms. She remembered, too, that they all had spoken well of him afterward and continued to remember him kindly, with the possible exception of Eleonora Duse, with whom he had carried on a long and erratic romance. "I could see in Luisa Baccara's face an example of the complete devotion the man inspired," Ester wrote. "As you may know, she remained with him until his death in 1938."

After coffee, when Luisa left the room briefly, Ester's journalistic instinct asserted itself, and she leaned across the table to ask the poet which of his many loves he considered the most nearly perfect. D'Annunzio laughed. "My most nearly perfect love?" he cried. "The most difficult one, of course! Eleonora! In addition to being a very great artist, she was a woman of the most exquisite sensibilty. She once wrote the most divine letter to her rival, the Marchioness Alessandra di Rudinì, widow of the Marquis Carlotti. *That* was another woman! An amazon, a virago! She ended her life as the mother superior of a convent in the French Alps. I had betrayed Eleonora with her in Florence. We had been on a hunting party in the afternoon and found ourselves staying that evening in the same hotel, in adjoining rooms. I decided to attempt the adventure, knocked on her door, and was admitted. But no sooner had we fallen into each other's arms than the woman opened a drawer of her night table and produced a pair of dueling pistols. She handed me one and said, 'The Marchioness di Rudinì does not engage in adventures. We will die together!' Naturally, I was compelled to make her a declaration of eternal love, and so I found myself embroiled with her. Eleonora was extremely jealous. She wrote this woman, proposing with the utmost seriousness and nobility to divide me with her six months at a time. Now, wasn't that divine? Who could resist such a woman?"

It was very late when Ester finally rose to go back to her hotel. D'Annunzio summoned the car and then saw her to the door and kissed her hand. It was only then that she remembered the brooch. Blushing with embarrassment, she thanked him profusely. D'Annunzio fixed her severely with his single eye. "Did you steal anything else?" he asked sternly. Ester must have looked stupefied, because he quickly smiled and patted her hand. "It was very stupid of you to have lost such a splendid opportunity—I have so many treasures," he said, waving her off toward the waiting car.

A few years later, I was dining with my grandmother in Rome and I happened to ask her about d'Annunzio's brooch.

"Ah, there is a strange story about that," she said. "You know, for a long time I thought I had lost it. The clasp had broken, and I had put the brooch somewhere, meaning to have it repaired. I think I had it in mind to bring it back to Italy with me one summer and give it to a little man I know on the Via Frattina. Anyway, I misplaced it, and it was several years before I found it, in a suitcase that had been mistakenly stored in the basement. About the time it turned up, someone told me that a famous Florentine jeweller had just moved to New York. I went to see him and showed him the brooch. The moment he saw it, he asked me where I had got it. I told him it had been given to me by Gabriele d'Annunzio and that the poet had designed and executed it himself. I showed him the inscription. 'Mastro Paragon Coppella was d'Annuzio. Didn't you know that?' I said. To my amazement, the jeweller then described to me exactly what sort of box the brooch had been in. 'I am sorry to disillusion you, Signora,' he concluded. 'But this brooch was made by us in Florence some years ago. It was one of many similar orders placed regularly with us by Gabriele d'Annunzio.'"

Mammina Ester sighed a little sadly. "So perhaps, *caro nipote*, he was a little bit of a fraud after all," she said. "Though certainly he will always be among the immortals."

CHAPTER FIVE

THE BEST AVAILABLE ENGINEER AND EXPERT

For a while I lived on a rooftop, in an artist's studio owned by an ancient aristocratic lady who taught piano and liked to paint in her spare time. It was an illegal construction, thrown up practically overnight to thwart the authorities, and it was made mostly of plaster. One wall and part of the ceiling consisted of a skylight that resembled the one Rodolfo gazed out of in *La Boheme,* and I could step outside and have an almost uninterrupted view of Rome in any direction. There was also a fireplace that worked very well and contributed heavily to the general aura of romance. I fell in love with the place at once.

Of course, there were disadvantages. The toilet was located diagonally across the rooftop from my front door and, on cold mornings or when it rained, I'd have to make a dash for it in my pajamas across thirty feet of open ground, then huddle, shivering, in a dank, icy, lightless cell that contained only a bare porcelain bowl, stripped in some dim past of its comforting wooden seat. I never quite got used to it, but, for the sake of atmosphere, I was willing to put up with it.

A more serious drawback became evident after the first real

downpour; the skylight leaked. I came home from a singing lesson late one afternoon, during a storm, and I found the water pouring in a steady stream down the inside of the glass and over my books and scores. The walls themselves were as damp as the interior of an abandoned mine shaft, and I could hear water gurgling like an underground brook beneath the wooden floor boards. When it finally stopped raining, two days later, I was perched on my bed in the middle of the room, with all my belongings about me on chairs and tables, hopelessly marooned and about to contract pneumonia. Then, for an added touch of horror, as the waters receded, scores of fat, black slugs struggled up through the cracks in the floor to dry themselves on my hearth. As soon as I felt brave enough to walk across the room, I descended in fury on my landlady.

"Signorino," she said, spreading her gaunt arms to embrace the world and all its injustices, "the quality of workmanship is not what it was. One summons plasterers, plumbers, architects, and masons, but society provides incompetents and thieves. I will do what I can, but these are not the Romans who built the aqueducts!"

"Signora, I think they are," I said.

"Ah, Signorino, you make fun of me," she said. "The times are not propitious to the working of miracles."

"Miracles are not required, Signora," I said, a little unkindly. "Mere competence and the proper tools will suffice."

"I will summon the best available engineer and expert," the Signora said, nodding stiffly as I bowed myself out of her presence.

The best available engineer and expert showed up the following afternoon; in fact, he was already on the premises when I got home. He was a short, stocky Roman of about fifty, and he was dressed in overalls, an undershirt, and a hat made out of a folded sheet of newspaper. He was squatting in a corner of my terrace, mixing some sort of cement in a bucket, and he did not answer my cordial greeting but merely looked up briefly, just long enough to fix me intently with an unfriendly pair of black eyes before returning to his work. I had the feeling I had been instantly judged and contemptuously dismissed. It was an unusual experience for me and I could not let it pass.

I walked up behind him and stared over his shoulder into the bucket. "Putty?" I asked.

The engineer and expert grunted. "What should it be?" he said. "Turds?"

I retreated a step or two. "What's the matter with you?" I demanded.

He stood up and I experienced a moment of panic; he barely came up to my shoulder, but he had the arms and chest of a blacksmith. I thought he might simply pick me up and heave me into the street.

"This is not even a permitted dwelling," he shouted, angrily waving his arms about. "It is made out of cheap plaster and rotten wood. Five times this year alone I have been summoned to keep it from being washed away, but it is as useless as attempting to sail the sea in a colander. Only an exploiting capitalist landlady would build such a place for persons to live in, and only a fool of an American would be cretin enough to inhabit it! *Porco Dio!*"

The vehemence of this outburst amazed me; I could not imagine from what depths of feeling it had arisen. "She is only a poor old lady who teaches piano and likes to paint," I said, after a short pause. "She needs money."

"We *all* need money!"

"Then you should be happy to be able to come here and work," I said.

"Work!" he said, spitting the word out like an expletive. "Work! You call this work? Patching a sieve with plaster? For me, a stone mason, a builder of monuments? To be summoned here like a peasant and paid a slave wage for being unable to fix the unfixable? It's exploitation, merely exploitation!"

"Then why do it?"

The engineer and expert turned his head and spat over the wall. "Spoken like a true American," he said. "Because we all need money, that's why. Do you see any building going on, American? There is no building. So stonemasons take handouts from capitaltalists to keep themselves alive doing jobs not fit for a child of twelve! *Merda!*"

He turned his back on me and bent down over the bucket again. I was angry, but I couldn't think of any way to turn the conversation in my favor, so I left him and went inside. I lay down on the bed and, a few minutes later, I saw him through the skylight take a ladder and place it against the wall. Soon his dark, apelike form was busy fiercely slapping putty along the outside edges of my window panes.

He showed up again the next morning, just as I was emerging in my bathrobe from the toilet, and he seemed even less cheerful than the day before. "Good morning," I said. "I have just concluded my capitalist ablutions in the restroom of the rich. I am about to attire myself in typical bourgeois clothing and sally forth to the exploitation of my fellow man." I raised my hand in the Fascist salute. "Down with the workers!"

He looked startled; I thought he might smile, but he caught himself in time. "Don't make bad jokes, American," he said, setting his bucket and tools down.

"You will excuse me, I am certain," I said, "considering that the source of the joke is reprehensible. From an exploiter everything is to be expected."

"True," he said. I started past him. "I will need to work inside today, when I have finished out here. You will be here?"

"No. I'll leave the door open."

He seemed surprised. "The *portiere* will come up?"

"What for?" I said, enjoying myself. "If the workers are not to be trusted in one's home, who is, eh?" I went inside and shut the door behind me.

When I came back that afternoon, he was standing on his ladder and caulking the inside seams. He did not pause in his work and I stood below him, watching him in silence for a few minutes. "Will you finish today?" I asked him at last.

"No," he said. "I will finish the window today. Tomorrow I will work on the walls. There are soft spots."

"What about the floor?"

He shrugged. "That is a carpenter's work, not a stonemason's," he said.

"Sorry," I said. "I didn't think—"

"But I will plug the holes along the edges," he continued unexpectedly. "That will help."

"Thank you," I said.

"But if I were you," he said, kneading more putty into the seams between the panes of glass, "I would inform the Signora that you are aware that this is an illegal dwelling and insist upon paying less rent."

"I don't think I can do that," I said. "I took it on the understanding that it was my risk."

"Did she tell you about the leaks?"

"No, but it doesn't matter. I'm alone here and I rented it for charm, not utility."

"You are a poor exploiter."

"I never said I was a good one."

I sat down on the bed and began leafing through some music I had just bought. The engineer and expert worked in silence for a few minutes and soon I forgot he was there. When he spoke again, the sound of his voice startled me nearly as much as the unexpected tone of gruff cordiality he had suddenly adopted. "You are a musician," he said, as if the discovery had magically opened a broad, well-travelled avenue between us. "My name is Pietro."

"Mine is Bill."

He still did not turn around. "You are American. How is it that you speak Italian?"

"My mother is Roman," I said. "I have many relatives here."

"Ah." Another silence, during which he continued to work with renewed concentration. Finally, he wiped his putty knife on his trousers, slipped it into his pocket, and climbed down from his perch. "You will come have a glass of wine with me?" he asked, gazing at me fiercely out of those bottomless eyes. "There is nothing more to be done here today."

I nodded and we went downstairs together.

This was the strange, unpromising way my friendship with Pietro began. It developed into a relationship that neither of us, I'm sure, ever fully understood, though I know mutual curiosity formed an integral part of it. To Pietro I was an exotic, the living embodiment of forces he had hated in the abstract most of his adult life—an American, a bourgeois, an aesthete—and I think he could not quite reconcile himself to the dismal fact that he liked me; he probed for weak spots, sounded me out on society, nature, the church, politics. When he found that we felt pretty much the same way about many of the worldly and spiritual issues of the day, he would lapse into long, morose silences during which I knew I was being weighed, measured, tested, all according to the abstractions he had nurtured over the years.

It might not have been so hard for him to arrive at some ultimate understanding of what I represented, if it hadn't been for the rigid structure of his faith. Pietro was a militant, dogmatic Communist and his allegiance to the Party went back into the Fascist era, when it had been neither comfortable nor convenient to be Red. In the end he would always find himself confronted, not by what he felt personally for me, but by the labels people of my class and background had always worn in his mind; I would have to be explained away by the catechism or the columns might crack and the temple come tumbling down. Pietro was in his fifties and it was too late for him to question allegiances, however blind, to which he had consecrated his life and for which he had actually suffered. "Twelve years in prisons and camps I did for the Fascists and capitalist exploiters," he growled at me that first evening, apropos of nothing at all, as if apologizing to himself for sharing a glass of wine with me. "Twelve years and no one, American, wipes those years away, you understand?" And so, when dogma would not come to his rescue, he'd find excuses for me: I was half Italian, I was an artist, I was an intellectual—in short, a freak, the exception that proves the Marxist rule.

I don't think we ever had a conversation. Pietro would ask questions, ponder my answers, then either remain silent for minutes at a time or begin to wave his arms about, pound his fists on the table, and shout slogans at me. "I was with Togliatti and Longo in the north," he'd bellow when the going got too rough. "We fought together and killed Fascists! We killed *men*, you understand? Are you telling me we were wrong? Are you telling me that, American?" And I would back down a little, because I soon realized that Togliatti and Longo were sacred names, not idly to be taken in vain; to have been with Togliatti in the north was to have been with Christ on the shores of the Sea of Galilee. One does not joke too much about God, not in dialogues with monks. I enjoyed and valued my friendship with Pietro—like the old peasant I had met on the boat coming over, he represented another link with a world I had long denied—and so it was no hardship to retreat, to remain silent, or to acquiesce. In any case, the most violent altercations always took place over the second or third litre of cold Frascati, and they had no permanent meaning beyond the immediate noise. Once Pietro even made me stand up with him and sing the "Internationale," while we brandished clenched fists in the air and shook them threateningly over the heads of the other drinkers in the wine shop. It was, I thought, merely playacting and therefore enjoyable; it meant nothing.

Pietro and I used to meet in the same wine shop, just up the street from my house, two or three times a week. He himself lived in Trastevere, a few blocks down the river bank from my quarter, but he never invited me to his house or introduced me to any of his neighbors. He didn't mind walking with me and I think he even enjoyed showing me off—it imbued him with an air of importance and mystery to be seen hobnobbing with the aristocratic enemy—but to have asked me into his house would have been too overt a sign of friendship, the sort of concrete, personal act that might demand definition, explanations. Later I realized that there was another aspect to it. Pietro lived alone, in the back room of an apartment he shared with a married cousin and six children; he had a nice class-consciousness about letting me see the humble circumstances of his life. Of course I never pressed him.

Occasionally, Pietro and I would go to a movie together and it was then, in the semi-darkness of the theatre, that he was usually at his best. He had a tough, cynical mind and a sarcastic, characteristically Roman tongue. The movies were almost always American ones, either Westerns or silly domestic comedies of the sort that became identified with Doris Day. Nothing could have seemed more remote or unreal to Italians then than these witless fantasies so out of touch with the realities of their own lives, which undoubtedly accounted for their popularity. Pietro would sit there, stare with disbelief at the unfolding action, and then pepper the air with his comments. He would inspire other wits in the audience to try and top him, and soon we would all be rocking with laughter at the insane dilemmas being faced by Joan Crawford, June Allyson, and Randolph Scott. There was one hot Sunday afternoon when we sat in a small, stuffy, third-run theatre and marvelled at the quick-trigger heroics of John Wayne. The place was packed with Roman families on their day off; fat mothers cradled babies on their laps and fathers stood along both side walls, holding older children in their arms or by the hand. The air was heavy with sweat, smoke, and tension as Wayne, his voice dubbed into a magnificent Latin baritone, urged a troop of mounted men in blue uniforms toward a showdown with hordes of murderous Apache, who lay in wait for him just beyond a ridge of barren mountains in the upper part of the screen. Unfortunately, before this climactic battle could take place, Wayne and his men encamped and there was what Hollywood movie buffs call a "wisdom scene" in the Old Colonel's tent. It seems that Wayne and the Old Colonel, played by some veteran actor like Charles Bickford, had been through the American Civil War together and it had been quite an experience for both of them. "*Ah, Colonello,*" Wayne said, articulating out of the side of his mouth in a flawless Tuscan accent, "what will history say of the campaign of the Shenandoah?" The old Colonel shook his head silently, but it was Pietro who supplied the definitive answer, speaking for everyone in that audience. *"Buh?"* he exclaimed, the sharp Roman noise of contempt and indifference exploding from his lips. Wayne's heroic soldiers rode off to their gallant encounter with the Apache to gales of scornful laughter.

One Saturday morning, Pietro appeared at my door and announced that he was going to give a party in my studio that evening. It was not going to be the usual sort of party I was accustomed to at all, he announced with a cheerful leer. He thought, however, that I would enjoy it, now that my acquaintanceship with him had served to break down a few of my more bourgeois prejudices. "My nephew Aldo is singing in the *varietà* tonight," he said. "There are several very beautiful girls in the *varietà*, with breasts like ripe oranges. Aldo will bring them here tonight, after the show. We will have a little music, a lot of wine and. . . ." He shrugged eloquently, his face alive with pleasurable anticipation. "We can go to see the show first, if you like. Aldo has a very beautiful voice. He is the best singer of *stornelli* on our street. We'll amuse ourselves, eh?"

The *varietà* Aldo had chosen to grace with his beautiful voice was being put on for two nights only, between showings of an old Totò movie, in a tiny, smelly, dirty little theatre behind the railroad station. The company, in addition to Aldo, consisted of an old *capo comico*, a straight man, an aging soubrette, and a chorus line of eight girls of assorted shapes and sizes. The *capo comico* told jokes in Roman dialect and played three boisterous off-color sketches with the straight man, the soubrette, and two of the more talented chorus girls. In between the comic scenes, the chorus line, skimpily dressed, lumbered awkwardly through several rudimentary dance routines and, led by the soubrette, paraded across the front of the stage and down a ramp around the orchestra pit, bouncing their ripe-orange breasts at the customers. During the second half of the program, Aldo, a thin young man with a very large Adam's apple, broad cheekbones, and a great mass of black, oily-looking curls, appeared, clutching a guitar. He was dressed in an ill-fitting dinner jacket, and he sang by tilting his head straight back in the air and aiming everything directly at the ceiling. He had a strong nasal tenor and could spin notes out endlessly, performing all the intricate improvised vocal turns required of a good singer of *stornelli*. "Songs of the people," Pietro explained to me during the applause after Aldo's first number. "Very old. This is the real music, the voice of the struggling masses. Aldo sings well—he can do anything with his voice—but his words are weak. Mere cynicism, not strong enough." I gathered from this description of his talent that Aldo was not a Communist.

After the show, Pietro and I went backstage and Aldo introduced us to the girls who were coming to our party. There were two of them and they were both named Maria; they were short and hairy, quite mousy-looking out of their spangled costumes, and they each had several gold teeth. Pietro was delighted with them. On our way back to my studio, as we boarded a streetcar and the girls stepped in ahead of us, their buttocks wiggling against the tight sheath of their skirts, Pietro nudged me heavily in the ribs. "What did I tell you, eh?" he whispered fiercely. "That Aldo, what an eye he has! Look at that! Melons and ripe oranges! *Popolane!* Girls of the people, American!"

The conversation all the way to my place remained scrupulously correct, even as we stood, packed tightly together, in the crowded trolley. We addressed each other formally in the third person singular, and I told the girls how beautiful I thought everything in Italy was. In my studio, the atmosphere became even more ritualistic, though neither Aldo nor Pietro seemed in the least concerned. They allowed the girls to converse with me, since I was the American exotic and the chief source of curiosity for them, and bustled about setting the stage. Aldo built a fire, then began uncorking wine flasks and spreading salami, *prosciutto*, cheese, and bread out on my desk; Pietro rearranged furniture, placing the bed and the couch against opposite walls and stacking my landlady's mounted canvases upright between chairs and wastebaskets around each area, so as to screen them off from the rest of the room. I saw all these arrangements going on in the background of the conversational minuet I was carrying on with the ladies by the skylight and I experienced several moments of real panic. The methodical preparation for what was evidently going to be an orgy seemed to have so little to do, to be so remote from my stilted talk about weather, famous landmarks, and ethnic habits. I imagined that we would all drink a lot of wine first, but I thought it would take a long time, two or three hours at least, to achieve the proper atmosphere of dissolution.

When he had finished laying out the food, Aldo sat down by the fire and began softly strumming his guitar. Pietro surveyed the results of his efforts, grunted with satisfaction, and joined the girls and me by the window. He had taken off his coat and tie, and his face looked flushed. *"Ciao, bella,"* he said to the nearest Maria and pinched her affectionately on the cheek.

"I'm hungry," she said, gazing eagerly at the food.

"Ah, so am I," said Pietro, steering her off toward the desk.

Aldo had begun to play a popular tango and I asked my Maria to dance. She nodded and we began to spin listlessly about the room, dancing between the canvas barriers. Moving about a foot apart, we had run out of conversation and I had no idea what to do next or how to achieve a feeling of intimacy with this little creature, whose head barely reached my armpit. I looked away from her and saw Pietro's Maria lean down over a plate of food she had been busily preparing for herself. Pietro was standing behind her, a little off to one side, and suddenly he reached out, grabbing his Maria by the buttocks and lifting her about a foot off the floor. "I'm hungry, too," he shouted, "but not for *prosciutto!"* The girl shrieked and Pietro spun her around, seized her in a bear hug, and rushed her across the floor toward the couch. They smashed through the improvised screen and collapsed on the bed, where they began happily to thrash about. *"Avanti, Americano!"* Pietro called out. "There's a bed, a girl, and privacy! Forward!"

I was paralyzed. Nothing in the preliminaries had prepared me for this onslaught, so I simply stood and stared helplessly at the extraordinary scene Pietro and his now willing partner were staging. But long before he even had the girl undressed, his massive, angry face appeared, glaring at me above a tangle of clothes and blankets. "Oh!" he exclaimed, waving me away and restoring the protective barrier of mounted canvases. "This is no circus, *amico mio!* You have your own piece!"

Aldo stopped playing. *"Ma che è? È pederasta questo?"* he demanded, indicating me.

Terrified, I retreated to the bed. Aldo began playing again, very softly, background music. From across the room the wild thrashing resumed, soon succeeded by long, significant pauses. It had all happened much too fast for me. Then I felt a small firm hand moving up my arm. I turned my head and found a round, smiling little face inches from my own, gazing at me out of warm, melting eyes. "It's not the first time, *tesoro?"* the girl whispered. "There is no need to be afraid."

"No, it's not the first time," I said, annoyed.

"Then you do not like me?"

"Of course I like you!"

"Then why don't we make love?"

Her arms, warm and clinging, went up around my neck and we sank into the covers together. I remember that Aldo, that musician of impeccable taste, switched just then to a garbled version of Ravel's "Bolero." *Well*, I thought, *there's something to be said for the Revolution after all!*

A few days after the orgy, the rains came again and lasted for nearly a week. The water did not come through the skylight this time (Pietro had done a first-rate job of caulking); it simply soaked through the walls. I would put my hand up against any part of the plaster and bring it away wet. I ran out of firewood and I soon despaired of even attempting to wade across the roof to the toilet. On the fourth day, I gave up, packed my clammy belongings, and moved across the river, into a cheap *pensione* off the Via Margutta. And so I lost track of Pietro for a while.

Later, after I'd gotten settled in my new neighborhood, I made an effort to go and see him. If he wasn't working, I'd find him somewhere around his old haunts, either in the wine shop or lounging about the streets. We'd greet each other effusively, slap each other on the back, reminisce about our wonderful party, and promise each other to do it again very soon. But for some reason we never did. I suppose it was because I became increasingly wrapped up in my own active life, which had nothing to do with Pietro and his street world of poverty, intermittent employment, and simple pleasures. We had never been able really to communicate across the gulf of time, upbringing, and social disparity that separated us, so that when it became an effort to meet, we eventually stopped trying. Occasionally, though, because Rome is a small city and one never quite loses track of anybody one has ever met, I would bump into him. We would always hail each other with grins and shouts of pleasure, spend a few minutes reminiscing, and part again, promising, of course, to get together in the near future.

The last time I saw him was on May Day, a couple of years after we first met. I was standing on a narrow sidewalk of the Corso, watching a Communist parade headed for a workers' rally in the Piazza del Popolo. Alcide De Gasperi's Christian Democratic government was then undergoing one of its periodic crises, and there had recently been considerable violent agitation throughout the country. Little had been done to solve any of Italy's chronic problems, especially unemployment and low wages, and the organized Left, a powerful alliance of Communists and Socialists, had been trying to seize power. Since they had been unable to gain it by the vote, they had been testing their strength in the streets, and you could tell that this crowd of marchers, shirt-sleeved and arrogant under its waving red banners, would make trouble if it could. The men wore red kerchiefs, sang and shook raised fists at us as they swept past on their way to the piazza, where Palmiro Togliatti would speak to them.

I was on my way to a singing lesson and had to get across the avenue, so I was standing in the front row of watchers, waiting for a break in the procession to scurry over. Suddenly, a large, hairy arm grabbed me by the shoulder and whisked me into the ranks of the marchers. I looked down into Pietro's sweaty, beaming face. "Hey, American," he shouted above the din of the crowd, "come with us! We're going to hear Togliatti and smash a few heads!"

I suppose I could have broken away from him, but I didn't. My sympathies have usually been left of center, I didn't much care for De Gasperi, and I had never been caught up in a movement before. It was a heady feeling to be part of a marching, singing throng, united in just protest against—what? Injustice, oppression, poverty, the status quo, all authority. Somebody grabbed my other arm and I was swept away. Linked together, singing, shouting, laughing, jeering, we poured down the Corso like the wave of the future and came dancing out into the piazza, where Togliatti, a tiny black speck high above our heads, a red flag with the hammer and sickle at his back, began to harangue us.

We were quite far away from the leader and unable to understand anything he said, but it didn't seem to matter. The marchers had come pouring into the piazza not to be convinced, but to roar approval. Pietro and I stood side by side and roared with the best of them. It was as if all honor, all truth, all courage, all justice had been concentrated on us, in that instant in time and never before in history. But it was only an instant, because something happened to change it. Togliatti was not interested in honor, truth, courage, and justice; he was interested in action and power, and the indistinct voice that screamed at us from a distance was the voice of hatred. The crowd felt it, stirred to its sinister music, and began to ebb and flow to its beat. I glanced at Pietro. His chin was raised, sweat poured down his face; he was shaking both fists over his head and howling like a beast. I became afraid and began to gaze about for possible avenues of escape.

Under the goading of that professional rabble-rousing voice, the irregular ebb and flow became a concerted surging movement that threatened to build rapidly into a tidal wave. Togliatti wanted that wave to spill out of the piazza, to roar angrily up the streets of the city, perhaps to sweep him into power on its crest, and his bitter voice screamed for it to happen. The crowd metamorphosed swiftly into a mob and began instinctively, blindly to organize itself; within minutes, I felt sure, it would begin to roll like a murderous avalanche through the middle of the city.

It was at this crucial moment that the police appeared; Mario Scelba, a tough, professional Sicilian cop who was then the Minister of the Interior, had been too quick even for Togliatti. His maroon-colored jeeps, packed with green-uniformed, club-swinging thugs, swooped suddenly in through the Porta Flaminia and began to spin into the center of the crowd, scattering waves of refugees against the walls of buildings, up the steps of churches, into every available doorway. Pietro and I ran with the rest. We took refuge in the narrow entrance of an apartment house, where we joined other screaming, enraged demonstrators. The jeeps soon reached the confines of the piazza, leaving a few huddled, bleeding forms on the cobblestones and a nest of marooned fugitives clustered like wasps about the Obelisk of Flaminius, while the rest of the mob streamed away in flight up the Corso, the Via del Babuino, the roads up into the Pincio, and out through the Porta Flaminia itself. The whole procedure had not taken more than ten minutes. Beside me, Pietro and several other tough-looking men were shouting insults at the police, but no one made any move to leave his refuge.

It was then that I noticed a lone adventurer. He was a thin, meek-looking little man in a dark clerk's suit and he had started to cross the piazza. We watched in amazed silence as one of the jeeps picked him out, came buzzing angrily up to him, and stopped inches from his bony knees. The little man glared angrily at the cops, then raised his cane and shouted, "Thirty years I've been crossing this piazza to my home! Imbeciles! Am I to be prevented now? Who has the right?" Then he calmly stepped around the jeep and proceeded on his way. One of the cops stood up and reached out for him, but a companion quickly hauled him back. The thousands of us huddled in our doorways and on steps watched his progress in silence. Another jeep swept past him, but no one touched him; he passed out through the Porta Flaminia unharmed. The incident broke all further resistance. Shamefaced, we came down from our posts and walked away. The cops sat stolidly in their jeeps, engines running, truncheons on their laps, and let us go.

Pietro and I said nothing to each other. It was too late now to go to my singing lesson and I walked him up to the banks of the Tiber. When it came time for us to part, I shook his hand and tried to banter with him in the old way. "I guess we are not all as brave as we thought, eh, Pietro?" I said, smiling.

He turned his head and spat. "Shut up, American," he said. "You know nothing about it. You are ignorant. You've never been beaten up. You've never seen a man die, or you'd have learned what fear is. We are not heroes or saints, American. We are only men. That old man is too old to care and, anyway, he is of the ruling classes, you could tell. A worker tries that and those Fascist worms will kill him. You know nothing. I am sorry for you."

Without another word or glance in my direction, he walked glumly and permanently out of my life.

CHAPTER SIX

A LITTLE FAT
IN THE THROAT

A few months after my own arrival in Rome, Arthur Valentine, an old friend of mine from New York, came to Italy to launch what he had always been certain would be a glorious operatic career. Since I had preceded him and had already embarked on my own course of vocal studies, it was only natural that Arthur, who had never been abroad, should expect me to help him. We had been childhood friends, and from the beginning our mutual passion for grand opera had linked us inseparably. Though, as Arthur and I grew up, we had seen each other less and less frequently, we had always made it a point to keep in touch and express interest in each other's activities.

Arthur was a fiercely dedicated soul. Whereas most of the young voice students I knew, myself included, would have been quite content to become merely good opera singers, Arthur wanted only to be a great one. From the very beginning, with a single-minded and unshakable faith in himself, he had consecrated his life to his career. Unlike most aspiring young singers, for instance, he never condescended to perform in public. "I'm not ready yet," he would say. If, at a party, somebody asked him to oblige with a song, he would adopt an expression of lofty indifference and firmly decline, because no true artist could possibly be expected to give the best of himself in such casual circumstances. His parents, who were the only people ever privileged to hear him sing, readily admitted that Arthur had a long way to go. "But the quality is beautiful," his mother would say. His father would nod agreement and add, "Yes, it's all a question of training. Arthur must study."

Since leaving New York I had not heard directly from Arthur. Once, however, a mutual acquaintance passing through Rome brought me word of him and I knew that he was still in New York, still diligently studying through the hot summer, still refusing to give any public exhibition of his talent. I remembered him saying once that seven to ten years was the minimum amount of time required to train a voice properly and that thirty was still young for a male singer. (Women's voices, Arthur conceded, matured more quickly.) "Caruso never had *his* high notes till he was thirty," he was fond of saying. It was thus made clear to everybody that, since he was only in his early twenties, he couldn't possibly be expected to perform anywhere yet and that everyone would simply have to be patient. Meanwhile, he continued to study privately with various teachers and lived at home with his parents. His father, a partner in an accounting firm, paid all his expenses and gave him a generous allowance, most of which was spent on opera tickets, scores, and rare old recordings of such luminaries from the golden age of song as Caruso, Bonci, Ruffo, Amato, and Chaliapin.

Sometime in August, I received a letter from him. It was full of glowing accounts of his progress and exuded that immense confidence in his destiny that had always characterized him. According to this letter, he was almost ready to make his debut and would, of course, begin his career in Italy, since, he said, there was no way for a young singer to break into opera in America. He planned to spend several years establishing himself in the principal European opera houses, after which, bolstered by his continental successes, he would return in triumph to New York and leading roles at the Metropolitan Opera House. Apparently I had been chosen to help him fulfill his destiny because the letter concluded by remarking how lucky it was that I was already in Rome. Would I please find him a place to live, prepare a budget of weekly living expenses to present to his father, and make a thorough survey of operatic conditions in Italy? He was arriving in late September, and I was to arrange to meet him at the boat in Naples.

I answered this letter as thoroughly as I could, though I'm afraid my survey of professional opera in Italy must have seemed sketchy to him. I had been studying hard myself for several months, but I was so far away from my own debut that I had no idea how one went about arranging for such an important event. Taking into account Arthur's Lucullan tastes, I reserved a large room for him at a Swiss *pensione* over the Spanish Steps, quarters far grander than the relatively grubby ones I then occupied in a tiny hotel on a back street off the Corso. I heard nothing further from him until shortly before his arrival and, on the day he was scheduled to dock, I took a bus down to Naples to meet him.

Except for the fact that he was losing his hair prematurely and had put on a good deal of weight, Arthur hadn't changed very much. The summer seemed only to have reinforced his confidence and lent authority to his pronouncements, which were now vast and definitive on all subjects. When I commented on his weight, he smiled happily. "All the great singers were too fat," he said, plucking at his double chin. "A little fat in the throat is an absolute must to cushion the tones."

On the way back to Rome, he ignored the scenery and talked enthusiastically about his plans. He intended to spend that winter perfecting his technique and working on his repertoire; in the spring he would begin to audition for the agents. He plied me with questions: Who were the best agents, the best accompanists, the best impresarios? Would the critics review his debut? Was there prejudice against foreign singers? I answered as best I could, and then it suddenly occurred to me that I had never heard Arthur sing.

"What kind of a voice have you?" I asked.

"I'm a lyric tenor," Arthur said. "Actually, the voice is big, almost dramatic, but the quality is soft—velvety, really—and I have a phenomenal top." He plucked thoughtfully at his chin. "You know," he added, "that's the secret of all great singing—hit the high note and hold it till they melt in their seats."

The first few days of Arthur's stay in Rome were hectic for me. He didn't know anyone and couldn't speak a word of Italian, so I felt obligated to look out for him. I was spending more time getting Arthur settled than I was on my own career, but I consoled myself with the thought that eventually Arthur would establish a routine of his own and I wouldn't have to see him so often. The main obstacle to this happier arrangement was Arthur's ignorance of the language, but here his operatic training helped. Of course, he couldn't go around addressing young women in Italian with such readily accessible phrases from the operatic repertoire as "sweet child of love" and "come, let us pledge our troth," but it was a start. And Arthur tackled the language problem with the same dedication he had brought to his voice training. It wasn't long before he was making himself understood, and, though his grammar was incredible, his pronunciation was accurate.

Gradually, as Arthur began to master Italian and meet some of the other American voice students in the city, I did begin to see less of him. But the respite was brief. My life had only just settled back into its own familiar routine when Arthur telephoned me one morning. "I've got to move out of this *pensione*," he announced. "Today!"

"Why?" I asked.

"They won't let me practice," he said.

I found out later that Arthur had rented an upright piano and had been in the habit of practicing his scales two hours each morning. Several of the tenants had complained, and Arthur had precipitated a crisis by refusing to alter his schedule to the afternoon, when no one would have been around to object. The plump Swiss woman who ran the *pensione* was very upset about it, but Arthur was adamant. Nothing was as important as the proper care of his voice, he said, and it required that he practice his scales in the morning. "I have to warm up the chords for the day," he told me.

By the afternoon, Arthur had found an apartment and he offered to share it with me. It was a large one in the Parioli, a fashionable residential area of villas and modern apartment houses, but Arthur assured me it would be well within our means. "It's very large and L-shaped and there's a piano," he told me. "It's owned by this very distinguished Bulgarian sculptress. Her husband disappeared during the war and she needs the money. We can have the large part of the L and she'll occupy the small part, which is just two rooms at the back, behind the kitchen. The only awkward thing is we'll have to share the bathroom, but that should be okay. She has a couple of kids, but they're at school and won't be in the way. We'll have the piano to boot. What do you say?" When I heard the price, it was still out of my reach, but Arthur would not accept my refusal. "Never mind," he said, "I'll pay two-thirds. I can afford it and this is too good a deal to pass up."

We moved in that evening. The Bulgarian sculptress was on hand to show us around and lay down the ground rules. She was a large, fluttery woman with a massive bosom, a baritone voice, and the manners of a dowager empress. "I am Ariadne von Pekov," she said in Italian, introducing herself to me at the door and thrusting a hand into my face for a ceremonial kiss. "You may call me simply Madame, though I am actually a good deal more. My husband was a Cavalier." She turned and grandly led the way through the rooms we were to occupy.

I began to think that Arthur had stumbled onto a good thing. Our part of the apartment consisted of two nicely furnished, good-sized bedrooms with small balconies, and a large sitting room, which contained the piano (a baby grand), a radio-phonograph, some easy chairs, a sofa, and one of Madame von Pekov's favorite works, a plaster statue of a naked Brunhild with breasts and thighs every bit as impressive as those of Madame herself. "I have left you this statue," she explained, patting its colossal buttocks affectionately with her open hand. "I hope you will not mind. There is no room for it in the back and I am very attached to it. One of my earliest masterpieces." We assured her that the statue would be safe in our care and that we were most happy with our living arrangements. At the end of the tour, Madame fixed us both with a severe eye and delivered her final pronouncement. "About women," she said. "I am an artist and a woman of the world, therefore I am fully aware of the needs of the flesh. Unfortunately, there is merely one bathroom and one front entrance. I am the mother of two impressionable children not yet at the age of discretion. I do not demand celibacy. You are not monks. All I must insist on is continence in the evenings and on weekends, when I and my children are in the house. During the day they are in school and I am out. The afternoons are propitious. However—" and she held up a large cautionary index finger—"at all times you must bear in mind that I am not occupying a bordello."

I was a little embarrassed by this speech, but Arthur, who had been bouncing around the apartment, humming happily to himself, waved a hand in the air. "No necessity to worrying, Madame," he said in his strange Italian, "I am here to studying the voice. Not time there is for flesh. Damaging it is to voice box and beauty of tone. House to remain among the virgins."

Oddly enough, this speech seemed to satisfy Madame von Pekov. She smiled, turned, and moved grandly away down the hall to her own quarters.

During the first few months Arthur and I shared the apartment, I never really heard him sing. To earn some extra money, I had begun to do some translating and free-lance reporting for several American newspapers and magazines, so I was usually out of the house on weekday mornings, when Arthur vocalized. On weekends he rested his chords. I never pressed him because I knew how he felt about it. "You can't just ask an artist to open his mouth and sing," he explained. "There has to be a mental preparation as well as a physical one. The rapport between an artist and his audience must be *simpatico*."

Though Arthur declined to sing, he was not at all reticent about airing his theories, which were all overwhelmingly absolute, and he was merciless about imitating the mannerisms and techniques of other singers. A baritone we knew was being taught to funnel pear-shaped tones through pursed lips, and for several days Arthur paced up and down the apartment, hooting. Another friend of ours believed in focusing the tone toward the bridge of the nose, and for a week or so Arthur went around holding a finger to his nose and making unpleasant nasal sounds. He would also perform these imitations in public, often in the corridors of Rome's Teatro dell'Opera, where young singers would gather from the cheap seats in the balcony between the acts of the opera to discuss the performances of the professionals onstage. Arthur spared nobody, not even the best singers of the day. According to him, no baritone since Mattia Battistini had ever had full command of his vocal resources, and it was a scandal that a supposedly first-rate opera house would tolerate the sort of caterwauling he was being subjected to during the current season. "I wouldn't think of appearing in public with the sort of limited technique these people have today," he once announced. "When I debut, I'll be in full control of everything I do." Needless to say, Arthur was not popular, but this didn't seem to matter to him; he cared only about being right.

He rarely talked about his own progress, but I knew that he was working very hard on his repertoire with a certain Maestro Campagno, one of the most expensive operatic coaches in the city. The week of his arrival I had arranged an audition for him with my own teacher, a celebrated retired baritone with a distinguished roster of pupils, but Arthur had telephoned me after singing for him to tell me that I had put myself into the hands of a charlatan. After that experience I had allowed Arthur to find his own way and somehow he had managed to place himself with Campagno. "It isn't that he knows much more than I do," Arthur had explained, "but at least he isn't messing around with my basic technique. And he has contacts with the opera house and a lot of impresarios, so he'll be useful later on." The only serious crisis Arthur had with the Maestro developed over a disagreement in the study of a duet from *Tosca* and it concerned the exact location of Arthur's passage note into the upper register. The Maestro maintained that it lay at F; Arthur was equally certain that he could pass only on F-sharp. But, just when an impasse seemed to have been reached and I expected at any moment to hear Maestro Campagno denounced as a quack, Arthur gave way. "The Maestro was right," he said cheerfully. "I can take those F's open, but the tone is too white."

One day, toward the end of winter, Arthur came home with a package under one arm and bounded into the living room. "I have a surprise for you," he announced. "You're going to hear me sing."

"What's the occasion?" I asked.

Arthur smiled broadly. "The Maestro and I agree that I'm almost ready."

"Ready to audition?"

"To debut," Arthur said. "I want you to listen to this." He ripped open the package, extracted a recording, and slapped it on the turntable of the phonograph. "You're going to flip," he added, waiting for the machine to warm up.

A few seconds later, a large, dark voice singing the serenade from *Cavalleria Rusticana* filled the room. My initial reaction was amazement that Arthur apparently really did have a good voice and knew how to use it. The quality was not unusually beautiful, but it was fairly impressive, especially on the high notes, which were well-focussed and ringing. When the last echoes had died away, I said, "That's pretty good, Arthur."

Arthur laughed. "Good? How did you like the top notes?"

"Fine, fine."

"It's like I told you," he said happily. "You have to whack them and sit there." He turned the record over. "Now listen to the duet."

Once again Arthur's top notes began to reverberate around the apartment, accompanied this time by an equally big soprano. "Katrinka Mirovic," Arthur said, when the record was over. "She also studies with the Maestro. You like her?"

"She's good," I admitted.

"She's a Yugoslav, and we've been working a lot together," Arthur said. "In fact, we're thinking of putting on a joint recital in a couple of months to get ourselves launched."

"Isn't that going to be expensive?"

"Sure," Arthur said, "but it's better than auditioning for agents and impresarios. This way, if we get the critics to attend, the agents will have to come to us and we can make our terms with the opera houses. I told Trinka all about it and she agrees with me. I'll have to pay for the whole thing, but it'll be worth it. She's good, don't you think?"

I had never before heard Arthur compliment another singer and he must have guessed what I was thinking, because he smiled and said, "Yes, Trinka and I have been dating. You'll like her a lot. She's a real artist." He grew suddenly solemn. "I'd appreciate it," he said, "if you could manage to be out on Thursday afternoons from now on."

He introduced her to me a couple of weeks later, but I never quite knew what to make of her. She spoke hardly any Italian and even less English, and she seemed to be totally uninterested in her surroundings. She was a large girl with a broad, flat face and small, black eyes all but hidden between a heavy brow and plump cheeks. She was evidently capable of sitting with bovine placidity for hours, because every time I met her she was planted like a huge bush on our sofa, her hands folded in her lap, her gaze focussed blankly on some point in the air not more than six inches from her nose. She must have been fond of Arthur, because they hardly ever missed a Thursday afternoon together in our apartment, though I had never even caught them holding hands. "That Katrinka," Arthur once confided to me, "she doesn't say much, but is she passionate! You ought to get yourself a steady girl, Bill. If you don't overdo it, it will do your voice good, add maturity to it."

Aside from his purely musical activities, Arthur might just as well have been living in New York, for all the interest he took in

Italy and Italian life. He had mastered enough of the language to get himself through the day and accomplish his objectives, but he had no curiosity at all about the land in which he was a temporary visitor. He had no Italian friends and seemed to regard his acquaintances with suspicion. When he wasn't with Katrinka, he spent most of his time in one of the two English-language movie houses or sitting, surrounded by other Americans, at Doney's, a large sidewalk café on the Via Veneto that was largely patronized by tourists. There he would order himself a Coca-Cola or a ginger ale and read the *Rome Daily American* or *Time* from cover to cover. He wrote long letters home in which he spoke exhaustively of his vocal progress and of his future plans, but, to judge by the portions he read aloud to me, his parents could safely have assumed that he was writing them from some provincial American capital in the Midwest. Arthur didn't even like Italian food and ate every night at the Club Americano, a smoky dive on the Via Gregoriana that sported a juke box and served up hamburgers and milk shakes. I often wondered what, if anything, Arthur thought about aside from opera.

Then, late one afternoon, he appeared in the apartment in a glow of enthusiasm. "Guess what?" he said. "The most extraordinary thing happened today! I got the best of an Italian."

"How's that?" I asked.

"Well," Arthur said, "I was sitting at Doney's this afternoon, having a Coke, when this Italian fellow came up to me and asked me if I spoke English. When I said I did, he introduced me to this other man, and they asked me if I could settle a problem for them. The other guy didn't speak English, see, so only one of them could do the talking."

"Arthur," I said, beginning to realize dimly where this conversation was leading, "Arthur, you didn't—"

Arthur cut me off with an impatient wave of the hand. "Wait a minute," he said, "let me finish. One of these guys was a sailor from some ship in Naples and he had to get back to it tonight because the boat sails out early tomorrow morning. The other guy was a customer. The sailor had just arrived from a trip to the Near East and he had this bolt of valuable cloth with him which this other fellow wanted to buy, see, so—"

"So because the sailor couldn't wait and the customer didn't have the money on him to pay for the cloth," I said, interrupting him, "they asked *you* to pay for the cloth until the customer could arrange to go home and get the money. And they gave you the bolt of cloth to hold as security until the customer could reimburse you. He's arranged to meet you later tonight or tomorrow morning."

Arthur gaped at me. "How did you know that?" he asked.

"For God's sake, Arthur," I said, "you've fallen for the oldest con game in the world."

"What do you mean?"

"The guy will never show up," I said.

"But I have the cloth."

"What did you pay for it?"

"Thirty thousand lire."

"The cloth is worthless, Arthur," I said, unable to repress a smile.

Arthur shook his head. "Don't be silly," he said. "I know cloth. First of all, the guy will probably show up tomorrow. I arranged to meet him right there, at Doney's. But if he doesn't, I'll have the cloth and I'll make myself a suit out of it."

I tried my best to look serious. "Arthur," I said, "believe me, the cloth is worthless."

"I have it right here," he said. "You want to see it? It's good cloth."

"I don't have to see it," I said. "I know it's no good."

"You don't know anything about cloth," Arthur said. "*I* do."

Arthur's reassurance began to irritate me a bit. "How much do you want to bet?" I asked him.

"Anything you like," he said. "I know cloth."

"I'll bet you another thirty thousand," I said.

"You're on," Arthur answered, stalking from the room.

The next day, after waiting nearly an hour on the Via Veneto for the purchaser to appear, we went to see a fashionable tailor on the Via Condotti. Arthur carried the precious bolt of cloth under his arm, but he had wrapped it carefully in tissue paper and wouldn't allow me to finger it. Inside the tailor shop, I introduced myself to the proprietor, a short, plump man with a fringe of graying hair above his ears. He had a small, oval face concentrated around a stubby nose, and a shrewd, closely set pair of eyes that blinked at us through thick spectacles and the smoke drifting up into his face from the stub of a burning cigarette that dangled from his lower lip. "My friend here," I said, "has acquired a valuable bolt of cloth from a gentleman on the Via Veneto."

I went on to explain how Arthur had acquired the cloth, and the tailor began to laugh. "The cloth is worthless," he said, grinning.

"My friend wishes to have a suit made from it," I said, with some relish.

"What for?" the tailor asked. "To make a mockery of himself?"

"It's good cloth," Arthur insisted.

"Permit me," the tailor said, taking the package from under Arthur's arm. He quickly ripped away the tissue paper, took a corner of the cloth between thumb and forefinger and rubbed briskly. He giggled. "It is made of dried grass," he said.

"I'll take it to another tailor who knows something about it," Arthur said angrily.

"Why would he lie to you, Arthur?" I asked.

The tailor removed the cigarette stub from his lower lip and applied the glowing end to a piece of the cloth. There was a whooshing sound and a little tongue of flame leapt up at us. The tailor dropped the cloth to the floor and ground the fire out beneath his foot.

"He's ruining the cloth," Arthur said.

"Let him take the cloth elsewhere and have a suit made from it," the tailor said affably. "But he must not wear it in public because, if by some unfortunate chance someone should flick cigarette ashes upon him, he would instantly become a human torch."

Arthur stamped out of the shop, leaving the precious cloth behind. That night I found an envelope on my bed containing thirty thousand lire. I took it and walked into his room. Arthur was lying on his bed, propped up against his pillows and studying an opera score. "Here," I said, dropping the envelope on his bureau, "you made a mistake. I don't want the money. You just made me a little sore."

Arthur did not look up from the score. "Keep it," he said. "I would have, if I'd won the bet. Take it now or I'll just have to give it back to you tomorrow."

"I'd rather just hear you say you'd made a mistake," I said. "Honestly, Arthur—"

"The only mistake I made," Arthur said, "was in trusting an Italian. But I'll never do *that* again. After Trinka and I make our debut and the impresarios begin to offer us contracts, I'll hire a good American lawyer, that's what I'll do. Actually, I'm glad this happened. It taught me a lesson."

I didn't think it had taught Arthur the sort of lesson he might have benefited from, but I knew it was useless to argue with him. I pocketed the money and left him alone, still invincible.

I went out of town on a story for a couple of weeks and came back to find Arthur and Katrinka busily preparing for their joint recital. Arthur had rented a hall in the Circolo Artistico, on the Via Margutta, a date had been announced, and a publicity release had been sent out to the newspapers. It stated that the young American tenor, Arturo Valentino, would be making his debut with the kind assistance of the noted Yugoslavian soprano, Katrinka Mirovic. Mr. Valentino would sing a group of Italian classical songs and German lieder. Miss Mirovic would sing two Rossini arias and a group of Serbian folk songs. Mr. Valentino and Miss Mirovic would then join forces in several operatic duets. Arthur showed me a letter from his father. "Everyone in the family is very excited," it read in part. "Please keep us posted and wire excerpts from all the reviews collect."

Arthur and Katrinka had been rehearsing regularly in the apartment, so I was able to keep in close touch with their progress, but this came to a sudden end one afternoon with the majestic appearance of Madame von Pekov in our living room. I was then alone in the apartment, and I was surprised to see Madame, who had been a model landlady and had kept strictly to her own end of the flat since we had taken possession. "You will excuse me, I am sure," she said, as I rose to my feet, "but it is necessary that I consult with you."

"Certainly, Madame," I answered. "Please sit down."

"I am here to inform you that these afternoon rehearsals must stop," Madame said, not budging from her stance in the doorway.

"Has Arthur been making too much noise? I thought it was all right to practice during the day," I said. "Miss Mirovic and he are preparing a joint recital—"

"I know nothing about such things," Madame said, "but you will recall that, when you both moved in, I made certain allowances and established certain procedures designed to protect my children from worldly contamination."

I nodded, wondering what indiscretion Arthur might have committed.

"On Saturday afternoon," Madame continued, "a forbidden hour, I returned home with my children to discover Signor Valentino and this woman in the bathtub, splashing water on each other. This is intolerable and must cease. You will understand that I am not a prude, but Miss Mirovic is no longer welcome in this house, and any repetition of the incident will require me to cancel our lease. I say this to you, because I do not wish to embarrass Signor Valentino, who was not aware of my presence in the apartment at the time. Fortunately, I was able to divert the attention of the children to other matters. I am sure you understand and I apologize for having to speak to you in this manner." She turned and sailed out of the room.

Katrinka disappeared from my life and so, for much of the time, did Arthur. I knew, however, that they had found another place to meet and that work on the concert program was proceeding apace. "It's going to be very exciting," Arthur told me. "Trinka has a great voice and I just know we're going to make a real splash with this debut."

I wasn't the only person in Rome eagerly awaiting Arthur's debut. He had become something of a celebrity in the closed-in world of the voice students, and there wasn't a young singer we knew in Rome who wasn't planning to be at the concert. I knew that Arthur would have to be very good, because his strong opinions and his self-confidence had not made him popular. He would be facing a highly critical audience and, I guessed, one quite prepared to derive pleasure from his possible failure. However, Arthur remained outwardly unperturbed. The night before the concert, he appeared in my bedroom and said, "Trinka's very nervous. I hope she doesn't mess up my debut. I think I'm going to be in the best voice of my life."

When, on the day of the concert, I arrived at the hall about half an hour early, I found the room nearly full. By the time Maestro Campagno, a tall, thin man with lean cheeks and a parrot's beak of a nose, appeared and seated himself at the piano, there were standees along the back wall and halfway up the sides of the room, which seated about three hundred persons. It was an extraordinary turnout for a debut by a couple of unknowns, and for the first time I began to worry a bit about Arthur. Everywhere I looked I saw a singer's face, and I remembered that Caruso himself had been chased out of Naples by just this kind of audience, during his debut at the San Carlo Opera House. Arthur was good but he was no Caruso.

Katrinka, gaudily attired in a voluminous purple dress that made her look as if she were peering out from the apex of a wigwam, now planted herself stolidly in front of the piano and launched impassively into Rossini. She sang without feeling, but her big soprano was impressive and she handled the complicated coloratura runs with ease. When she had completed her opening group of songs and lumbered offstage, the room echoed to solid applause and several shouted "bravos." I reflected that Arthur had worried unnecessarily about her nerves; she seemed to have none.

There was a curiously long pause before Arthur finally appeared. I saw Maestro Campagno suddenly turn on his piano stool and gesticulate urgently toward the wings. It had become ominously quiet in the hall. Someone at the back of the room snickered, but, just when I began to think something must have happened, Arthur, looking intense in a dark-blue business suit, emerged and took his place in front of the piano.

Even before he opened his mouth I could tell he was in trouble. His eyes stared blankly over the audience out of a sickly pale face and his hands clutched at each other convulsively at belt level. Maestro Campagno had to strike a loud chord several times to prod him, and an endless minute passed before Arthur emitted a sound. When he did finally begin to sing, I couldn't believe my ears. That dark, rich voice I had grown used to hearing around the apartment had somehow become reedy and white, with thin, flattened top notes and little volume. Nor did it improve with time. Arthur strolled on and offstage like a somnambulist, and in his duets with Katrinka he was all but drowned out. After his opening group, people began to drift silently away, and the room was half-empty when the concert came mercifully to an end.

I was sure Arthur was ill and, after it was all over, I rushed backstage. He was nowhere to be found. Katrinka's angry, red face peered at me out of a dressing room. "Dot Ortoor!" she said. "Vot *ein* fiasco! *Und* me he tells not to be narvoos! *Ein* fiasco!"

I ignored her and caught up in the foyer to Maestro Campagno, who was calmly putting on his overcoat and shaking his head sadly. "Where's Arthur?" I asked.

The Maestro shrugged. "He rushed away," he said.

"What happened, Maestro?" I asked. "Was he sick? That wasn't his voice we heard out there."

The Maestro smiled grimly. "Signorino, I will tell you something," he said. "To talk about singing and to sing in a room, that is one thing; to face that great beast which is the public is another. Your friend Arturo had to be pushed onto the stage. He is not alone. I, too, was one of the great studio singers of my era, but in the theatre—" and here the Maestro sadly turned his palms out. "There is no explaining it, Signorino."

Arthur and I never discussed his career again, but in the weeks succeeding his debut I noticed several significant changes. Cigarette butts began appearing in our ashtrays, and he stayed out late at night. He continued to study, but there was no more talk of a debut or of his plans to audition for anyone. His personality improved a good deal. He stopped criticizing other singers and, though he had stopped dating Katrinka, he once said to me, "She's going to have a career, you know. Not a great career—she has no taste—but an adequate one. She has guts." And on another occasion, I overheard him talking to another American singer during an intermission at the Teatro dell'Opera. "You don't like the man's technique?" Arthur said. "All right, he may not have much technique, but he isn't afraid to stand up there and sing. That's half the battle." Then, shortly before Thanksgiving, I came home from another trip to find him gone. He had left me a note, thanking me for everything and saying that he wanted to get home for the holidays.

I didn't see him again for several years, not till I was back in New York. I had heard that he had gone into his father's accounting firm and was doing quite well. One day I walked into a cocktail party and spotted him among a group of people I didn't know. "Yes, I made my debut in Rome," he was saying, "but you know something funny? I didn't have it. In fact, I was so nervous I don't even remember going on. It's just one of those things no man can prepare for."

CHAPTER SEVEN

OPEN SEASON
ON TURKS

he first decent apartment I lived in during this period of my life was acquired by a systematic campaign of terror that I still look back on with mingled awe and shame. The events all seem somewhat preposterous and childish to me now, but I remember that at the time, in the midst of an acute housing shortage, nothing seemed as important to me as the acquisition of a private room free from the depressing communal atmosphere of a cheap *pensione.* I could never, on the small monthly allowance I received under the government's G.I. Bill of Rights, even have aspired to anything as elegant as the entire floor of a *palazzo,* if it hadn't been for my chance meeting with Max Daniels.

I had been in Rome about a year when I first met Max, early in the spring of 1949. I had gone up to register for another term of courses at the Fraschini Institute and I found him in the lobby, a dark, stocky figure in a seersucker suit and a battered straw hat. He was holding a load of books on his lap and gazing with mild interest at the harassed young woman behind a school desk who was doing her best to cope with a noisy crowd of American applicants. I sat down beside him to await my turn with the forms and he immediately struck up a conversation. "My name is Daniels," he announced abruptly. "Max Daniels."

We shook hands and one of the books slid off his lap. He cursed and scooped it quickly off the floor. "Where can I unload these?" he asked.

I must have looked blank.

"Sell them," he elaborated.

"Any secondhand bookstore," I said. "There are several of them up the street. I'll show you."

"Thanks."

His abrupt, nonchalant manner and the cocky Western twang of his speech intrigued me. Most of my American acquaintances in Rome were Easterners, or at least educated in Eastern schools, and they all seemed to fit quite well into their Italian surroundings. Max, on the other hand, exuded an atmosphere of total Americanism, an aura that immediately called up visions of endless prairies basking benevolently under the watchful eye of the Tribune Tower. I couldn't imagine what he was doing in Rome.

"Did you just get here?" I asked.

"Yes."

"From where?"

He smiled. "From the heart of the old U.S.A., Chicago."

"Staying long?"

"What I've seen, I like," he said. "You know, it's really something for a provincial like me to find himself chasing the ghost of old Cesare Borgia down these streets. Wop is becoming a very big word in my vocabulary."

He didn't yet know what he was going to study and when I asked him about the books, he said, "Who knows? They give me a book allowance and I need the money. Seventy-five bucks a month can't take you very far, even in old Italia. I took the biggest books I could find."

"But why Italy?" I asked.

He shrugged. "It's in the wind, isn't it?"

After we had filled out all the forms and handed them in to the registrar, we strolled out together and headed for the street with the secondhand bookstores. Max was having trouble with the books and I helped him carry them. In my load I spotted an edition of Manzoni's *I Promessi Sposi*. To make conversation, I commented on what a fine novel it was and the influence it had had on Italian literature.

"The Italians can't make it as thinkers," was his answer. "I tried Dante. Boy, *there* was a real *fool*."

I was still mulling that one over when we entered the first bookstore. Eventually, we entered them all; and with me haggling and Max deciding, we separated the clerks from about twelve thousand lire. After emerging into the street again, Max suggested a beer and I took him to a German place I knew about on the Piazza Santi Apostoli. We sat down at one of the sidewalk tables and ordered a round of dark.

"Thanks for helping me with the books," Max said. "Now tell me about the Fraschini."

"What do you want to know?"

"The only thing that matters—how does it work?"

I told him what I knew. Until the influx of post-war American students, the Fraschini Institute had been only a shabby business and secretarial school down whose dim, sordid corridors padded impoverished lower-middle-class Italians in quest of enough shorthand and bookkeeping to improve their hopeless economic status as government clerks. (Rome, like Washington, is primarily inhabited by civil servants.) Then word of the American government's generosity to studious veterans of world conflicts seeped through to Signora Fraschini, the agile, middle-aged lady who ran the school. She went to the American Embassy and placed her institute at the service of greater learning. Her timing was flawless and she proved to be flexible in her approach. Unlike the rigid and established schools, the Fraschini allowed you to enroll your own teacher on its faculty, thus qualifying everybody for the benefits. We came to her to study Italian, French, and German; painting and literature; history and economics; music and drama. The Fraschini Institute was swamped with American undergraduates and Signora Fraschini prospered. She rented an entire building to accommodate her school. Even those of us who were really studying something registered with her because we needed the official credits to qualify for all the money.

Max listened attentively to my brief analysis, punctuating it with nods and brief grunts to show that he understood fully, then switched topics. "And what are you up to?" he asked.

"I'm studying voice," I told him. "I'm a lyric tenor."

He nodded again. "Where are you living?"

"I'm sharing two rooms with a friend in a *pensione*," I said. "He's also a singer. It works out pretty well."

"Well, I know about an apartment," Max said. "The Hungarian who changes my money told me about it. It's big, three bedrooms, and it has balconies, lots of furniture, and reeks with Mediterranean charm. There's also a grand piano in good shape."

"How much?"

"Sixty Italian grands a month," Max said. "They'll take less if we pay in dollars."

"No kidding?"

"On my G.I. money I can't begin to carry it alone, but split three ways it would be a cinch."

"It's too good," I said. "There must be something wrong with it."

"There is," he said. "A couple of tenacious Turks."

It turned out that one room in the apartment, an otherwise most desirable one, was occupied by a pair of Turks who had been living there since before the war. According to Italian law, the owners found themselves unable to evict the Turks, who were paying a ridiculously low rental based on the pre-war value of the lira, though they were free to rent out the rest of the apartment. The Turks, who had a very good thing, were deaf to threats, entreaties, even bribery. The Italian landlord and his wife were frantic.

"Well, I guess it's out," I said.

"Don't you believe it," Max said. "Trust in American ingenuity. Now, what about your friend?"

"Walter? He'll love it. At the *pensione* they only let us sing an hour a day. Here we could practice any time."

"That's the idea," Max said.

The next morning we hunted up Max's Hungarian money-changer and went up to see the apartment, which proved to be every bit as good as Max had said it was. It occupied the top floor of a small Renaissance *palazzo* in one of the older sections of the city. The main entrance, off the living room, had a view over the Tiber and the rooms were enormous, with towering ceilings and walls on which were hung great, dark paintings teeming with saintly women and plump cherubs. The furniture was hideous but comfortable, and I found the piano to be only half a tone flat and basically sound. The Italian owners, an ancient count and his invalid wife, shuffled anxiously around behind us and seemed pathetically eager to woo us. We didn't see the Turks, but we knew they were there because we heard them muttering behind a closed door that led into one of the bedrooms. Once, on our way back from inspecting the kitchen, I turned around and caught the count in the act of shaking his fist and mouthing imprecations at the hostile door.

I wasn't at all sure what we were going to do about the Turks, but Max was serene and Walter, who had been testing the acoustics in the living room, was enthusiastic. He tried a scale up to B-flat and sat on it, cupping both hands behind his ears to get the full effect. "My God!" he said. "I sound like Caruso in here!"

Max chuckled. "Can you sing any higher, Pondrus?" he asked.

"It's Pondru," Walter said stiffly. "Like the French. You don't pronounce the final s."

"Sure. How high can you go?"

"E-flat over high C," Walter said. "I have nearly three octaves."

"Fine. And how long do you practice every day?"

"Well, that depends," Walter said. "I'd like to get in at least a couple of hours a day."

"Fine, fine," Max said, and rubbed his hands together.

None of this was making much sense to me. The count was standing there with a puzzled and slightly pained expression on his face, clasping and unclasping his hands. "Well, do we take it?" I asked.

"What do you say, Walter?" Max said.

"I'm for it."

"What about the Turks?" I asked.

Max brushed them aside. "Forget about them," he said. "They'll be gone in no time."

Before such quiet confidence my own doubts evaporated and I broke the news to the count, who immediately produced a lease, which we all signed. Max tipped the Hungarian money-changer and the apartment was ours, almost. That same afternoon we started to move in. Max took one bedroom, while Walter and I arranged to share the other one. The Turks remained invisible behind their locked door. After dinner, on the evening of our first day in the apartment, Max launched his campaign.

"I've seen them," he said.

"Who?"

"The Turks. I suggested they move out."

"What did they say?"

"They wouldn't discuss it with me," he said cheerfully. "Actually slammed the door in my face."

"What do they look like?"

"I don't know," Max said. "Middle-aged, surly professorial types."

"Well, I suppose if they won't move out, we can live around them," I said.

"Don't be ridiculous," Max said. "Sing, Walter."

"Now?"

"Of course."

Pondrus went over to the piano, struck a chord, and went up and down the scale.

"Not there," Max said. "Over here, where they can get the full benefit."

Walter went out into the hallway opposite the locked door and began running through his full repertoire of vocal exercises. "Boy," he observed during a momentary lull, "the acoustics out here are even better!" After the exercises, I sat down at the piano and we alternated in a few arias. Walter's voice wasn't very pretty and it occasionally strayed from the pitch, but it was robust. Max beamed, especially on the high notes, which Walter had a habit of holding as long as his breath lasted.

After more than an hour of this, just as Walter was going up for the first C-sharp in *A te, o cara*, Max suddenly began to wave him away from the door. No sooner had he retreated into the living room, than I saw the door violently flung open. A swarthy, enraged face protruded into the hallway and began to shout at us in what sounded like a blend of Turkish and Italian. After several minutes, the face withdrew and the door slammed shut again.

"That's the one with the beard," Max said. "You can see that it's going to be open season on Turks."

And that was only the beginning. Max threw himself into the siege with such dedication and fiendish intensity, sweeping us along in his wake, that the beleaguered Turks in their bedroom fortress found themselves all but cut off from the outside world. I never really understood what cold, inner flame drove Max to such collegiate excesses. He certainly never spent any time studying and was never seen at the Fraschini except on the days when checks were due. His whole life in Rome revolved around the situation in our apartment. It was as if the exhumation of the Turks was essential to his vision of himself as the American superman asserting his superiority over inferior peoples. But whatever the reasons, he never let up for a moment.

Not only were the Turks isolated in their one legal room (bathroom doors were kept locked at all times, the telephone in the foyer was disconnected, and an electrician was imported to separate them from access to heat and light), but they came and went in constant peril. Max rigged up a series of fearful traps (buckets, bricks, ball bearings, glue) and equipped us with artillery (tennis balls, marbles, hydraulic bicycle pumps). But his masterpiece was a dart game. From almost any part of our living room we could hurl our tiny missiles at a target erected in the front hall through which the Turks—pudgy, scurrying figures in dark suits, shielding themselves behind briefcases and magazines, foulmouthed and frenzied in their haste—were forced to pass in and out in order to keep alive. And then there was always Walter, our ace of trumps, his voice either raised in spontaneous song or recalled in electronic splendor through the amplifier of his gramophone.

It lasted almost a week. Early on the morning of the seventh day, the Turks cracked. It seems a miracle to me now that they lasted as long as they did under the weight of such an assault.

They capitulated on a Sunday morning, though not without one last desperate attempt to safeguard their low-cost stronghold. Max had persuaded Walter and me to invite all of our musical friends up for a sort of informal breakfast concert. We planned a long and varied program that got underway shortly after eight o'clock with the Triumphal March from *Aida*. We had about twenty voices for it, if you include Max and myself, and everyone sang loudly. It was such a success we ran through it twice before getting into the Tomb Scene from *Ernani*. Then followed excerpts from *Rigoletto* and *Traviata*. We had barely gotten into the swing of the Sextet from *Lucia* (Walter was flatting badly) when one of the Turks, the one with the beard again, came bursting out into the hallway and dashed past us toward the street, one hand busily tucking in his shirttails.

Of course we were prepared for this. When the police arrived, the irate Turk in the rear, they were confronted by a tranquil scene: Max, Walter, and I in solitude, sipping morning coffee to muted Mozart from the gramophone. Heated accusations from both Turks, suspicious questions from the confused officers, puzzled denials and calm assurances from us, the sudden planned appearance and emphatic support of our vengeful count, and the inevitable ensued—within half an hour we were all grouped in hostile array before a stern, irritated magistrate.

What seemed to be the trouble? the magistrate wanted to know.

The Turks shouted accusations and pointed fingers at us; we denied everything and were supported by the count.

The Turks were entitled to their privacy, the magistrate said. Had we invaded it?

No indeed.

What about the dart game? the Turks screamed.

An unfortunate accident, we said.

The obstacle course? The telephone? The locked doors? The singing? Above all, the singing?

Were we not entitled to live in the apartment as we chose? we asked. Were not the Turks entitled only to their own room? Why should they be allowed to dictate how people were to behave in an apartment over which they had no jurisdiction?

The magistrate nodded sympathetically.

The Turks screamed.

The magistrate berated them for their behavior in court.

Obvious paranoid types, said Max.

We are men of the world, said the count to the magistrate, and explained his position. Was not the count a respectable landlord? And was not the law in Italy bound by tradition and inclination to support the rights of the few over the many? Were not the rights of property sacred? Were not these upstanding young men *artisti* as well as representatives of the greatest and most generous ally in the world? What, after all, were the Turks? Foreigners, pagans, profiteers, and disturbers of the peace, Sunday's sacred peace at that.

The magistrate dismissed the charges.

The Turks became hysterical.

The magistrate exploded. A lecture was read and a fine was levied, accompanied by threats of prosecution and imprisonment. Case dismissed.

Neither Walter nor I had contributed much to these proceedings, but out in the street Walter turned to us and said, "You know, I think we were wrong."

"You sing," Max said, with a brief smile, "I'll dance."

The Turks moved out that afternoon and we never saw them again. I moved into the liberated bedroom and we settled with relief into a more tranquil routine. Once his mission had been accomplished, Max quickly lost interest in the apartment and we rarely saw him. After a few months he moved out and I heard that he had gone into partnership with the Hungarian money-changer. He spent a lot of time in Positano and Capri, though he always stopped by the Fraschini every month to pick up his credits. Walter and I spent a pleasant year in that apartment but at the end of it, the count wanted too much money and forced us to move out. I don't think he liked us very much and I can't say I blame him.

CHAPTER EIGHT

A SERIOUS GAME

L ike most Americans, I grew up believing that we are the only people in the world who really understand the romance of business. I used to assume that if we could only export our shiningly positive approach to money, our creative ingenuity, and, above all, our know-how, we could easily prevent the world's populations from succumbing to the horrors of Communism and other forms of tyranny. What we needed abroad, thought I, were fewer well-meaning but fuzzy-minded diplomats and more dynamic, idealistic businessmen, forward-looking fellows who would really get things done. I now realize, of course, that my childlike trust in native virtues was naive, to say the least, attributable perhaps to my incredible ignorance of money matters. Anyway, it wasn't until after I'd arrived in Rome and had almost become a partner in an international business scheme that I caught a glimpse of the abyss that separates two worlds.

During the time that Max, Walter, and I shared an apartment, I became aware that Max was involved in a number of business ventures that struck me at the time as quixotic. He plunged into them, however, with enthusiasm and unfailing optimism, apparently convinced that he would make his fortune in Italy. He was totally uninterested in whatever he was supposed to be studying at the Fraschini and he hardly ever went to class. He would only appear regularly at the school toward the end of each month, when study credits were recorded and checks were due. Most of his time was devoted to promoting his mysterious ventures and "deals," any one of which, he assured us, could come through in a big way and make him rich. Walter and I hardly ever saw him in the apartment; we'd catch glimpses of him around town, often in the company of his rather seedy Hungarian money-changer, Lazslo, and we'd hear occasional reports on the progress of his various enterprises. With his cocky, aggressive manner, Max soon came to typify for me the adventurous spirit of American capitalism and I was convinced he would make good. "It's the American century," he liked to say, "and everybody's dancing to the American tune."

One day, after an absence of several weeks, Max showed up at the apartment in the late afternoon and found me alone in the living room. I remember looking up from a magazine to find him in the doorway, smiling and rubbing his hands briskly together.

"Well, Caruso," he said, striding into the room and throwing himself into a chair, "still warbling away?"

"Oh, yes," I said. "And what have you been up to?"

"This and that," he answered, "this and that. Mostly I've been gambolling Dionysiacally about the rocks of fair Capri. Unfortunately, I ran out of lire."

"And how are all your projects working out?"

Max cocked an index finger into the air. "*The* project," he said quietly. "I'm going to open a night club."

"In Rome?"

"Of course," he said, "and I've got just the place. It's a cellar, full of strange magic nooks. We'll decorate it to suit the mood and drop a few of my Hungarians into it for flavor."

"But what kind of a night club?" I asked. "Mostly for music or—"

"The music of the spheres," Max said, cutting me off. "It can't miss."

The place Max had found had once been a German beer cellar. After the war it had been taken over by a series of Italian entrepreneurs who had opened a series of unsuccessful little clubs, all of which had folded. Max explained why: "You open a joint and play it for chic and you know what happens? All the chic people come and sit around staring at each other's clothes and sipping sherry while you go broke." After the failure of chic, the locale had been used as a cheap bar where men went to pick up girls. Inevitably, the police had closed it up, jailed the proprietor, and now it languished, waiting for someone else to try again.

"What makes you think you can make a go of it?" I asked.

"Don't you see?" Max said. "Magic, that's the secret of any successful club. You get the right sense of unreality in a place and everybody drinks. I've got it all figured out. Now all we need is the dough."

"How much do you think it will take?"

"About ten million lire," he said. "That's enough to take over the lease and the license, fix up the place, and get it open for drinking. The finer little touches can be added later, when the money starts to pour in."

"That's quite a chunk of capital."

"Are you kidding?" Max said. "It works out to only fifteen grand in real money. And for a whole night club."

"Do you have a prospect?"

"One beaut," he said. "He's done some speculating on the market through Lazslo and he might be willing to invest. All we have to do is convince him that the idea is sound, which is where you come in."

"Me?"

Max nodded. "The guy is an Italian citizen, but his father was American and he's a little confused about his identity, especially in the morning. Now, I can handle the American side—that will to success—but we need somebody to handle the Italian half. I have a feeling this guy panics easily and he'll need a lot of graceful Latin phrases to keep his mind off the horror of the actual business transaction." Max smiled at me. "And you speak a very reassuring Italian phrase."

"I still don't know what you want me to do."

"It's easy," Max said. "I want you standing by at all the negotiations. You're also half Italian, and if Pietro Lincoln—"

"What's his name?"

"Pietro Lincoln," Max said happily. "It's a boff, isn't it?"

"But what do I do?"

"You stick right beside him," Max said, suddenly very serious. "You'll be in the most Italian outfit you can assemble, one of those tight little suits with black, pointed shoes, and every time Lincoln starts to waver under the strain of having to be an American and write a check, you rush right over and prop him up again."

"How, for God's sake?" I shouted.

"Take it easy," Max said quietly. "All you have to bear in mind is that Italy is the land where people say yes when they really mean no." He paused and cocked a finger at me. "Do you understand the enormity of what we're asking Lincoln to do? He's to *risk* his capital for a *reasonable* return. Now, we know he's part American and that's what Lazslo and I are counting on. We also know his father is from Chicago, and that's another break. Breeding counts and the big American wind blows out of Chicago. But at some point along the way Lincoln is going to lose faith and become an Italian and that's where you come in."

"Why—why couldn't Lazslo handle him?" I said weakly. "He speaks better Italian than I do."

"A Hungarian?" Max said, amazed. "They're the most unreassuring people in the world. If you want magic, call on the Hungarians or the Irish. But what Pietro Lincoln is going to want is security. That's the last thing a Hungarian can promise." He stood up and began to pace restlessly about the room. "Besides, Lazslo is helpless with desire. His girl's a singer and he wants her to work in the club. We can't risk being too eager."

My head was spinning with the complexity of all this racial logic, but Max was impervious to my confusion. He gave me detailed instructions on where to meet the following morning for our first session with Lincoln and then he clapped me affectionately on the shoulder. "And there's five percent in it for you," he announced. "That's the way it's played in the big time."

The next morning, at eleven o'clock, I went to the address Max had given me, which turned out to be a grimy little coffee bar on one of the side streets off the Via Veneto. Max, Lazslo, and an exotic-looking girl were sitting expectantly at a corner table. I was wearing my only Italian suit, a black, single-breasted one I had bought in Naples, and I could see Max scanning me appraisingly.

"Where are the shoes?" he asked as I joined them.

I confessed I didn't own any Italian shoes.

Max shook his head over my offending Florsheims. "No little pointed ones? Hell, if Pietro looks down, he'll know he's alone."

"I'll go buy some," I said.

"There isn't time today," Max snapped. "Anyway, all we're

going to do is show Lincoln the place. Get some before the next meeting. And watch your necktie," he added, frowning. "That one leans a little to Princeton. Go buy yourself one of those raw silk jobs they sell on the Via Condotti. You've got to *look* authentic."

I sat down and Lazslo, looking very blue in the morning light, shook my hand limply and introduced me to the girl. She was slender and white, as frail and delicate-looking as expensive porcelain, with enormous light-blue eyes and a mass of frizzy, copper-colored hair. "How are you?" she asked in a strange little voice, extending a long, transparent hand. "You call me Poochie, all right?"

I squeezed her hand and told her I'd be delighted to call her Poochie. Max beamed and leaned back in his chair. "Oh, the magic, the magic," he said happily.

"Is not this exciting?" Poochie said. "I will sing very many very beautiful gypsy songs and make everybody cry."

Lazslo shook his head and looked at his watch. "Signor Lincoln comes not on time," he said.

Max seemed confident. "Capital is committed to making talent wait—a little," he said. "Cheer up, Lazslo." He turned to me. "Lazslo gets better as the day grows older," he said. "Hungarians are not much good before noon."

Poochie laughed sweetly, a sound of tinkling bells in distant meadows. "Oh, I am exquisite in the morning," she said and looked at Max. "Now?"

Max looked at his watch. "Now," he said.

Poochie opened her purse and withdrew a long, black cigarette holder. She stuck an Egyptian cigarette into it and Lazslo lit it for her.

"I want her to be working that holder when Pietro Lincoln arrives," Max explained. "It may make him wonder what's going on down at the other end."

Poochie inhaled ecstatically and began to puff clouds of pungent smoke into our faces. I sat there, trying to look properly ethnic, but I began to be assailed by doubts. Even in my Italian suit, no one, in the more than two years I had been living in Italy, had ever mistaken me for anything but an American. I was about to bring this problem up with Max when Pietro Lincoln arrived.

My back was to the door and I hadn't seen him come in, but suddenly he was there, standing by our table, bobbing his head up and down. Lazslo rose suavely to the occasion. "Ah, Signor

Lincoln," he said expansively, his Hungarian accent thickening on each succeeding syllable, "how charming that you should come."

Max and I stood up and shook Pietro Lincoln's hand; Poochie flicked ashes on the floor and displayed thirty-two marvellous teeth. Pietro Lincoln surveyed the teeth with amazement and sat down. Lazslo ordered a round of aperitifs and Max immediately leaned forward over the table and began to sell his dream. I settled back in my chair and looked at our capitalist.

He was a soft, round young man, probably in his thirties, with bright red cheeks that looked freshly scrubbed and a wide, pink mouth that seemed affable enough. His eyes were brown, small, and set alarmingly close together over a nose that violently contradicted the rest of his features; it was long and moist, pointed like a tapir's, and it seemed to be sniffing for guidance in all directions. His most extraordinary features were his eyebrows; they were thin and delicate, they looked plucked, and they were in constant motion. Whenever he spoke, they would execute a hypnotizing, grotesque little dance above his face, first shooting wildly up almost to the edge of his hairline, then plunging heavily down to shield his eyes, rising again to knit ferociously above the length of his nose. I began to have the feeling that perhaps Pietro Lincoln wasn't quite up to Max's extravagant hopes for him, but I had to admit that everything did seem to be going splendidly.

Max had been talking steadily, seriously, very convincingly about his plan for the club. He described it, I remember, as a haven for the weary and the oppressed, where thousands of exhausted fugitives from mundane realities would bask contentedly in an atmosphere that would represent a most felicitous blending of two world cultures. "What we have to offer is dreams," he said enthusiastically, "and that's what the world wants. Am I right?"

Pietro Lincoln nodded and executed his eyebrow dance. "Yes, yes, that is most interesting," he said. "And what is the investment required?"

"Fifteen million lire," Max said softly. "A trifle when you think of all we can accomplish."

Pietro Lincoln smiled, flung his eyebrows at the ceiling, caught them, knotted them securely above his nose and murmured in Italian, "Fifteen million lire. Yes, not a small sum. . . ."

Max whirled on me and I suddenly realized that my ethnic

moment had come. I had no idea what was required, but I rose valiantly to the defense of my five percent. I cleared my throat and smiled stupidly. "Why don't we go and inspect the location?" I said, also in Italian. "I believe it is very nearby."

Startled, Pietro Lincoln glanced at me, then he nodded and quickly stood up. "An excellent idea," he said. "Let us go."

On our way out, Max caught me by the arm and grinned conspiratorially. "You nailed him," he whispered. "Just keep doing it. Every time he starts to fade away into his Latin mystique, bomb him."

I nodded helplessly and we hurried after the others.

At first glance, the place Max had selected to lure the Italians into dreamland seemed highly unlikely. It consisted of several small, dark underground rooms with tiny barred windows looking out onto the street at sidewalk level. The floors and walls were filthy; great mounds of battered tables and chairs had been heaped untidily in various corners. The caretaker who showed us around, a sour old man with a face like a puckered orange, was dressed in old army fatigue pants and a torn undershirt. He shuffled along ahead of us from room to room, turning dim light bulbs on and off and casting contemptuous glances back into our faces as we peered hopefully into the gloom.

Max realized we were in trouble and wasted no time. When we reached the largest of the rooms, he turned to face Pietro Lincoln and flung his arms out at the walls. "Let me tell you about the murals I've got planned," he said. "Filmy girls in cloche hats seen through hazy pink mists, nymphs and satyrs gambolling in exotic foliage, elves and leprechauns bounding through primeval forests. . . ."

Max talked faster and faster. He filled the shabby rooms with his romantic visions, peopled them with the fantastic creatures of his imagination, forcing us to see not a string of dingy little rooms full of rubbish, but a chain of warm, cozy caverns echoing to haunting music and crowded with swarms of entranced customers, all eating and drinking expensively. For his pièce de résistance, he turned to Poochie.

"Can't you picture her?" he asked in a whisper. "A symphony of shimmering sequins, she stands motionless in a dim spot, she sings the ancient Magyar songs of despair and betrayal, of earthly love, heavenly torment." He turned back to face Pietro Lincoln, who seemed to have turned into a statue, and added, "There isn't a Hungarian gypsy alive, Pietro, who can't take you right out of this world!"

"Oh, isn't he a sweetie," Poochie chirped.

Abruptly, Pietro Lincoln began to shift his feet back and forth. "Yes, yes," he said hoarsely, "I see clearly what you mean."

"Then it's all set?" Max asked.

"We will see," Pietro said. "I must consult—"

"You do understand the metaphysic of the place?" Max asked. "The need for escape? The appeal of magic? The touch of hands in outer space?"

"Oh, perfectly," Pietro said, edging toward the door. "Telephone me tomorrow and we will make another appointment."

Out on the sidewalk again, after Pietro Lincoln had climbed into a taxi and driven away, Max laughed and rubbed his hands briskly together. "Bingo!" he said.

"Do you really think he'll put up the money?" I asked.

"Couldn't you tell?" Max said. "He only tried to wop out once."

"He left in a great hurry," Lazslo observed.

Max turned on him. "Lazslo, you're going to have to learn to subdue that Middle European gloom," he said. "I tell you, it's in the bag. Now all we have to do is make a date to sign contracts."

The next day, Max informed me that he had had some difficulty getting through to Pietro Lincoln, but an appointment had indeed been made for the following Monday morning, at Lincoln's apartment. Max and Lazslo went to work drawing up legal documents and, at Max's insistence, I went out and bought a raw-silk necktie and an expensive pair of handmade shoes.

Pietro Lincoln lived in an ultramodern apartment house, a huge, rust-colored ocean liner of a building in one of the most fashionable Roman suburbs. Once again dressed in my Neapolitan suit and mincing painfully along in my tight new shoes, I followed Max and Lazslo, who was carrying a heavy briefcase full of papers, into the elevator. "Remember now," Max said as we rode up, "be charming, but stick to business. No coffee-drinking or other frivolities until the papers are signed. And let me do the talking."

The door of Pietro Lincoln's apartment was opened by a tiny, dark creature of indeterminate sex who ushered us into an austere, barren room at the end of a long corridor and abandoned us. In the middle of the room, there was a walnut conference table surrounded by heavy wooden chairs, straight-backed, stiff, and elaborately carved; on the walls hung English hunting prints. There were no other furnishings. We sat down in the uncomfortable chairs and waited.

After twenty minutes, during which we heard no sound of movement from the rest of the apartment, Max opened the door and stuck his head into the hallway. He looked up and down, then shut the door and returned to his seat.

"I knew it," Lazslo said uneasily.

Max glanced at him scornfully, folded his arms, and stared imperiously at the door.

Finally, after another twenty minutes, as Lazslo became more and more depressed, we heard a murmur of voices and a rapid shuffling of feet out in the corridor. Suddenly, the door burst open and four beaming penguins, exuding an aroma of expensive cologne, waddled into the room and bowed.

"*Buon giorno*," said the first penguin, clasping Max's hand and smiling broadly. "Commander Giovanni Squarcialancia at your service." He turned and gestured expansively at the other penguins. "My colleagues," he said. "Great Officer Rienzi, Cavalier Giusepponi, Baron Pomodori."

Max looked stunned. "Where is Mr. Lincoln?" he asked.

The Commander held up a plump index finger and shook it slowly back and forth. "Ah, our dear Pietro," he said. "He has gone to Frascati for the day. Naturally, he would not wish to sign the contracts without our approval."

"Why not?"

"Because, my dear Signor Daniels," the Commander said, "there is a considerable amount of money involved and a considerable risk. We must scrutinize the documents. We must be reassured that all is in perfect order. Of course, you understand."

"Of course," Max said grimly. "When do you think we could expect the money?"

"My dear young gentleman," the Commander said, "let us first peruse the documents."

"Max," Lazslo said very gently, "these gentlemen are Mr. Lincoln's lawyers."

"We're going all the way," Max said grimly and sat down at the table. "Show them the contracts, Lazslo."

It took only an hour. The penguins clustered at one end of the table, passed the documents back and forth to each other, peered at them, clucked over them, nodded, shook heads, pointed fingers, held whispered consultations, glanced suspiciously at each of us in turn, and did everything, in fact, except hold them up to the light. Finally, the Commander gathered up the documents into a large untidy heap and sat down directly across from Max. The other penguins rose and rearranged themselves in adjoining chairs.

"It is impossible," said Squarcialancia, and the other penguins all nodded dolefully.

"Why?" Max asked.

The Commander shrugged. "There is no guarantee that the money will ever be returned," he said.

"We're not asking for a loan," Max said. "This is an investment."

"For only fifty percent?" the Commander said, astounded.

"That's the American way," said Max.

The Commander sighed. "It is not *our* way," he said. "Truly I am dismembered with grief." His colleagues nodded sympathetically.

Max stood up. "When will Pietro be back from Frascati?" he asked.

The Commander made an open, helpless gesture with his hands. "Perhaps this evening," he said, "perhaps tomorrow morning. But, my dear sir, it is useless. Clearly the documents are not in order."

"There is no safeguard," said Great Officer Rienzi.

"There are no securities," said Cavalier Giusepponi.

"There are not even deposits," said Baron Pomodori.

The Commander smiled apologetically. "What can we do?" he said. "Nothing is certain, all is vagueness. Believe me, I am desolated."

Without another word, Max stormed out of the room, his face white with rage. Lazslo quickly stuffed all the papers back into his briefcase and hurried after him. I lingered long enough to shake hands with all the apologetic penguins, and then I also left.

However, on my way out the front door, I happened to turn my head and look back. There, at the very end of the corridor, stood Pietro Lincoln. He was dressed in slacks, sandals, and an open-necked sports shirt, and his whole face seemed to be in motion, the extraordinary eyebrows pumping like pistons. When he saw me staring at him, he smiled, bowed slightly, and retreated behind a door.

Downstairs, I found Lazslo waiting for me. "Where's Max?" I asked breathlessly.

Lazslo looked forlorn. "He didn't wait," he said. "He was too upset."

"Lincoln's up there!" I said. "He was hiding from us."

Lazslo nodded. "Of course."

I started to say something, and then I stopped. My head was full of questions, but I couldn't seem to sort any of them out. I must have looked every bit as bewildered as I felt, because Lazslo smiled sadly and patted me awkwardly on the arm.

"Poor Max," he said. "With him, it is always the same, you know. He seizes on some wonderful idea, like this night club, and he builds it up in his mind until he makes of it an ideal, almost a religion. It becomes an end in itself. But to us in Europe, you see, life is not a crusade, but only a serious game for rather humble stakes—jobs, money, a little pleasure." He sighed. "You didn't notice? Not once, in all these talks, did he ever discuss the simple question of profits. How can we be surprised that Mr. Lincoln, who is frightened, should retreat behind his lawyers? A very dynamic people, you Americans, but you do not distinguish between your ideals and your self-interest. It is a little sad."

Some weeks later, Max left Rome and went back to America. I haven't heard from him in years and I don't know what happened to him. I suspect, however, that at home he was able at last to put his enthusiasm and sense of destiny to good use. Any day now, in fact, I expect to bump into him, probably somewhere along Madison Avenue or Rodeo Drive, and I won't be at all surprised to hear that he's doing very well.

CHAPTER NINE

VOICES

I don't think I began to understand Rome and my own involvement in Italian life until I moved to an apartment on the fourth floor of a run-down Renaissance *palazzo* at one end of a piazza called the Campo de' Fiori. The piazza is in the middle of the old papal city, surrounded by narrow, twisting little streets that thread their way among blocks of ancient houses dating back, many of them, to the fourteenth century. The rooms of my apartment were huge, with beamed and frescoed ceilings, thick walls, and tiled floors, and there was also a terrace, awash in flowers and trellised ivy. I slept, or tried to, in a front room with a large window looking out over the piazza. At first, I was startled by the noise. There were lulls, but never long periods of uninterrupted silence. In the very early morning hours, I would sometimes be awakened by the explosive buzzing of a motor scooter, the rumbling of cart wheels over the cobblestones, the crash of some unbelievably heavy object onto the pavement. Mostly, however, even at night, the sounds consisted of voices, individual and concerted, blending into and succeeding each other in a never ending choral composition of pure cacophony. It was astonishing.

Actually, the sheer volume of sound at certain periods of the day didn't surprise me. I had known all along that the Campo de' Fiori was the site, six days a week, of a large open-air market. I would get up in the morning and open my shutters to look down over a sea of gray canvas umbrellas sheltering perhaps as many as two hundred stands. A great crowd of shoppers ambled and pushed down narrow aisles between long rows of heaped edibles of all kinds. Directly beneath my window alone, at the north-western end of the piazza, I counted thirteen venders of vegeta-bles and several selling preserves, cheeses, and sausages. On my way across the piazza to a café where I often had breakfast and read the morning paper, I would pass pushcarts of fresh vegeta-bles piled into great green mounds, tables buried under soft white and brown mushrooms, pyramids of cherries, apples, oranges sliced open to reveal their dripping interiors, pears, apricots, bunches of white and green asparagus, enormous beets and onions, tiny round potatoes, huge heads of fresh lettuce, green and red peppers, artichokes, tomatoes, carrots, wild strawberries. Along one whole side of the piazza stretched a seemingly endless line of butcher stands, behind which the butchers themselves, in soiled white smocks, wielded their cleavers and large flat knives under the plucked bodies of chickens and the bloody carcasses of lambs and kids hanging in rows from steel hooks. There were also bunches of pigs' feet, chunks of tripe, chains of plump sausages. At the far end of the piazza, the fishmongers presided over damp boxes and baskets of the day's catch—fish of all shapes, flaming red, blue, and silver, soft masses of squid and small octopuses, mountains of white-and-gray minnows with tiny, dead bright-button eyes, dozens of small dark-red clawless Mediterranean lob-sters. And scattered along the periphery of these crowded rows of comestibles were still other stands, selling pots and pans, dishes, glassware, cheap toys, shoes, and clothing. The stone face of the piazza, roughly rectangular and about the same size as a football field, disappeared every morning of the week but Sundays and holidays under the umbrellas, the tons of merchandise, the shuf-fling feet of thousands of shoppers.

The voices to which I awoke and which filled my room nearly every morning arose, of course, from this market. Not yet fully awake, I'd hear them soaring up from the sea of gray umbrellas, as indistinguishable at first as waves beating against a rocky shore-line. After a while, however, I began to recognize rhythms and tones, endlessly repeated, and eventually I became able to pick out the individual calls of certain vendors. These voices, whether male or female, all had some characteristics in common; they were loud, flat, and rough, with the peculiar hoarseness of the carnival barker. I'd lie in bed sometimes and listen for each one, and soon, through the dull roaring of that human sea, I could string the solo voices together, make of them a leitmotiv for the entire market.

"Ah, Signore," the voices would call into my room, "look at these trays for a hundred lire! Signori, look at this stuff! A hundred lire! You can't buy anything you don't taste! Kid today! There's kid today! Look at this beauty, Signori! Look at this! The most in apricots—take a look! If you don't taste them, I won't sell them to you! Beautiful tomatoes, fresh zucchini, look here! Beautiful, beautiful and sweet, Signora! Beets, a hundred lire for such beets! These oranges, Signori—have you ever seen such oranges? Eggs to drink! Eggs to drink! Courage! Courage! Come over here! Look at these sweet little carrots! Signora, you see anything better than these? Wow, look at these strawberries! Come here, they're special, really special! Cherries, cherries as hard as rocks! Fish! Alive they are! Alive! Hey, hey, hey, look at these pearls! Hey, over here! Over here! A hundred lire! You won't taste them, I won't sell them to you!"

Later, threading my way through the market to the café or the newsstand, I was able to associate the individual voices with faces, gestures, expressions. The vegetable stands were mostly tended by women, stocky and strong, with rough hands and copper-colored faces beaten and lined by the sun. They were country people who had come directly from their farms to sell their produce in the piazza, and they had been up since two or three o'clock in the morning. Some wore gold bands in their ears, and their teeth were often astonishingly white; they called their wares out over the heads of the buyers, and exchanged snatches of shouted gossip with each other between official bellowings. They stood flatfooted on the cobblestones, and occasionally they'd lean over to rearrange their displays, seeming at the same time to caress their mounds of vegetables and piles of fruit, running stubby, dirt-caked fingers over their oranges and apples, peppers and cauliflowers and potatoes. They looked tired, their faces creased and worn, but proud, rooted to the same earth from which their fat, fresh vegetables had sprung.

The butchers and fishmongers were mostly as white as their

damp smocks, with fat, round faces and strong, hairy arms. They were city people, and many of them lived in the quarter. They had been up since before dawn, having driven several miles out to the city's general market, in the Via Ostiense, near the Porta San Paolo, where they had bought the naked carcasses and heaps of silvery fish they were now carving, chopping up, and selling. The fishmongers had wet, red hands; every few minutes they'd snatch up pails of water and sprinkle the day's catch, keeping it fresh-looking and clean against the sun and dirt of the piazza.

The vendors of pots and pans and clothing and cheap house-wares seemed more nervous, more frantic than the others. Their cries were pitched higher and were often couched in the form of challenges, as if the buyers who thronged past had every right to be suspicious and needed to be strongly convinced that they might be passing up some brilliant bargain. These salesmen of gaudy and cheap and slightly shoddy products had the anxious, mobile faces of small-time con men. They, too, belonged to the quarter, but they looked as if they rode the cold winds of chance; they tended to bounce, to scurry rapidly from one end of their displays to the other, to be ready to snatch something out for an unwary passerby who might be persuaded to succumb to the lure of a cheap pair of sandals, a bright yellow-and-green plastic toy, a monstrous purple lamp, a hideously painted bust of the Virgin. They hovered over their wares in family groups of two and three, the women as agile and shifty as the men, and I always had the feeling as I passed them that they had sneaked in unbidden, having acquired their merchandise from the back of a pickup truck or a looted warehouse. At the sound of a siren or the sight of a police-man's uniform, I expected them to be off, packing up and scurry-ing away down the nearest side street.

From my window, I began to spend ten or fifteen minutes at a time staring down over this bustling morning scene. I never grew tired of it. Sometimes I'd pull a chair up to the sill and sit down to watch. Occasionally, from some nearby window, a Roman matron would lean out, lowering an empty basket on a string to a child dispatched on the morning's errands. Later, the basket would be hauled back up, full of vegetables and fruit, milk and cheese, with perhaps the carcass of a chicken stuck into it, the scrawny neck and lifeless head dangling over the side. And often the basket would go back down for a second trip, carried briefly away into the crowd by a solemn urchin clutching a wad of lire in one grimy hand.

Despite the sea of gray umbrellas, the piazza was always full of color as well as sound. The merchandise, in all its gaudy hues, glittered brightly in the open spaces. Above, the sky on a sunny day blazed a deep blue, and the rays of the sun struck the façades of the old houses and *palazzi* that lined the square, with their dark-orange and amber walls, brown shutters, and terraces blooming with flowers and vines and green shrubs. Directly below me, a small stone fountain in the shape of a soup tureen splashed gaily, its waters teeming with bits of refuse—peelings, lettuce leaves, rotten fruit—dumped there by passing vendors. In the very center of the piazza, towering on a pedestal of stone over the umbrellas and the crowd, loomed a great bronze statue, blackened by time; this was the hooded figure of Giordano Bruno, who was burned alive in the piazza on February 17, 1600. Sinister and calm in his monk's robe, his head bowed and shaded by a cowl, and his hands folded in front of him over a book, Bruno seemed to emphasize the vitality of his surroundings by his very indifference and silence.

The plaque at the base of the statue, which was designed by a sculptor named Ettore Ferrati, gives the date of its dedication—June 9, 1889—and carries the following inscription: "To Bruno/ The Century By Him Divined/ Here/ Where the Pyre Burned." Actually, according to the reference books I began to consult on the subject, the pyre on which Bruno died did not arise in the very center of the piazza but at the corner of the Via de' Balestrari, at the southeastern end. He was one of the first to be burned alive there, but by no means the last. In fact, I discovered that a great many Jews and other heretics were put to death in the Campo de' Fiori, and that the piazza was the site of at least one other gruesome practice. The Via della Corda, a dark and narrow little street running parallel to the Via de' Balestrari, was named after an instrument of torture once employed at the corner of the street and the piazza. People caught cheating in the grain and fodder market that occupied the piazza were bound at the wrists and hoisted into the air by means of a large pulley. A heavy weight was attached to their ankles, thus stretching their bodies to the utmost, and they were then allowed to fall toward the ground just far enough to jerk their arms and legs out of their sockets. This barbarous punishment was not definitively abolished until the winter of 1816.

Of all the victims who suffered and died in the Campo de' Fiori, Bruno was the most famous and certainly the most interesting. Like all the great religious rebels and reformers, he began by being orthodox. By the time he was seventeen—in 1565—he had become a Dominican monk, in the Monastery of San Domenico in Naples, and some seven years later he was ordained a priest. Unfortunately for his personal welfare, he had an inquisitive and ranging mind. He read poetry and the pagan as well as the Christian philosophers, especially Heraclitus, Parmenides, Lucretius, and the very dangerous Copernicus. He began to have doubts about dogma, especially concerning the Trinity and the Incarnation. In 1576, he moved to Rome, but he left almost at once and wandered about Liguria, Piedmont, the Veneto, and Lombardy for about two years. He went to Switzerland and became a Calvinist, but he soon rebelled against this new orthodoxy as well. In France, he acquired a reputation for his philosophical and scientific treatises, as well as for his championship of the Copernican system. Civil war drove him out of France to London, and he continued to wander about Europe until he showed up in Italy again in the spring of 1591, at the invitation of a Venetian aristocrat, Giovanni Mocenigo. Bruno must have had a difficult personality. He persistently refused to make the smallest compromise, and offended nearly everyone he met. Mocenigo was no exception, and in May, 1592, he denounced Bruno to the Inquisition. During his trial, Bruno defended himself by insisting on the distinction between "philosophical reason according to principles and natural light" and "truth according to the light of faith." On July 30, however, he declared himself penitent and ready to submit. All might have worked out well, but Pope Clement VIII suddenly demanded that Bruno be handed over to him. Bruno arrived in Rome in February, 1593, and was immediately clapped into prison. The new trial he was subjected to dragged on for seven years. The Roman authorities demanded from him not only a retraction on the ground of faith but also a complete denial of his own philosophy. Bruno hesitated, but eventually stood firm. On January 20, 1600, the Pope ordered sentence to be carried out, and three weeks later Bruno, as "an impenitent, tenacious, and obstinate heretic," was turned over to the secular court. He and all his works were condemned to be burned. When the verdict was read to him,

Bruno said, "Perhaps you tremble more in pronouncing the sentence than I in receiving it." From then until the moment of his death, he didn't waver. On his way to the pyre on the day of his execution, he turned his head away and refused to kiss a crucifix offered to him.

Bruno's death and the other autos-da-fé and tortures practiced for so long in the Campo de' Fiori eventually gave the place a bad name. The guidebooks hardly mention it, and I soon discovered that it was all but impossible to find any postcards or souvenirs depicting it. Until 1889, there had been nothing in the piazza to commemorate Bruno's death, and the statue was not erected until long after the end of papal government in Rome and only at the instigation of a determined band of scholars and students. It was as if the authorities had determined to blot out some of the more uncomfortable pages of history. And yet the Campo de' Fiori had been for nearly three hundred years the very heart of Rome. From the second half of the fifteenth century to the end of the seventeenth, the most celebrated names and faces of Renaissance Rome graced its cobblestones and side streets.

"Campo de' Fiori," literally translated, means "Field of Flowers," but the place may have been named after Flora, the beautiful Roman mistress of Pompey the Great, whose theatre and curia and surrounding gardens once occupied the eastern end of the piazza and the neighboring Piazza del Biscione. (It was in one of the halls of Pompey's curia that Julius Caesar was struck down.) It is also possible that the piazza got its name from another Roman lady, Terenzia, who dedicated part of what was probably then an open field to a lascivious entertainment she had thought up and instituted called the Floral Games. The historian Gregorovius, when he looked into the question, provided a much more prosaic, and very likely accurate, explanation for the name. "Cardinal Scarampi, in 1456, was the first to build in the Campo de' Fiori," he wrote. "This piazza, where the Theatre of Pompey once stood, then occupied considerably more space than it does today. It took its name from the field that completely covered it and, until the time of Eugenius, it had served as a place of pasture for livestock. A few houses faced it from one side, and from the other it stretched more or less openly away toward the Tiber. Scarampi . . . had it paved."

Houses, shops, and inns rose on all sides, and the piazza began to flourish as a center of trade and social life. Papal bulls and other

official proclamations were posted there, which meant that anyone who wanted to keep abreast of the day's events had at some
point to pass by. Religious processions on their way from the Vatican to the basilicas of San Giovanni in Laterano, Santa Maria
Maggiore, and San Marco passed through the piazza, as did most
of the foreign officials and nobles who entered the city in order to
visit the papal court, directly across the Tiber. To facilitate all this
traffic, Pope Sixtus IV opened a new street into the piazza—the
Florida, now called the Via del Pellegrino—and later Rodrigo Borgia, after he became Pope Alexander VI, widened and improved
several of the nine other streets converging on the Campo. These
side streets, as well as the piazza itself, were lined with the small
shops of groups of artisans who had banded together to ply a common trade. Often the streets were named after the principal activity carried on in them. The makers of trunks, hats, coats, and cross-
bows flourished in the streets of the Baullari, the Cappellari, the
Giubbonari, and the Balestrari, while the Vicolo del Gallo took its
name from the presence of a popular tavern. Nothing, unfortunately, remains to commemorate the fact that in the middle of the
sixteenth century the city's first two editors, Antonio Blado and
Antonio Salamanca, opened their printing establishments either
in the piazza itself or in one of the surrounding streets.

In 1579, Pope Gregory XIII built a fountain in the center of the
piazza, just about where Bruno's statue now stands. Because of low
water pressure in the area, it had to be built six feet below street
level, and, like the one directly under my window, it was in the
shape of a tureen, made of white marble and with four spouts. The
people of the quarter called it "the soup bowl." In 1622, Pope
Gregory XV had an inscription carved on it. *"Ama Dio e non fallire/
Fa del bene e lassa dire,"* it read, urging everyone to love God, do
good, and mind his own business. In the nineteenth century, Pope
Gregory's soup bowl was dug up and moved to the Piazza della
Chiesa Nuova, after which the much smaller and quite similar one
was built at my end of the Campo. The occasion was the arrival in
the piazza, in November, 1869, of the daily open-air market,
which had for four centuries been carried on in the nearby Piazza
Navona. Before that, it had been in existence at the foot of the
Campidoglio for at least two hundred years, and very probably it
can trace its origins back to Republican Rome. The municipal government had decided to move the market because extensive
repairs and innovations had to be undertaken in the Piazza

Navona, whose three great fountains—two of them by Bernini—
were already among the most cherished tourist sights of Rome.
When the transfer was made, the Campo de' Fiori had long since
ceased to be the center of the city. For a century and a half, the
Campo had been deteriorating until it was little more than an
open space in a crowded quarter whose streets thronged with the
poor and with people earning a hard living on the fringes of life.

The coming of the market partly restored the piazza's importance, luring shoppers from all the surrounding quarters, and
even from newer and richer sections well beyond the boundaries
of the medieval city. It did not, however, bring the rich back into
the crumbling *palazzi* or make the area quite respectable. Thieves
and prostitutes reportedly haunted the foul and narrow streets
leading into the piazza, and the entire quarter acquired a slightly
romantic but dubious reputation as the center of Rome's petty
underworld. Much later, Mussolini planned to open up the whole
area by ramming a modern avenue through entire blocks of old
houses. The war prevented him from carrying out this plan and
many of the others he had formulated for the modernization of
the city. It was only ten or twelve years after the war, when well-
to-do Romans started buying and remodeling apartments in the
old, long-neglected great Renaissance houses of the city, that the
raucous low life of the piazza began to be tempered by the presence of a few respectable families. The preponderant voices, however, remained those of the real "Romans from Rome," living out
their lives in the quarter as they always had, oblivious of history.

Many other voices besides those of the market invaded my
room. The most insistent and violent one belonged, I guessed, to
a woman in her thirties. She lived in one of the apartments near
the corner of the Via dei Cappellari, somewhere behind the lines
of laundry that hung, dripping relentlessly, across the street. Her
voice was shrill and hard and piercing; it would come soaring
across the piazza from behind the wall of laundry like a battle cry
from the ranks of an army advancing behind flapping pennants.
"Ah, Massimo-o-o!" it would scream. "Massimo-o-o, where the
hell are you, you dirty monkey? Get the hell up here right this
minute! Massimo-o-o! If you aren't home in two minutes, you little
bastard, I'll break your head! Massimo-o-o, imbecile! You hear me?
Get up here right now before I come down and break your arm!
Ah, Massimo-o-o! Massimo-o-o! *Cretino! Imbecille! A' vie' qua-a-a!*"

These tirades often became so vituperative, menacing, and foul-mouthed that I'd find myself wondering how the woman could keep it up. I'd go to the window and gaze down into the piazza, hoping to spot Massimo among the hordes of children swarming through the market or, on Sunday, around the base of Bruno's statue. The voice would scream on, threatening mayhem and the vengeance of Heaven on the object of its wrath, but no little boy would separate himself from his fellows and go running across the cobblestones. At least, I never noticed him.

Massimo apparently did hear, however, and eventually he would come home. The voice would cease its screaming imprecations and remain silent for some time. After a while, though, I'd hear it again—usually around two o'clock in the afternoon, when the market had closed up and the commercial uproar had abated somewhat. The intensity and depth of emotion would still be evident in the voice, but the tone would have altered dramatically. "Massimo! Massimo!" I would hear it shout. "Treasure of my heart, flower of my life, why don't you eat? Eat, eat! You want to die of hunger? You want your mother to perish of grief? You want your papa to die of shame, to tell me I don't cook like I used to? My love, my sweet, my angel, have another tomato, eat your bread, drink your milk. Eat, eat, love of my life! Here, Mama will give you a big hug and kiss! You eat now! Massimo-o-o! *Tesoro! Amore! Mangia, che ti fa bene! Cocco! Angelo!*"

I tried often to imagine what Massimo looked like. I saw a small boy of seven or eight with dirty knees and scuffed shoes, black hair and eyes, red cheeks, and sturdy shoulders, but too fat for his age. I'd see him climb the stairs to the sound of threats and fury, bursting in to be met by a hug and a light cuff and a mound of steaming spaghetti. Who, anywhere around the Campo de' Fiori, would not have heard of him? At the newsstand, I once idly inquired about him, but the young man who sold me my newspaper couldn't identify him, either. "Ah, Signore, it could be any one of them," he said, indicating with a flick of his hand a crowd of urchins then engaged in kicking a soccer ball around the piazza. "Massimo? A common enough name. And here everyone shouts from the windows all the time. Do you not notice?"

This young man's name was Remo. He and his family had been tending their stand, on the corner of the Via dei Baullari, for thirty-five years. They would take turns sitting like benevolent

gnomes inside a very small wooden booth festooned with magazines and newspapers. Nothing escaped their vigilant attention.
Remo rarely smiled, and he thought that life in the piazza had
deteriorated a good deal since he first began to observe its goings
on. "Ah, Signore," he said to me one day, "you like this market?
It is not what it was. No, indeed it isn't. On Saturdays you had to
fight your way into the piazza, that's what I remember. Now—"
He shrugged. "Now it's nothing. People are moving out. The ones
who were brought up in this quarter, they do not like the old *palazzi*. When they have money, they move away. The rich and the
foreigners are moving into the buildings now, but they don't buy
in the market. They go to the supermarkets in the Parioli—drive
all the way out there rather than buy in the piazza. No, it's not
what it was." He was unhappy, too, about the crime in the area.
"Dirty people," he said. "*Gentaccia*, that's what they are. The quarter is full of them. Every thief in town lives here. Do you have a
car?"

I told him I didn't.

"That's lucky for you," he said. "It would be stolen. Don't trust
anyone you meet in the piazza. Anyone can see you're an American." At the time, I had seen no evidence of crime in the piazza,
and I paid no attention to Remo's advice.

One night at about 2 A.M., I was awakened by the sound of loud
masculine laughter and conversation outside my window. I
looked down and saw a group of men directly below. They were
talking and joking, making no effort to keep from disturbing the
neighborhood. I shouted down at them to keep quiet. One of them
looked up briefly, but otherwise they paid no attention. Their
hoarse, merry voices continued to resound in the night air. After
about ten more minutes of this, I went to the kitchen and came
back with a large pot full of water. I asked them one more time to
keep quiet, but I was ignored. I then leaned out the window and
poured cold water on their heads. Bellowing and cursing, they
quickly scattered out and regrouped beyond the fountain, out in
the piazza and well out of range. Through the slats of my shutters
I saw them conferring angrily and occasionally pointing up
toward my window. Slightly uneasy, I went back to bed.

The next morning, when I stepped out into the piazza, I was
greeted by a young tough in wrinkled slacks and a torn jersey. He
was unshaven, with close-set eyes and a snarl of oily-looking

curls, and he had evidently been lounging against the wall of my building, waiting for me. "Hey, you," he said hoarsely. "Hey, are you the one who threw water on us last night?"

The market was in full swing and the piazza was crowded with people. I made up my mind not to be intimidated. "Yes," I said. "You woke me up."

The youth shook his head gravely. "That was a very stupid thing to do."

"Listen," I said. "I have some rights. I asked you twice to keep quiet and you paid no attention. You have no right to wake everybody up."

"And you have no right to throw water on people."

This seemed a rather weak rejoinder to me, so I pressed my luck a little. "I could have called the police, you know."

The tough smiled, revealing a bright row of gold teeth. "No, no," he said, shaking his head. "You would not do that. No one in this quarter would do such a stupid thing. You have to live here—no?"

"I don't live here all the time," I said. "Besides, I don't like to be threatened."

The tough smiled again and spread his hands out wide. "Threatening you? Who is threatening you, Signore? I? I merely wish to protest against being doused with water in the middle of the night, that's all. That's not unreasonable, is it?"

"Mario, introduce me to the gentleman," I heard someone say.

I turned, and was confronted by a short, stocky, bald Roman in a rumpled but well-tailored brown suit. He had a round, affable face with large brown eyes and a strong, prominent, straight nose. He was smiling broadly. "Mario does not know my name," I said, and I introduced myself.

"Of course he does," the new arrival declared. "You are the American on the fourth floor. Everyone knows who you are. I myself have often seen you in the piazza. Pleased to meet you. My name is Domenico. My friends call me Memmo."

"Were you also in the piazza last night?" I asked.

Memmo laughed. "Alas, yes," he admitted. "Luckily, you missed me. Mario, here, was soaked. That probably accounts for his sour face." He turned to Mario and clapped him roughly on the shoulder. "Hey, Mario, cheer up! The bath did you good, eh? The first one you've had in weeks."

Mario made an effort to smile, but it did not seem entirely genuine. I concentrated on Memmo. "I'm sorry about it," I said. "But I was tired and I wanted to get to sleep. You were directly under my window, and I asked you all several times to be quiet."

"Right," Memmo said. "Quite right. I think we will not chat there again. However, *caro Signore*"—he took my arm confidentially and pulled me a few feet off to one side—"don't do such a thing again. For your own good, Signore. No one would harm you, of course—*Dio mio*, an American!—but Mario and his friends can play such tricks, Signore! The apartment is so full of beautiful things. I have not seen it, but I know that it is. Apartments can be broken into, Signore, and even the most beautiful object can be made to disappear. What is the sense in playing tricks on people like Mario, eh?"

I looked back at Mario, who was still standing by the entrance to the building and regarding me sourly. "And you?" I asked. "What about you?"

"I?" he said. "Oh, I'm a friend of Mario's. He runs little errands for me. I have a shop here, just around the corner. You've passed it many times. Electrical equipment—radios, iceboxes, toasters, things like that. You've seen my shop, haven't you?"

I said that I had passed it often.

"Well, of course you have," Memmo said. "It's a very well-known store. Everyone in the neighborhood knows me. Ask anyone."

"It's very kind of you to warn me," I said.

Memmo looked astonished. "Warn you?" he said. "Signore, I would not think of presuming to warn you. Still, it is important that you know how things are here on the piazza, eh?"

"Yes, I understand," I said. "Thanks very much."

"Forget it," Memmo said. "Forget the whole thing. And don't worry about Mario. Nothing will happen. Come and see me in the shop. Drop in any time—right there, just around the corner." He shook my hand and departed in the direction of his store. As he went, I saw him nod almost imperceptibly to Mario, who went off with him, not casting so much as a backward glance in my direction.

A couple of days later, I did drop in on Memmo. From the outside, the store looked like any other small shop dealing in electrical housewares, but since my encounter with Mario and Memmo and our oblique conversation, I had become curious about it. When I stepped inside the door, I discovered that the place was all but empty of merchandise. The window display featured a cheap washing machine and a secondhand refrigerator, but except for a couple of toasters and a small radio or two the store looked cleaned out. Mario and a couple of other shady-looking young men lounged against the walls, smoking American cigarettes, while Memmo sat behind a small wooden desk. He had been talking into the telephone, but he hung up immediately when I came in. "*Ah, buon giorno, buon giorno,*" he said, coming out from behind his desk and rubbing his hands briskly together. "How nice to see you! Thank you for dropping in."

"Business seems to be a little slow," I said.

"On the contrary," Memmo answered, smiling broadly. "Business could not be better."

"You've sold everything in the shop, then?"

"Well, not quite," Memmo said. "Come back here."

Memmo led me back to his desk, opened a top drawer, and pulled out a large, flat box full of Swiss wristwatches. "Look at this," he said, holding one up by the strap. "Fifty thousand lire, this watch costs. I sell it for thirty. Would you like it?"

I told Memmo that I already had a watch.

He put the box back in the drawer and closed it. "Well, then, how about this?" he opened another drawer and showed me a pile of cigarette lighters. "Or these?" He produced boxes of cufflinks, tie clasps, studs, men's and women's bracelets, earrings, electric razors, razor blades, small bottles of cheap cologne, key rings, charms. Finally, with an elaborate little flourish of one hand, he opened still another drawer and took out a long, thin, expensive-looking case. "Perhaps there is a lady in your life?" He opened the box to reveal a handsome pearl necklace. "For you," he said, "for my friend the American, only a hundred thousand lire, eh?"

"No, thanks," I said. "I can't afford it."

Memmo sighed, cheerfully stuffed the box back into the drawer, and closed it.

"You seem to be selling everything here," I said.

Memmo smiled and shrugged. "Well, Signore, I believe in floating with the traffic, eh? What you Americans call, I believe, the law of supply and demand."

"How can you afford to sell these things so cheaply?" I asked.

"Signore, we have our own direct sources of supply," Memmo said. "We eliminate the middleman, as you would say. We import everything directly. You understand?"

"I think so," I said.

After that, I became increasingly aware of Memmo and his boys. Mario and half a dozen other young toughs strolled in and out of the shop, and several times I noticed them peddling objects through the marketplace. Once, I found Mario and a friend presiding at the corner of the Via dei Baullari over a large stack of shoeboxes. They were selling sandals for five hundred lire a pair—a ridiculously low price. Occasionally, they would operate out of the back of a panel truck, selling everything from shirts to hardware. I never saw Memmo anywhere except inside his store, usually on the phone or in deep conversation with one of his young men.

One day, at the newsstand, I asked Remo about Memmo and his friends. Remo glanced sharply at me, then looked around to see if we were alone. "Stay away from them, Signore," he said in an undertone. "They are no good, that bunch. I let everything I hear go in one ear and out the other. It is better that way. But I tell you this, Signore—the police drop in there from time to time, and it is not to pass the hours chatting. Memmo wasn't around for a long time last year, and that Mario—you know him?"

I said that I did.

"A bad one," Remo said. "He was a carpenter. Then he killed a man one day just because the fellow clapped him too hard on the back, or something. He did three and a half years. A hood, *un vero teppista*. Don't have anything to do with them."

"But who are they? Are they from around here?"

"All from this quarter, Signore, every one of them," Remo said sadly. "They give it a bad name. All over Rome, people say the Campo de' Fiori is a den of thieves. Memmo and his crowd— they're responsible for that. It's really too bad."

Weekdays, life on the piazza was conducted according to a specific rhythm, and there was only one period of real silence. Sometime between 2 and 3 A.M., the pulse of the quarter would suddenly stop. For anywhere from ten minutes to a half hour, the voices would be stilled and no other noise would be heard. The piazza seemed then to be holding its breath. The pale-yellow light of a few street lamps would cast shadows along the damp cobblestones and throw into relief the small balconies and terraces, the cornices and moldings of the old buildings. At such times, the smell of the piazza would be very strong—an odor of earth and old stone and dampness and decay. The figure of Bruno, on its pedestal, would dominate its surroundings then as it did at no other time.

The respite was invariably brief. It would be shattered by the sound of an iron shutter being unlocked and rolled up, by the buzzing of a motor scooter, by the slam of a heavy wooden door, by the clatter of planks being unstacked, by the rumble of iron-clad wheels over the cobblestones. Soon the first pushcarts would appear, loaded high with boards, and the piazza would be alive with voices—those of the *facchini*, the market's porters, greeting each other and murmuring guttural instructions. Laboriously, seeming to work at half speed in the dim light, they would begin to erect the stands and counters from which the day's merchandise would be sold. As they worked, the first trucks arrived from the outlying farms, disgorging their sturdy women and their mounds of fresh fruit and vegetables. The first butcher would appear with a load of raw meat, and wait impatiently for his counter to be erected; often, if his stand was in the early stages of construction, he'd go off in search of hot coffee and a roll. The arriving venders and the porters had little to say to each other; their relationship had long since been clearly established by custom, and they seldom had much in common. The vendors represented capital, and many of them came from the country or other parts of the city. To them, the piazza was merely a marketplace for their goods. The porters, on the other hand, the builders of *bancarelle*, all came from the quarter. They lived in the narrow streets and alleys that fanned out from the piazza, in cluttered rooms and tiny apartments full of women and small children. They kept their planks and pushcarts in ground-floor rooms along the Via del Pellegrino, the Vicolo del Gallo, the Via della Corda, sometimes around the corner in the Piazza Farnese. Every morning they were up and at work by three o'clock, ready to toil for hours like mules for between five hundred and a thousand lire a day. Their voices— harsh, tired, cynical, resigned—seemed to speak for all the poor of the quarter. By eight o'clock, when the clamor of the market filled my ears, they would have vanished back into their burrows.

Five hours later, in the strong heat of the midday sun, the porters would reappear and begin to raze all that they had built. As the crowd of shoppers thinned out and the vendors packed up their goods, the porters hauled down umbrellas and awnings, carefully dismantled the stands, loaded the loose boards onto their pushcarts, and trundled them back to their storage bins. The stone face of the piazza gradually reappeared, filthy with refuse—an empty expanse strewn with the leavings of a careless army. The voices of the quarter sounded now from the open windows and doorways of the surrounding houses—the voices of mothers and young children, of fathers home for the midday meal, of young men swarming back on their scooters and bicycles from the tasks of the morning. To all these merely human noises was added the discordant hum of jostling traffic, shifting the emphasis but in no way diminishing the habitual uproar of the piazza.

Then a large blue open truck would enter the Campo and park to one side. From it a dozen men dressed in faded and stained blue smocks would descend and fan out over the stones. Some, armed with huge brooms, would sweep the refuse into sizable heaps; others would shovel the garbage into the truck. Then the piazza would be carefully and thoroughly hosed down. Only the fountain would be ignored, and left half choked with the day's leavings. By the time the street cleaners had departed, the piazza, under a fierce sun, would have begun to dry out and acquire a hard, baked look. Half a dozen flower stalls, submerged earlier by the flowing tide of the market, would stand out brightly along the Via dei Baullari. And at my end of the Campo two or three white-jacketed waiters would appear and begin setting up tables and chairs on the sidewalk directly across from the fountain.

These tables, bounded by portable plants and hedges, belonged to a restaurant called La Carbonara, which occupied two stories of the building next to mine. It was too expensive for most people of the quarter, and was patronized mainly by Romans from other sections of the city and by foreign tourists who had found it listed in their travel brochures or chanced upon it on their way to the Piazza Farnese. The foreigners were always the first to arrive, at midday, and they would settle themselves at the outdoor tables, under the hot sun and in full view of the unlovely fountain. The Italians never arrived much before one-thirty and always ate inside, away from the noise and between cool, whitewashed walls. At lunch, La Carbonara catered to a hard core of regulars. I used to eat there two or three times a week, and I soon got to know the regulars. They sat alone or in small groups, but they all knew each other and exchanged conversation. The king of the place was a huge butcher named Nando. He came later than the others, never arriving before two o'clock, and his entrance always enlivened the room. He would stand in the doorway, blocking it completely with his enormous bulk, and banter obscenely in street dialect with his friends, who would call out insults from the surrounding tables. He would take some time to decide where and with whom he would sit, then move heavily toward a proffered chair and sink into it, resting his massive hands on the table and lowering himself with the grace of an elephant submerging in a pool. Often he would bring along a choice cut of meat for himself, slap it down on the table, then turn it over to the waiter, giving him precise instructions on how it was to be prepared. *"Carissimi,"* he would say, addressing the room at large, "look at this obscene cut of good beef, a real steak, not the obscene pieces of obscene rubber they serve everywhere these days. That's meat, *cari amici.* You think I'd eat anywhere if I didn't bring my own meat? I'd be an obscene idiot to risk my guts in any obscene den of obscene thieves." Then he'd order a litre of wine and attack the bread, stuffing great chunks of it into his mouth and spraying crumbs all over the table-cloth. Nando made everybody cheerful. Diners who had never seen him before would look up startled and listen in amazement to the Rabelaisian exchanges his arrival evoked, but then they would relax and enjoy the good humor Nando engendered. Once, however, two middle-aged English ladies in severe suits and flat-heeled walking shoes, who evidently understood an unusual amount of street slang, rose from their corner table and hurried disapprovingly away. Their departure spread a pall over La Carbonara. "Well, look at that!" Nando finally said, tearing off another large chunk of bread. "A couple of frigid witches who wouldn't know a good piece of meat if they saw one." Everyone roared, and the English ladies were quickly forgotten.

Among the other luncheon regulars was a jeweller named Roberto. He was in his sixties and always sat by himself, at a rear table in a corner of the room. He ate voraciously, leaning over his plate and stuffing pasta into his mouth. I suspected that he lunched at La Carbonara every day only because of Nando. The entrance of the butcher never failed to galvanize Roberto. He would look up from his food and hurl the opening insult across the room. Sometimes the exchanges became so vehement that Roberto, carried away, would soar to his feet and prop himself up against his chair as he fired coarse witticisms at the butcher. In its intensity, his expression resembled that of a sports fan outraged by a referee's decision. Such an outburst ended as soon as Nando chose to break it off, at which point Roberto would immediately subside into his chair and return to his food. He never spoke to anyone else in the restaurant. I gathered that Roberto and Nando liked each other, but I never saw any evidence of real friendship. They never ate together. I once asked Nando about Roberto. The butcher shrugged. "A little crazy, that's all," he said mysteriously. "But a good man. He has a heart."

The jolliest table was the one presided over by Franco, a plump, curly-haired young man who dealt in dubious antiques on the Via dei Coronari, a few blocks away. He ate with his mistress, a handsome, dark-haired woman a few years older than he was, her teenage son, her older sister, and various friends in the antique business. There was always room for one more at Franco's table. Franco sat at the head of the table, beaming on the company, pouring wine for the latest arrivals, and presiding over spirited discussions of the day's events. Whenever Nando chose to honor Franco's table with his presence, Franco would commandeer a special bottle of wine in his honor, ply him with small delicacies, roar with laughter at his jokes, listen to his every word as to an oracle. Nando's bulk caused seating problems at Franco's crowded table, generally compelling later arrivals to sit well out into the aisles, partly hidden behind the first line of eaters. "Ah, Nando, Nando!" I'd hear Franco say. "You rogue, tell us what you did today! Tell us who you swindled! Tell us about your life, Nando, you king of butchers!"

The end of the lunch hour in La Carbonara was usually signalled by the arrival of a thin, furtive-looking creature dressed in a baggy black or gray suit, who would enter the restaurant nodding and bobbing to everyone he saw. His pockets bulged with small articles and crumpled pieces of paper, mostly receipts or bills of sale. This raven of a man, Otello, was a buyer of other people's failures. He would read the newspapers for announcements of bankruptcies, and would scurry off to present himself as a possible purchaser of whatever the victim had to sell. We never knew what he would show up with, but almost always it was some pathetic symbol of disaster—a wristwatch with a worn leather strap, a wedding ring, an antique brooch, a silver cigarette case. He would go from table to table, producing these objects from his pockets in the hope of a quick sale. He was tolerated, and sometimes Franco would ask him to have coffee at his table, but I noticed that Nando never spoke to him and that Otello was never asked to eat with anyone. A waiter would eventually appear with his order, and Otello would go off to dine by himself. When the others departed, he would still be there, a scrawny, solitary figure nibbling away at a salad or a small piece of meat. His digestion was bad.

By the middle of the afternoon, the tempo of life in the Campo de' Fiori, after the relative calm of the luncheon break, would be speeding up again. The shops, closed for three hours, would reopen and traffic would pour through the piazza along the Via dei Baullari as the inhabitants of the quarter returned to their jobs. After four o'clock, the children, just released from school, would chase each other around the fountain, run shouting down the side streets, play games in the doorways and against the walls of the houses. Women would appear in the windows and on the terraces, pausing to observe and enjoy the surge of life below them. During this time of day, the voices in the piazza were exclusively those of the quarter; they sounded the harsh accents of the old city. Toward evening, long shadows would strike down across the piazza, and swallows would wheel and dart over the tops of the buildings. The noise of homeward-bound traffic dominated all other sounds. The children would gradually vanish from the scene, to be replaced by men just home from work and pausing, before rejoining their families, for a smoke, a chat, a last-minute errand in the shops. Outside La Carbonara, the waiters would be back at work, unstacking the outdoor tables and resetting them for the dinner hour. Around the statue of Bruno old men would gather, to sit smoking and observing in silence the end of the day.

The night never brought peace to the Campo. A noisy car or scooter would suddenly roar across it; a band of boisterous young men would gather at the corner of some street; radios and phonographs would send music out through open windows; a sound truck advertising the fortunes of a political party or the virtues of a laundry soap would circle the piazza, blaring exhortations; a mother would shout from a window at an errant husband or a tardy child. Even La Carbonara would contribute a voice or two. Once, I was awakened by the sound of a family dinner party that had degenerated into a violent quarrel, and on another occasion I watched from my window while a group of young German tourists arose from a table to go fishing in the fountains. A pretty girl in slacks, using the remains of an umbrella she had found somewhere, sat on the lip of the soup bowl and salvaged broken boxes, tin cans, and rotting heads of lettuce while her companions cheered her on, greeting the appearance of each new treasure with yelps and applause. Only after 2 A.M., with La Carbonara closed for the night, the coffee bars and shops tightly shuttered, the last carouser safely at home, perhaps just as a night policeman, on his bicycle, began a slow round of locked doors and barred windows—only then would there come that brief time of absolute silence.

On Sundays, despite the absence of the market, the Campo remained a riot of color and sound. I would awaken to the ringing of bells as the churches summoned the faithful to Mass. Through my shutters I would hear the voices of children already at play. When I opened the shutters, I would see them scampering across the cobblestones after each other, wheeling and darting with the same abandon as the flocks of swallows over the rooftops. At the far end, the older boys usually organized a soccer game and played ferociously, watched by a crowd of loafers around the pedestal of Bruno's statue. Just beyond, against a corner of the Palazzo Righetti, a gang of men would be gambling with coins by flinging them against the wall and hoping to land them within a hand's length of each other. Savage arguments often broke out, but could not be heard over the tumult of the soccer game. The piazza on such mornings took on a carnival air.

On Sunday afternoons, however, public functions would intrude. During my stay, a municipal election campaign was just getting under way. I came home one afternoon to find that long, thin banners advertising the virtues of seven or eight political parties had been strung across the piazza or plastered to the walls of buildings. The following Sunday, around lunchtime, a small speaker's stand draped in red banners was erected behind Bruno's back. Sound trucks and tiny Fiats equipped with loudspeakers began touring the piazza and the surrounding streets, urging the people of the quarter to attend a Communist rally at five o'clock that afternoon. The din they made would certainly have cost them my vote, but no one seemed to pay much attention.

Shortly after five o'clock, a cluster of loudspeakers above the stand began to blare out a medley of Communist songs, and a small crowd gathered. A thin, intense-looking young man in horn-rimmed glasses appeared on the platform and screamed into a microphone, "Rome is the paradise of speculators!" He proceeded to expound at length on the various problems of the city, all of which, he said, were the direct result of collusion between the corrupt Demo-Christian city government and the great, exploiting noble families, such as the Torlonia and the Borghese, whom he described as pillars of capitalism and Fascism. He spoke for an hour, his glasses periodically sliding down to the end of his nose, his hair falling forward over his eyes as he shook his head for emphasis each time he spat out one of the hated names. Less than two hundred people listened to what he had to say, and many of them wandered away long before he had finished. They were mostly the middle-aged and the old—shabbily dressed; there were almost no young people.

By seven o'clock, the Communists had gone, taking their platform, their loudspeakers, and their banners with them. The young men reappeared, and a few of them began kicking a ball lazily back and forth. I sat at Bruno's feet and watched a gang of small boys engaged in a wild game of tag at my end of the piazza. The light began to fade and the street lamps went on. Voices from the terraces and open windows sounded faint and peculiarly distant in the twilight. I was about to get up when I became aware of something unusual going on near the corner of the Via dei Cappellari. People were pouring out of the street, pausing occasionally to look back. Two parallel rows of flickering lights came bobbing down the narrow alley, and a chorus of chanting voices soared out from beneath the lines of drying laundry. A double file of boys dressed in white surplices and holding lighted candles now appeared, and behind them walked a priest, leading the chanting. Six men supporting a painted statue of the Madonna followed, and after them came a small crowd, mainly of women with shawls or kerchiefs over their heads, each holding a candle and singing. The procession entered the Campo, but it quickly turned left and headed off toward the Piazza della Cancelleria. It was making a tour of the churches in the quarter on the occasion of some saint's day. Everyone in the piazza paused to watch it pass, but it made no more lasting an impression on the Campo than the Communist rally of a few hours before.

I decided to have an *espresso,* and I walked across the piazza toward the café. It was nearly dark now, but still too early for dinner. I threaded my way among the soccer players and through groups of men and women with babies and small children. Suddenly a group of young boys came bursting out of the Via dei Giubbonari, laughing and shouting and bumping heedlessly into everyone. One of them, a sturdy urchin of seven or eight with a round face and a mass of black curls, slammed head-on into me. I grabbed his shoulder and smiled at him as he looked up at me. "Ah, Massimo!" I heard a familiar voice say. "Massimo! What the hell are you doing? Don't you know better than to go around bumping into people? Ask the Signore's pardon! Massimo! *Cretino!*" I looked around, but in the growing darkness I couldn't identify the speaker. The boy shook off my hand and shot past me, zigzagging away across the crowded piazza. The terrible voice followed. "Ah, Massimo-o-o! Massimo-o-o!" it screamed. "Wait till I get you home! Wait till I get my hands on you! Massimo! You lousy little brat! *Mascalzone! Farabutto!* Ah, Massimo-o-o!"

I never did pick out the mother. She remained, like so many others, a disembodied solo voice within the music of the piazza.

CHAPTER TEN

ARRIVEDERCI, ROMA

Coming home very late, on a warm spring night in 1951, and crossing the broad, silent expanse of Rome's Piazza del Popolo, I met a friend of mine named Denny March. He was sitting by himself at the foot of the Obelisk of Flaminius, in the very center of the piazza, and he hailed me out of the shadows as I went past. I joined him and together we sat there for an hour or so and talked. Denny was going home, back to New York, and he was distressed about it. He had come to Italy about the same time I had, in the spring of 1947, and ostensibly for the same reason, to study singing, but now he was leaving and he wasn't sure why. True, like most of us who had arrived with high hopes and confidence in our talent, he had had eventually to face the fact that he would never have the great operatic career he had promised himself, but he had managed to earn his living in Italy as a part-time movie actor, voice dubber, and night club comic. It had never occurred to him to leave, not until a long hiatus between paying jobs had convinced him that he could only strike it rich back in America. "I wasn't really getting anywhere here," he said, "so what else could I do?"

But he hadn't convinced himself and he didn't want to be alone again that night. He had been unable to sleep and had left his *pensione* near the Piazza di Spagna to pace the Roman streets, had wound up here, in the shadow of the towering obelisk, alone in the deserted piazza. We talked and talked about all the things that had happened to us during these four years in Italy and suddenly, sitting there and staring out over the gleaming cobblestones, in the warmth of a Roman night sky, seeing the dark tops of trees above the parapet of the Pincio, smelling the sweet ageless smell of the Roman stones, the smell of an ancient basilica split open and left to bake for centuries in the hot sun, Denny, a tough boy from a good slum in lower Manhattan, began to cry. "Why the hell am I going?" he said, more to himself than to me. "Why? I love this place. I thought I'd never leave it."

A few months later I, too, left and the same anguished question echoed in my head. Why was *I* leaving? Like Denny, I had practical reasons—my G.I. Bill of Rights had run out and I had also given up the idea of a singing career. (I could hit the high notes, all right, but my voice was too small to fill a major opera house.) I had begun to write but I wasn't making quite enough as a free-lance stringer and translator to get along. Still, all these considerations could have been surmounted. Italy, after all, had a much greater claim on me than on Denny. I was half Italian, almost a native Roman by now, and I realized that part of me had always remained rooted in Italy. Since coming back I had reclaimed a portion of myself and now, in leaving again, I had become painfully aware of what my years here had come to mean to me. Not that I wanted to become Italian now or that I had filled myself with fashionable contempt for my own country; it was only that I had accepted so much from Italy, had taken so much for granted, that suddenly I was no longer sure if what I expected from my future in America was really worth what I was giving up. I remember standing at the rail of the liner *Independence* and watching the Neapolitan shoreline recede: below me the blue water of the bay; in the distance the pink-and-white houses of Naples, the black slopes of Vesuvius. Had it been only a few years ago that I had arrived here, in this same harbor on an equally beautiful day? I shut my eyes and immediately my head was filled with the sights and sounds of those years, a whirling kaleidoscope of scenes and faces, all the colors of a time deeply savored. It was a game I would learn to play often and one I sometimes still indulge in, whenever I am not in Rome . . .

I sit on a terrace in a fashionable restaurant overlooking the harbor of Palermo. I have been stuffed with macaroni cooked in the Sicilian style, with cheese and raisins, and I am a little drunk from the heavy black wine my host pours for me. He is an aging Sicilian baron to whom people bow on the street and say "kiss your hand" to. "Giuliano?" he now says, with a laugh. "They will never catch him." He waves toward the barren hills behind us. "He sinks into the rocks," he says. "I hope they do not catch him. We need someone to keep the fear of God in these peasants." And one day later I stand on the narrow balcony of a room overlooking a dark, dirty street in Partinico, a wretched town on the other side of those barren hills that shield Palermo. Beside me stands a colonel of carabinieri. He is from the north, middle-aged, mustached, and serious. "We will catch this bandit," he tells me, "despite the fact that we get no help from these peasants. To them we are *sbirri*, spies. *We* are the enemy, not the bandit who robs them." An old woman goes past underneath our balcony. She is dressed in black and wears a shawl over her head. "She is going to the water fountain in the piazza," the colonel tells me. "To the spot where three weeks ago her husband and five other men were shot down by the gang. It was midday. She was there, along with perhaps three hundred other persons. She has seen or heard nothing. No one else admits being there at the time. . . . "

Or I am dining with a girl at a popular restaurant on the water in Naples. It is *Ferragosto*, the beginning of the summer holiday, and it is impossible to find a hotel room anywhere. My girl and I have missed the last boat for Capri and we are prepared to sit out the night right where we are. The headwaiter comes over. He has hired a boat for us. Only ten thousand lire, fifteen dollars! We accept. The boat arrives. It is a skiff and it is rowed by a lean, very old man in torn pants and a jersey full of holes. We laugh and climb in. The boat smells of fish but it is spotlessly clean. The old man stands up in front of us and begins to row, leaning forward on the heavy oars and allowing the full weight of his thrusting torso to propel us over the water. It is a slow business, but we don't care. We sit in the bottom of the boat, our arms around each other and leaning back against the seat. The old man begins to hum to himself, to set himself a rhythm. We will arrive at dawn. Above us the stars seem to move down and engulf us. I have never been so happy before . . .

Or, on another spring night, I am standing on a terrace in Capri. In my vest pocket I have my toothbrush and I have not been home for three days. I cannot even remember where I slept last. The party I am at is being given by an English lady who has been having an unfortunate affair with an Egyptian rug dealer. Everyone is waiting for the writer, Sinclair Lewis, to arrive. It is expected that he will show up as mean and drunk as he was the night before at somebody else's party. It is a very hot night for May. To my left, an Italian war ace, who is supposed to have shot down countless English and American bombers and who now designs women's clothes, is sounding off on the virtues of Fascism. His audience, composed mainly of Americans, is listening to him politely. On my right, someone is arranging a picnic for the following day. A motor launch will pick the guests up at the Piccola Marina and will deposit them, along with baskets of fruit and bottles of champagne, on the rocks near the Green Grotto. There will be swimming and sunbathing and perhaps love-making in the open, under blue skies and a hot sun. I am looking around for a drink to speed the evening to a conclusion when my hostess begins to laugh. She leans way back and shrieks. Unfortunately, she is top-heavy and the laugh carries her too far over. We stand amazed as she topples from the terrace and crashes into the vineyard some feet below. No permanent damage has been done, but the party is over and so is my stay on Capri . . .

Or I stroll the medieval streets of Siena and see the Swedish girls, like great coveys of blond grouse, dancing away before me, pursued by the slim ferret shapes of the town's young blades. The Swedish girls and I, all students at the private musical academy of Count Chigi Saracini, have just returned from a hilarious outing to the little town of San Gemignano where, in the main piazza, at the foot of the town's thirteen noble towers, we have heard an open-air performance of *Il Trovatore* in which the tenor has cracked a high C and, upon being loudly condemned, has invited some member of the audience to step up and do better. (There were no takers, but the performance ended in a near riot of flying seat cushions.) Now the girls and I have descended from the bus to find the young men waiting, as they wait every night for their northern goddesses. And soon, perhaps in a few minutes, the girls will pair off, one to a blade, and vanish arm in arm around the corners of the dark, silent streets. The summer is nearly over and my own goddess has already gone home, to her husband and children in Stockholm. I will walk back alone to my room in a villa on a slope above the brown rolling hills of a Tuscan valley . . .

Or I sit at a café table across from an uncle, whom I'll call Umberto. He has a long, lean face with pale cheeks, high, arched eyebrows and thinning gray hair combed straight back and close to the skull. Zio Umberto is a failure, bitter about the eclipse of the books he has written and the poverty the war has brought him. I am sad for him because I remember how he was in my childhood. On his rooftop terrace he had kept a pair of pet black snakes. The reptiles had lived in a drain and as a child I had watched, awestruck, from a window as their long, glistening bodies had glided slowly into the sunlight. Zio Umberto had also kept the amputated small toe of one of his feet in a bottle of formaldehyde and he had been fond of showing it to me. "You see, Billino," he had said to me, turning the bottle slowly around in the light so that the toe could be observed bobbing gently in the fluid, "an absolutely useless organ. I had it cut off to prove to everyone exactly how useless it is." He used to fry noodles in melted butter and he had once turned the garden hose on a neighborhood bully who had been tormenting me. Now he is a bitter old man who sits at café tables and complains of the absence of something he calls order in public life. I listen to him because it is my way of mourning his past glory . . .

It was a wonderful game I learned to play that morning, at the rail of the ship taking me home. The patterns of my Italian kaleidoscope seemed endless and I had only to close my eyes to summon them up. They linked me indissolubly to my Italian heritage and confirmed daily the gifts Italy had showered upon me. During those four and a half years I had not been fully aware of what was happening to me and I had not been properly appreciative. I had begun by rejecting so much in Italian society, mainly the abstract political and religious props I had quickly identified in my mind with the square-pillared slabs of Fascist architecture and the ornate baroque of Roman churches, all pretentious front. I had been impatient with Italy's failure to achieve true democratic reform and social justice, and I would become enraged when my Italian friends and relatives would settle placidly, as many of them did, for one of the more established dogmas of left or right, or

were simply swept away by the new wave of laissez-faire capitalism that had begun to engulf the country. It wasn't until I left Italy
that I was able to forgive the Italians for not being Puritan social
reformers and to realize how much I had benefited from what
they were.

In any case, now that I was going home, I would have plenty
of time to play the game I learned that morning, plenty of time to
remember and to speculate on what it had all meant to me. I went
to the stern of the ship and stared back at this country I had come
to love as dearly as my own. I remained there until long after the
mist-shrouded cone of the volcano had sunk out of sight and the
empty sea had enclosed us. I could not tear myself away from the
rail.

I was crying, I realized, but not because I had shut myself off
from a world I didn't understand and had not wanted to be part
of, but because I knew now that, like my mother, I had at last
become a citizen of two worlds. As one of my street people
observes later in this narrative, the stink of Rome's ancient stones
was in my bones. I could no longer imagine it any other way and
I was sure I would always come back. What hurt was that I didn't
know exactly when.

INTERMEZZO

I spent most of the next ten years in New York. I did come back to Italy in 1952 with my first wife, but we left after less than a year, partly because, like many American women, my wife had difficulty adapting to the restrictive ground rules of life for females in a Latin country, and also because I was unhappy in my job. I was running a public relations office in Rome for an outfit called Italian Films Export, a semi-official entity supported by the Italian film industry, which was eager to expand the production and distribution of Italian movies in the U.S. My job was to think up feature-story ideas for English-language publications, assign photographers to take pictures of film celebrities, gather up all the publishable gossip I could about the Italian movie world, and feed all this chatter and gloss back to New York, from where our home office would try to place it.

The worst part of the job was having to be nice to visiting members of the American entertainment press, some of whom expected me to do most of their work for them as well as be lavishly wined and dined. The low point was a visit to Rome by the columnist Leonard Lyons, a pompous little man who expected me to supply his wife with a car and driver so she could go shopping in comfort and who informed me that his literary style had been molded on a careful study of the essays of Addison and Steele. I lasted about seven months in this work and fled back to America with relief.

Except for a couple of brief visits, nine years were to pass before I returned to Italy, this time with two daughters as well as my wife in tow. Since 1956 I had been on the staff of *The New Yorker*, first as a fiction editor for three and a half years, then as a staff writer. I had also written several novels. I planned to live in Italy and to write magazine pieces from there, mainly for *The New Yorker*, while also continuing to turn out fiction, short and long. We settled into an apartment in the Aventino, in one of the loveliest residential sections of Old Rome. (I used to delight in giving instructions to visitors bound for our place from the center of the city: "From the Piazza Venezia, go down the Via of the Imperial Forums, turn right at the Colosseum, go past the Arch of Constantine toward the Circus Maximus and the Baths of Caracalla. Just before you reach the Pyramid of Cestius, turn left. . . . ") From there I began to write not only about what I had already experienced, but mainly about what I now observed.

I immediately found changes much more startling to me than the ones that had occurred in my own country, because I felt, as I still do, that the onrush of modern capitalism was organic to the American social structure but not to the Italian. I remember, for instance, being shocked by Federico Fellini's movie *La Dolce Vita*, not because of the extent of the social corruption depicted in the film but by the fact that that corruption was so peculiarly American—the photographers, the movie-industry shenanigans, the night life, the child with her ear attuned to the jukebox. The Romans, after all, had been pretty handy at orgies and such, and I found it alarming that in the film a pallid American striptease had been substituted for the glories of the ancient romp. I would have preferred to see the Italians go to hell in their own way, but at least to remain true to my concept of them. Ever since then I have continued to be amazed by Italy. I have also been charmed, delighted, occasionally horrified, but never bored. Although, for personal reasons, we did not remain permanently in Italy this time either, but left again after about a year, I have continued ever since 1962 to come back on a more or less regular basis, usually for a stay of a few months at a time. I always find plenty to write about and I'm sure I always will; Italy is a cornucopia for any journalist.

The tone of these pieces is, I think, quite different in style and approach from the earlier ones, mainly because I was (and am) no longer involved in a voyage of self-discovery, as far as Italy is concerned. The first-person pronoun is less evident here and certainly less important as an arbiter of events. What I wanted to do (what I'm *still* trying to do) was simply to report what I thought was going on and why, and what the Italians themselves felt about it. I have done very little updating, but left these selections pretty much as I first wrote them, even though the point of view is clearly one of reminiscence.

PART TWO

PART
TWO

CHAPTER ONE

IL BOOM

S oon after I got back to Rome, in December 1961, an old friend of mine, an American who had lived in the city for a long time, remarked that many things had changed in the nine years since I'd left. "After the war, there was a lot of political excitement in the air, but the pace of life was slow and easy," he said. "Now no one gives a damn about politics, except the politicians, and the pace has become a gallop after material goods. For the first time in my life as an American in Italy, I feel like an effete Athenian among ancient Romans."

It was certainly true that the Romans were apathetic toward the political situation. Not even Premier Amintore Fanfani's much discussed "opening to the left"—the formation of a new governing coalition, based upon assurances of support from the Socialists—had caused much excitement, though it was actually the most revolutionary political development of the sixteen years since the Christian Democrats had come into power. In forming his new government, Fanfani had turned his back on his old allies, the Liberals, whose party had become associated almost exclusively with the interests of big business, and risked everything on the word of Pietro Nenni, the wily old Socialist leader, who had promised to back the government if it carried out its announced intention of nationalizing the production of electric power and doing something about Italy's ever-present unemployment problem. But these matters seemed to excite hardly anyone, and the reason, as my friend pointed out, was that Italy was enjoying a solid business boom. It was hard for people to concentrate on the ins and outs of coalitions when everybody was trying to get rich and when conditions were so good that practically nobody had to struggle to survive. For the first time in the country's history, *il benessere*—Italy's equivalent of a chicken in every pot—seemed to be truly within reach.

The most obvious sign of *"il boom"* was Rome's fantastic traffic problem. No one knew what to do about it. The city had issued license plates for more than five hundred thousand cars, and it often appeared that all of them were trying to use the same street at the same time. The swarms of motor scooters and bicycles that I remembered had been replaced by even larger swarms of tiny Fiats, whose drivers seemed to be fanatically engaged in day-long Dodgem games without rules and with nothing at stake but their lives. Of all the world's large cities, Rome, with its spidery network of narrow, irregular streets, its cluttered piazzas, its monuments and ruins, and its abrupt hills and winding river, was perhaps least suited to the automobile age. "Where are we going to put all these cars?" an article in the daily *Paese Sera* inquired. "Rome risks being stuffed full from one day to the next; complete immobility in her main arteries, which even now are unable to cope with the increasing rhythm of traffic, threatens to become a reality at any moment." The story went on to predict that people would soon have to resort to rafts—bought, like their automobiles, on the installment plan—and pole their way to work along the Tiber.

Despite constant acrimonious criticism in the press ("CITY AND STATE INERT AGAINST THE INCREASING CHAOS" was a typical headline), the authorities had probably done as well as could be expected with an impossible situation. A network of new roads had been built to accommodate the vehicular tides flowing throughout the city, and every street, every avenue had its forest of traffic signs. That old nemesis, the traffic cop with his book of tickets, was becoming an all too familiar figure. (Foreigners, especially tourists, were gently treated. Instead of a ticket, they usually received a little blue slip printed in four languages, in which they were welcomed to Rome, "the most cherished goal of international tourism," informed that they had violated a provision of the highway code, and that "the communal authorities are quite convinced that this infringement was unintentional and wish you a very happy stay in Rome.") However, there were few stop lights at intersections, and the burden of deciding who had the right of way remained with the driver, who usually shouldered it with sangfroid and a terrifying indifference to the consequences of error.

The main system that had been adopted to keep the traffic flowing was the basically simple one of moving everyone in a circle to the right. Unfortunately, in Rome this didn't always work; the driver often arrived within sight of his destination only to run up against the disheartening little blue sign with a white arrow pointing off to the right, and, upon obeying it, became enmeshed in another tangle of one-way streets and dead ends, or trapped in a jammed piazza between a church, a fountain, a public building, and a national monument, until at last, by a system of trial and error, he escaped, sometimes finding himself back at his original starting point. Furthermore, one-way streets in Rome had a habit of changing their direction (along with their name) every eight or ten blocks, and until one became used to it, it could be unnerving to find oneself heading directly into a wave of cars coming the opposite way. The local traffic system had its drawbacks, all right, but no one could deny that there was a certain competitive zest to driving in Rome that was absent from American cities.

The triumph of the automobile, with all that it implied in the way of an industrial boom, was, of course, not merely a Roman but a national phenomenon. Indeed, Rome itself had benefited less from *il* boom than many much smaller towns. Rome was still primarily a city of civil servants and store clerks, and the average income was lower than it was in many other Italian cities. Nevertheless, the earnings of the average Roman had more than doubled in the past six years, and the superficial evidences of the new *benessere*, which actually radiated from Milan, were all readily visible. In addition to automobiles, people were buying radios, television and hi-fi sets, washing machines, and refrigerators. Shop windows were filled with goods, and despite the relatively high price of everything they displayed, the stores were doing a brisk business. There were now several American-style supermarkets, plus a couple of laundromats, and it was considered chic to be seen in them. Good restaurants had always prospered in Rome (Romans rarely entertained at home in the evening, preferring to make an excursion en masse to some favorite culinary spot, where the food was likely to be superb and astonishingly cheap), but now the city's theatres and night clubs were also thriving. This was regarded as an extraordinary step forward, since the *real* Romans had a centuries-old reputation for wangling free theatre tickets and for being able to nurse a single sweet vermouth through an entire evening at a ringside table in the most fashionable club in town. Reluctance to waste money on either entertainment or art had always been characteristic of this city, in which everyone knew someone who had a cousin who worked in a Ministerial office and could get it for you free. Few were the plays that ran more than four weeks in the old days, but now a mere four-week run of anything was considered a failure. And nothing about the new Roman affluence impressed me as much as the sight of an entire middle-class family out on the town and drinking whisky at a dollar or more a shot in some fancy *boîte*.

Despite Italy's high birth rate and the difficulties of emigration, there was less unemployment, and consequently (another sure sign of better times) everyone was complaining about the servant problem. Domestics, it seemed, were harder to find than ever before, demanded more money, wanted to live in homes of their own, and were joining a labor union. Only wealthy Roman households could afford to pay a servant more than fifty dollars a month, lower wages than even a minor store clerk could earn. The situation troubled an impoverished Roman nobleman, who confided to me that he still had a maid who had been with his family for many years but that even she had begun to ask for a better deal. "Wherever social and economic justice occur," he confided to me, "there life will become a little less gracious."

The most striking aspect of *il* boom was its identification in the Roman mind with the American way of life, as it was usually reflected on local movie screens and in popular picture magazines. Stores and other businesses had begun to advertise their wares in English, and unlimited installment buying was the order of the day. American fashions and American crazes were adopted immediately and wholeheartedly—often to an extent that would have been considered embarrassing at home. *Il* Twist was red hot, but it had by no means driven out the rock 'n' roll combos—consisting of young men with pompadour haircuts and named something like "I Crazy Boys"—that had become standard fixtures in all the night clubs. Practically every musical television program was modelled on the Ed Sullivan Show. American words, phrases, and bits of slang had crept into the Italian language; I remember overhearing one day a young Roman buck greet a friend he was meeting for an aperitif with *"Buona sera,* man, *che fai per il* weekend?"

Physically, too, quite apart from the network of new roads and the ever-present sign of clogged traffic, the city had changed a great deal. The center of Rome, with its famous landmarks, had been defended from the real-estate speculators by stringent laws designed to guarantee the city's historical integrity, but in the outlying residential areas there was chaos. Along the Via Cassia and on Monte Mario, in sections that used to be open countryside dotted with small private villas, great slabs of terraced apartments now rose, piled carelessly on the hillsides, like children's bright-colored blocks; the Parioli, once a quiet, fashionable quarter, had become a tangle of streets and villas; and to the south serried rows of institutional-looking buildings, the apartment houses of the new bourgeoisie, marched across barren acres of upturned brown earth toward the Alban Hills. Rome had become a city of builders, on a scale not even imagined since the time of the Caesars.

All this building and earning and buying and selling seemed to go on, and to be growing, quite independently of what the government did or didn't do. *Il benessere* had become a state of mind, a goal—something that every citizen now felt entitled to achieve and therefore avidly pursued. Naturally, in this climate of "anything goes" there had been some abuses and a few spectacular scandals. The current one, which had begun to come to light about the time of my return, and had led to a parliamentary investigation, had to do with the construction, then still incomplete, of Rome's new airport on a marshy tract at Fiumicino, a few miles north of Ostia. The case had a flavor that was typically Roman, because so many of the people caught up in it turned out to be linked to one another by ties of family and friendship as well as by business interests. At the center was the curious figure of an Air Force colonel named Giuseppe Amici, whose family seemed to have had an interest in the swampland chosen for the airport. In 1951, Colonel Amici, then a major, had been appointed by the Ministry of Public Works to supervise the construction of the airport, and, according to the parliamentary inquiry into the matter, for seven years he had apparently been in complete charge, accountable to no one, spending money and assigning building contracts as he pleased. During all that time, the Colonel had been either a partner or a large investor in several building firms that had been doing a handsome business with the airport. The result was that the new airport, whose cost had been originally estimated at twenty-four million dollars, had already cost nearly fifty million and would probably cost another forty or so before it was finished.

However, it was when one began to unravel the thread of family connections that the Fiumicino affair became fascinating and characteristic. The private secretary of a Cabinet Minister in charge of certain aspects of construction at the airport was the cousin of a building contractor's wife, who happened to be in business with the Minister's wife; the Cabinet Minister who appointed Colonel Amici to his post had as *his* secretary an Air Force general, who also happened to be the Minister's brother-in-law; Mrs. Amici had gone into business with the wife of an important official in the Ministry of Public Works; Arturo Amici, the Colonel's son, had formed a business partnership with Anselmo Fusari, the Colonel's driver, who, in turn, had invested large sums of money in two business concerns holding contracts with the airport. The voluminous parliamentary report began to read like one of Stendhal's Italian novels—a feudal tale of characters linked by the interests and irresistible attractions of blood. "It is a picturesque quadrille," the writer Eugenio Scalfari observed in a series of articles in the independent weekly *Espresso*, "a saraband of wives, cousins, ex-dependents, in-laws, split into opposing ranks that meet, quarrel and make up, vary the projects, change the direction of the airstrips, make and unmake prices and contracts." Scalfari went on to ask, "Are we faced with an isolated episode, however scandalous and grave? Or are we faced with the crisis of a system and its institutions, which are evidently unable to function and to defend themselves from private interests?" In a long, bitter editorial, *L'Osservatore Romano*, the Vatican newspaper, commented, "There is nothing to say—public and private morality have been deeply wounded."

Despite the extreme seriousness of these views, very few people in Rome believed that anything would ever really be done about the Fiumicino scandal. The consensus among my more cynical friends seemed to be that the case would die away in time and be forgotten, and that if it should ever reach the courts, the accused would know how to protect themselves, procrastinating and throwing up a dense smoke screen of documents to confuse the issue. This is precisely what eventually happened, but then, as one Roman financier informed me in private, "The airport will never be finished, not until everyone involved has earned himself at least a little villa by the sea or an Alfa-Romeo."

The most interesting man I met in Rome soon after my return was Pier Paolo Pasolini, a thirty-nine-year-old novelist, poet, critic, translator, scriptwriter, and professional philologist. A thin, intense, soft-spoken, bespectacled homosexual, he was blessed with a genius for arousing controversy. He had just made his first film, *Accattone*, and it was causing an uproar. Its release was held up for a while by government censorship, and it had been under attack, as well as defended, by various officials, literary men, and celebrities in general. It was also making a great deal of money. Filmed at a cost of about a hundred and thirty thousand dollars, it had already earned more than twice that amount during the first three weeks of its local run.

Pasolini's subject matter, which he had already explored at length in two best-selling novels, *Ragazzi di Vita* and *Una Vita Violenta*, was the sordid, brutal world of the Roman *borgate*—a world where grace and hope had yielded to extreme cruelty and indifference, and a resignation that went beyond mere despair. The *borgate* were squalid Roman communities—shantytowns, many of them—inhabited by more than two hundred thousand people, whom Pasolini himself described as a subproletariat. Hardly anyone succeeded in escaping from the *borgate*, and the few who did were soon replaced by others—the poorest of the peasants who had begun flocking to the city from their country villages in the hope of finding jobs. Pasolini was born in Bologna, but he had lived in Rome for the past twelve years and obviously knew his background well. When he had first moved here, he had been penniless, and the people he had lived among then were the people he portrayed in his books and his movie. "The world of the *borgate* is pre-Christian," he said. "It has been preserved by the structure of the Papacy, which imposed itself upon this culture and froze it protectively in time. The face of it is baroque, but the understructure is simple; it is built not on love, but on a code of honor." "*Accattone*" means "beggar," in the most literal sense, but it has a nastier connotation, implying something of the thief, or the hustler—something underhanded and mean. In the movie, it was the nickname of a small-time pimp, whose sole ambition was to have a girl who would be able to keep him in style—dress him flashily, and buy him cars and jewelry. It was the only way he could envision escaping the hunger and poverty he had known all his life, but he is undone by his inability not to love the one creature he could exploit. The part was beautifully played by Franco Citti, whose rough features succeeded in exactly rendering the character's weakness, sloth, and sensuality but also conveyed an inner vitality and a capacity for irony and ferociously honest introspection. "We're all a bunch of bums, we're all done with, they've shoved us aside!" he says in the film. "We only count if we have a thousand lire in our pockets. Without that, we're nothing." It was not a cry of despair but a hard statement of truth.

Like many young Italian writers, Pasolini had worked for the movies from time to time, but *Accattone* had given him his first chance to direct. Knowing nothing of technical matters, he had made rough sketches beforehand of each scene as he saw it in his head, consulted with his camera crew, and then simply went ahead and shot it, never making more than two or three takes of any one episode or varying the position of the camera. The result was a stationary, brutal directness that complemented the subject matter. The film was full of the sights and sounds, the heat—even, it seemed, the smells—of the *borgate*. And the language spoken was not merely *romanaccio*, the dialect of the slums, but a language created by Pasolini—an odd, poetic blending of pure Italian with words and phrases of authentic slang.

It is hard to understand now why the film should have been so bitterly denounced at the time. It was neither pornographic nor immoral, nor did it grind any political axes. It blamed no one and attacked no one. Pasolini was accused of being a Communist, of trying to be a second Jean Genêt, and of wanting to be the Italian Rimbaud, but he thought of himself as a crusading moralist who in his work had chosen to impose a morality on a world that had none. (In *Accattone,* he used the music of Bach to underline the dreary squabbles of his pimps and prostitutes, thus reminding everyone of the essential beauty of humanity beneath even the most bestial veneer.) He himself was to become a victim of it. Some months ago, he was found murdered in his car, abandoned near a stretch of empty beach north of Ostia.

CHAPTER TWO

THE MORAL CAPITAL OF SWITZERLAND

T he oddest thing to me about Milan is that although it has changed more drastically over the years than any other large Italian city—and is, in fact, constantly changing at a feverish pace—it always gives me the same comfortable, unchanged impression when I return after an absence. I find it is still predominantly a city of grays and browns; of large, elegant-looking *palazzi* with broad French windows; of narrow avenues paved with maroon stone blocks, along which green trolleys rumble; of fogs and rain and sudden extremes of humid cold and heat. If I stroll down the Via Manzoni past La Scala, stop for coffee at one of the cafés in the Victor Emmanuel Gallery, or wander out into the vast Piazza del Duomo for a look at the familiar Gothic spires of the cathedral, all seems exactly as I remembered it, and the reason for this was first explained to me by an Italian architect I met there. "The city is a huge cobweb," he said. "At its center, in medieval Milan, crouches the Duomo, and everything moves centripetally toward it. If, like most casual visitors, you stay within the circle of the old city moat, then the place *is* much the same. It's outside the moat that things are happening."

My failure to admire everything that is new and different about the city annoys my Milanese friends, who are always eager to point out all the improvements that have been made since my last visit. Most Milanese are intensely chauvinistic, and naively proud of their city's modern achievements, and nothing delights them so much as the sight of a new building or the sound of a new statistic. I had lived in the city for about six months in 1950–51, but I had not been back since. No sooner had I appeared this time than I found myself being whisked about in a car by three Milanese businessmen whose sole purpose, apparently, was to impress me, and they succeeded. Milan, which was badly damaged by bombs during the war, had been rebuilding ever since—chaotically, tirelessly, and seemingly without the slightest thought for aesthetic considerations, or even for basic urban needs. Around the perimeter of the cobweb, entire countrysides had been swallowed up by blocks of apartment houses, unrelieved by parks or open spaces. There seemed to be no zoning codes or rules of any kind. An office building rose amid slums, a new apartment house contained suites of offices, a night club flourished in the basement of a bombed-out ruin.

Immediately after the war, a local newspaper took a poll of its readers, asking what they most wanted to see in the Milan that was about to rise from the rubble. A good many of them rather surprisingly chose a skyscraper, and Milan now had several of them, despite the fact that the city is surrounded by the almost unlimited flat real estate of the Po plain, and has no more pressing need for such edifices than do the American plains cities that also feel they must have them. Between the main railroad station and the Piazza della Repubblica, to the southwest, the Pirelli and Galfa Buildings, both thirty-one stories and the city's tallest, soared above a forest of lesser glass-and-steel structures that might have been transplanted directly from Park Avenue. Between the Piazza della Repubblica and the Porta Garibaldi, about five blocks to the west, the city administration had begun to build a so-called Centro Direzionale, a kind of city-within-a-city that would include more skyscrapers, more office buildings, and a few luxury apartment houses and hotels, along with parks, movie theatres, supermarkets, and shops. The Centro Direzionale, as its name implied, was intended to relieve the crushing congestion in the center of town—though this concept was viewed skeptically by some of the more knowledgeable citizens. "It it one thing to build a new center," one of my businessmen guides explained, "but it is another to make a real Milanese go there. We all have this strange idea that every day, at least once, we must walk through the Victor Emmanuel Gallery or stand in front of the Duomo. Perhaps it is because we have so few other permanent things here. Anyway, every day at lunchtime I bet you will see people going right from the new *centro* to the old, and the old *centro* will be even more crowded than before."

Although the skyscrapers were the most striking symbols of *il* boom, the Milanese were even prouder of their new subway, which was first proposed in 1905 and had been under construction since 1957. From one end of the city to the other, you repeatedly came across devastated piazzas and streets where furious digging was going on. All day long in front of the Duomo itself, knots of vociferous sidewalk superintendents peered down into the subway excavations, often exchanging banter with the workers below. The Milanese didn't seem to care so much about what the new subway system could do for them as for the simple fact of its existence. One heard from all sides that it was to be the newest, the fastest, the cleanest, and the best—and, above all, that it was being built without any help from the government, and against appalling odds. "Milan rests on water, you know," one of my guides confided to me as we stood staring down at an uncompleted station platform. "All you have to do is go down five or six feet to find it. What a problem! But it just goes to show that here in Milan we can do what can't be done anywhere else in Italy."

This has always been a frequently recurring theme in Milan, where the hometown booster spirit often seems as impassioned as that of certain cities in Texas. Everything in and around the city is touted as superb, fabulous, colossal, incredible, miraculous, or (rarely) merely great. The enthusiasm is shared, in varying degrees, by non-Milanese. A well-known Florentine writer once told me in Rome, "Milan is the only serious city in Italy," and a French visitor was quoted in a local magazine as having said that Milan had "a verve that London has lost, Paris is losing, and New York can never have." An American management consultant who had offices in Milan and in several other large European cities maintained vehemently that the Milanese were by far the most dynamic people on the Continent to do business with. The Milanese themselves are always able to muster a lot of statistical evidence in support of their superlatives, and it may well be true, as a local economist once observed, that "if the Lombard industries should come to a halt, the entire economic life of the nation would be paralyzed."

Seventy-five thousand firms, including a couple of dozen of the country's biggest, such as Montecatini Chemical and Pirelli Rubber, were then providing employment for nearly eight hundred thousand people in the city area. The Milan stock exchange handled five-eighths of the country's securities transactions, and the Milanese controlled a quarter of Italy's active capital and paid a quarter of its taxes. The average income of the million and a half Milanese was the highest in Italy, there was a telephone for every three inhabitants, there were nearly three hundred thousand automobiles, and there was hardly any unemployment. The want-ad columns of the *Corriere della Sera* were full of requests for skilled workers and domestic servants. And according to an article I read in the weekly *Epoca*, the Milanese were not only richer and happier than other Italians but also luckier; in the Totocalcio, the national lottery based on the results of weekend soccer games, the Milanese won more—a total of about a million dollars—than the citizens of any other place.

Milan's astonishing concentration of wealth and industry was partly the result of the city's favored position in the middle of the lush Po valley, but it was also, to some extent, attributable to the Milanese character. In an essay published in the *Corriere*, Indro Montanelli, a well-known Italian writer and journalist, described the Milanese businessman as "a courageous and tenacious fighter with an almost infallible nose and very quick reflexes, who at a certain point falls in love with what he is doing and does it more out of love than self-interest. Work drugs him. . . . He is terrified of Sunday, because then he doesn't know what to do with himself." Nor, Montanelli went on to say, was it a question of family, since fewer than a hundred thousand local citizens could trace their Milanese ancestry back more than a couple of generations. Apparently, it was all due to the magic effect on character of the city itself, and it was often pointed out to me that most of Milan's great fortunes had been made by humble people who had come to it from elsewhere and started from scratch.

During the past few years, *il boom* had created both a new middle class and a new stratum of the genuinely rich—people who had made their millions and were now chiefly preoccupied with spending them as ostentatiously as possible. It had, for instance, become important to entertain lavishly, though the Milanese was traditionally an early-to-bed, early-to-rise sobersides. Debutante parties, which had recently become de rigueur among this group, had been known to require the services of two orchestras, one white and one black. (Parties could be given for a variety of reasons. A well-known opera singer threw one to celebrate making his first billion lire.) Regulation possessions include a Mercedes-Benz or a Cadillac, a motorboat, a box at La Scala, a collection of abstract paintings, appropriate furs and jewels for one's wife, and at least one very valuable antique or objet d'art. Stories about the gaffes perpetrated by the new rich were as common as those about our own oil tycoons. A typical report going the rounds concerned a young matron who set out to acquire her first modern canvas. She was shown a Picasso, and asked its price. When she was informed that it cost eight million lire, she said, "Too bad, I wanted something for ten," and walked out of the gallery. Another tale concerned a cheese king who had ordered a cabin cruiser he had seen in a magazine ad. When the boat arrived, he had it trucked to Santa Margherita, on the Gulf of Genoa, and launched. At once, the owner decided that the locale was wrong; the yacht didn't look right in so large a body of water. So he had it carted to Lake Garda and refloated, but again the effect was discouraging; the boat looked insignificant against the backdrop of the Alps. Consequently, he had a special pool dug for it in the garden of his country villa, just north of Milan, and he now happily entertained his friends aboard it on weekends. Great wealth also produced more profound problems, of course. Though the local businessmen worked all day long, their wives, surrounded by domestics, did not, and the varieties of malaise nurtured by too much leisure had become a boon to the medical profession; Milan, in fact, was the only city in Italy with a thriving psychiatric practice. A common neurosis was the *crisi di parcheggio*, an hysteria brought on by inability to find a parking space in the middle of town.

A most serious concomitant of Milan's prosperity was the rush of people from other parts of Italy to find work. About eighty thousand immigrants were coming every year and every day more of them could be seen pouring bewilderedly out of the long trains of second-class coaches that arrived hourly at the central railroad station. Contrary to the popular impression, most of these new citizens came not from Sicily, nor from the equally arid southern tip of the Italian boot, but from the impoverished agricultural areas and stagnant villages of the nearby Veneto, to the east. Still, it seemed as if every other voice one heard in the streets and restaurants had the broad, slow inflections of the south. The more established Milanese referred to the southerners as "*terroni*," meaning people who were overly attached to outmoded peasant customs, but the use of the term was ordinarily more affectionate than opprobrious. In any case, according to the Milanese, the *terroni* were soon as happily engaged in the pursuit of profit as everyone else. The process of adjustment, however, could be painful and ugly. For one thing, despite all the building that was going on, the city couldn't begin to provide accommodations for all these new people. Many had to settle somewhere outside of town, and every day a quarter of a million workers had to spend several hours getting to and from their jobs. Some of them, in order to be at work by seven or eight o'clock, had to rise at four, and did not get home till late at night.

Home itself could be a horror. Though Milan's slums were far less noisome than those of Naples, Palermo, or Rome, they existed, and as many as thirty people had been known to share a small, bare apartment or a couple of rooms in the so-called "ant-heap *pensioni*" that flourished on the outskirts. The immigrants did their best to cope patiently with these conditions. The usual procedure was for the man of the house to come first, look for work, and get settled; then he sent for his family. Sometimes, however, he had to bring his family with him, and then he had to find immediate shelter. Ingenious methods had been devised to meet this demand. In the woods and fields of Brianza, a once exclusive residential area north of the city, the landscape teemed with one-room shacks and bungalows, most of them built by unemployed carpenters and stonemasons from the Veneto. Because these structures had been put up illegally, and were periodically condemned by the police, they were designed so that they could be dismantled and reassembled in a matter of hours. The authorities found themselves nearly helpless to eliminate the Brianza community because it was capable of reestablishing itself nightly. The going price for one of its portable and squalid homes was about two hundred dollars.

A traditional dominant theme in Milan's attitude toward the rest of the world is resentment of Rome. There is nothing new about this—the Milanese have never forgiven Cavour for his insistence on making Rome the capital of his united Italy, and they still revere Napoleon for having established *his* Italian capital here—but as Milan's post-war power and influence grew, so did its traditional umbrage. The local feeling about Rome, then and now, is a compound of distrust, envy, and contempt, comparable to the reactions of Chicagoans vis-à-vis New York. Whenever anything goes wrong, the Milanese are likely to blame Rome, and "S.P.Q.R." is translated locally as *"Sono Porci Questi Romani"* ("They are pigs, these Romans"). Since Rome is, after all, the seat of government, the Milanese are inclined to believe that all governmental regulation of commerce is a heinous conspiracy to defraud them of the fruits of their genius. "Politics is a Roman industry, and the only one they have," a friend of mine said to me one day. "We make the money, and they steal it." The Milanese have long been indifferent to politics, and, consequently, are almost unrepresented in the government Ministries, where, they feel, most of the damage is done. They are likely to point with pride to all that their city is accomplishing without government help or interference—then it was the subway, two new airports, public housing, and so on—and they invariably claim that they could do much more if Rome would just leave them alone. At the time the European Common Market was being created, the city administration published a handsomely illustrated brochure in four languages touting Milan as "the Seat of European Institutions" and in which a lead article proclaimed boldly that Milan was "a capital in search of a country."

Quite apart from all the rational explanations for the Milanese grudge against Rome may lie a deeper cause. This is the gulf that separates two distinct mentalities—both Italian, but worlds apart. I once overheard a discussion between two elderly, distinguished women, one from Rome, one from Milan, on the relative merits of their hometowns. The Roman lady had been maintaining loudly that Milan was not an Italian city at all, but the moral capital of Switzerland. The Milanese matriarch's firm, final word was "I never go to Rome. Everything is so old there."

CHAPTER THREE

THE OLD
DONKEY'S SKIN

O ne of the recurring themes in Italian life is the inefficiency of the Civil Service. I was reminded of it soon after my return to Rome by the series of scandals that broke out involving one branch or another of this arm of the central government. First there was the one involving a maladministration of public funds for the construction of Rome's new airport, at Fiumicino, and this was soon followed by several equally lurid ones, most notably in the customs service, the Health Department, and the state banana monopoly. Every few months, year in and year out, the attention of the country is periodically focussed on the antiquated, self-perpetuating bureaucracies that for many decades have functioned, for all practical purposes, independently of the public interest and all political institutions. Anyone who has ever entered a Roman Ministry in an attempt to carry out the simplest civic chore—requesting a passport, say, or seeking out the proper authority to deal with some humdrum business problem—can testify to the atmosphere of confusion, sloth, and sheer ignorance that prevails in the Kafkaesque corridors of the handsome old *palazzi* in which the institutions of the state have proliferated.

In an article in the weekly *L'Europeo*, Luigi Barzini, a writer who is also a Member of Parliament (or was then), once compared the structure of the Civil Service to the skin of a very old donkey, covered with wrinkles, bumps, and half-healed sores. He pointed out that more than a million persons depend directly upon this decrepit organism for a living, and that the cost of maintaining it amounts to about half the country's entire budget. Yet its employees are badly selected, badly used, and badly paid. There is an almost total absence of discipline, and this, according to Barzini, is partly due to the fact that no one who doesn't steal at least a billion lire or kill his superior can be fired. "The offices in which these people are distributed were not created for reasons of efficiency," Barzini noted. "They exist by chance—they were born during the unification of Italy, or they were created by Fascism, to meet some organic exigency or to set up someone protected by a powerful Minister. Once created, an office cannot be easily abolished. It struggles ferociously to survive, invents new tasks for itself, camouflages itself, disappears from view, changes its name." And Barzini went on to remind his readers that right up to 1954 there was an office devoted to paying reparations for the damage caused by the march of Garibaldi's thousand Red Shirts through Sicily in 1860. "We can be grateful for the barbarian invasions," he observed. "Otherwise, we'd have somewhere in Rome a press office for the Vestal Virgins."

Periodically, the government attempts to reform this institution, or at least talks about doing so, but for some reason nothing is ever done. This is probably because the consequences of any drastic reform would be politically disastrous in Rome, which is still largely a city of civil servants, many of them in minor posts and all of them sadly underpaid. The public's dislike and distrust of its government employees is more than matched by the discontent of the employees themselves, who unite from time to time in strikes that paralyze the transportation systems, the post offices, the schools, and other essential services. The scandals themselves never lead to anything, either, since it has long been a Roman axiom that *i pezzi grossi*—the big shots—never go to jail. "The absence of a sense of the state, of belonging to a political society, as apart from the broader aspect of being Italian, is generally regarded as the principal source of Italy's political troubles," a British correspondent once commented in the *Economist*. He went on to point out that the fact that the immediate representatives of the state are hardly of the best doesn't help matters.

The Romans themselves, of course, know how to get around having to deal with the bureaucracy. The usual method is a judicious use of *la bustarella*—an envelope stuffed with money—that gets passed under the table to the right person. Other, more ingenious methods have also been adopted, with varying degrees of success. An English woman I know, a longtime resident of Rome, used her good looks. She had been waiting in vain for months for a permit to install an elevator in her apartment house. Since she lived on the top floor of an old building on the Via della Croce, near the Piazza di Spagna, and it had taken her nearly two years to get the other apartment owners in her building to agree to put in an elevator, she had become increasingly exasperated by the silence emanating from the city government, without whose consent she could do nothing. Her building was an old one in the historic center of the city, which is protected from change by a host of restrictive government regulations. My friend got up one morning, put on one of her handsomest outfits, and descended on city hall. It took her about an hour to locate the proper office, which she remembers as a large rectangular room in which half a dozen old men dressed in shabby-looking business suits were rearranging what looked like stacks of papyrus scrolls, reading pornographic comic books, and sipping coffee. Her entrance into this tomb made a dazzling effect. She announced her business, gave her address, and stated that, if she were given her permit within three days, she would reward the man who brought it to her with a leisurely afternoon of bliss in her company. The elevator has since been installed and functions perfectly.

Most *statali*, as civil servants are called, have at least two jobs, since the pay is too low to support them. Many of them work as waiters in restaurants and cafés or help to run small family enterprises on the side. A few are artists and writers who can find no other means of support. Perhaps the most celebrated *statale* of all time was the Roman poet Giuseppe Gioacchino Belli, who was the first of the great vulgar poets who wrote in *romanesco*—the city's sharp, spicy dialect—and his laudable ambition was "to paint the whole moral and civil life and religion of our Roman people." He showed himself to be characteristically Roman by distrusting his own talent and trying fanatically to reform his own nature, without the least success.

Belli was born in Rome in 1791, had a miserable childhood, and escaped from poverty by marrying a rich woman ten years his senior. He wrote his first dialect verses around 1820, but the bulk of his work was composed between 1830 and 1849. The revolutionary winds of 1848 and the dramatic events of the short-lived Roman Republic dismayed and depressed him. He became a misanthropic recluse and, after the restoration of the Papal government, a humorless supporter of the status quo. He got himself appointed theatrical censor of the city government, and soon made himself an unenviable reputation as a pedant and a bigot.

The Rome of Belli's time was a small, cheerful city of fewer than a hundred and fifty thousand people, asleep among its green hills and tumbled ruins and wholly unprepared by inclination and recent history for the agitations of the political events that were soon to overwhelm it. In illustrations of the time, all the familiar monuments, from the Trinità dei Monti and the Spanish Steps to the Colosseum and the unreconstructed Forum, are seen as if through a haze of improbable memories. Children gambol around the Triton in the Piazza Barberini, trees shade the Palatine, peasants spread their country wares in the archways of the palaces where medieval princes and their ladies once walked. The visual impression is of a city exhausted by its past glories and ready to sink with a sigh beneath the cypresses and the vineyards of the soft, surrounding hills.

Belli, of course, knew better. In his verses he depicted the vitality of a city on the eve of its rebirth. There is hardly a section of old Rome that the poet did not celebrate in one or another of his two thousand poems, and in all of them one can sense the surge of life beneath the ancient charm, which evidently cloaked a more piquant reality. Unfortunately, Belli, once he became a *statale*, repudiated all the work that was to make him immortal. Being unable to undertake the task himself, he asked a friend of his, a monsignor, to collect his verses and destroy them. Dialect poetry was not highly regarded in those days, and little of Belli's work had been published, but his poems were very frequently recited at public gatherings—much to the author's discomfiture and alarm, since they tended to be openly skeptical in tone, and were invariably scornful of the clergy. Luckily, the monsignor turned out to be a far more cultivated and broadminded person than Belli himself; he collected the verses and carefully preserved them. When the poet died, in the city he had loved even while he castigated it with his wry wit, it was about to become the capital of a new nation, and its people have remembered him only for the sometimes bitter but loving truths he sang of them. Like many other Roman *statali*, he had managed, without really wanting to, to live two lives.

CHAPTER FOUR

EIGHTY MILLION IMPORTANT PIECES

 few years ago, an American woman emerging with a party of fellow tourists from an exhausting morning spent tramping about the ancient Roman forums was heard to remark that in some places the grass grew so tall that it reminded her of a safari she and her husband had once taken through the African bush. "I could have sworn I saw a lion," she said.

From time to time, stories appear in Roman newspapers not only about the height of the grass in the various forums but also about the general stage of decay and disrepair afflicting many of the city's most famous monuments. "Urgent work is needed, on restoration of roofs, columns and pavements," one such story stated a few years ago. "A city like Rome has a million problems every day and ours always take second place to things like roads and building construction. But, on the whole, the communal monuments are all in salvageable condition. That is to say, they're not in a disastrous state."

Few outside experts would agree with this estimate of the situation. In fact, eminent individual citizens and such private organizations as Italia Nostra, which concerns itself not only with the country's cultural and artistic patrimony but also its ecology in general, have been predicting for years the total destruction of the great outdoor museum that is Italy to most foreign visitors. "I go to Pompei and I find that the most complete, unique document of an ancient civilization is falling to pieces under the weeds because there are no funds to maintain it," Professor Ranuccio Bianchi Bandinelli, a well-known historian and archeologist, once commented. "I go to Milan and I find that the Duomo is crumbling because the water-bearing strata have been unbalanced by the surrounding excavations made to aid the speculations of the building industry. I come to Rome and the walls of the Palatine and the Roman Forum are collapsing. It's the rains."

The Professor made it clear in his statement that the rains he was referring to alluded to a veritable deluge over the past twenty-five years of a class of people in power and the earning of money at the expense of the nation's heritage. In all of Italy, as an article in Milan's *Corriere della Sera* pointed out, the amount of money spent to preserve urban historic centers and works of art is roughly what it costs to build about twenty miles of *autostrada*. Nor, according to Antonio Cederna, the author of the piece, can the blame for this situation be laid simply on a chronic lack of funds, the scarcity of technical means, or the bureaucratic inaction that results merely from slipshod administration. "What is now clear, instead," he wrote, "is that the blameworthy inertia demonstrated by the governments of this past quarter-century is an intentional one and that no attempt is going to be made to remedy this disastrous situation. Thus it will be possible to continue to favor all those who profit from the plundering of our cultural wealth."

Hard words, but no one in authority has since dared publicly to challenge them. Nor has anyone denied that what the experts have been saying for some time now about the condition of the country's great monuments is accurate. Outside of Rome, in addition to the Duomo of Milan and the ruins of Pompei, the most celebrated invalids are the Tower of Pisa, which needs shoring up against a dangerously accelerating rate of incline; the Golden Doors of the Baptistery in Florence, which were badly damaged by the flood of 1966 and are corroding; the great bronze Horses of San Marco, rotting in the polluted air, and since removed from their pedestals; and the entire city of Venice itself, whose state of decay has been an international *cause célèbre* for years.

Until Italy's leading newspapers and magazines began to write extensively on the subject a few years ago, little or nothing had been done to carry out any of the major repairs and restorations recommended by various government-appointed committees in 1956, 1965, and 1968, and even since then, with the press still playing Cassandra almost daily, not much gets accomplished. Additional funds to save Venice, for instance, have been voted by the parliament, but no one can seem to agree on how or by whom they should be spent. Indro Montanelli, whose scathing series of articles in the *Corriere* in the early seventies did much to focus attention on the inaction of Venice's municipal authorities, was brought to trial by them on various charges, including slander. The case dragged on for months in a Milanese court until Montanelli was at last acquitted. The fact of the trial itself, however, did little to whip up enthusiasm for future similar crusades by other, less established writers. It has since become very clear that the only time the authorities respond or move with any alacrity is when the press manages to get the word through to the outside world.

This is the main reason why many concerned Italians were delighted when, soon after the Palatine and the Imperial Forum had been temporarily closed a few years ago to all visitors because of cave-ins and danger from falling chunks of stone, an American millionaire named Thomas Merrick, from Long Beach, California, offered to buy the Colosseum, then also undergoing worried examination by the experts. Mr. Merrick declared to the press that he was quite serious and promptly despatched a handsome blonde to Rome to negotiate the purchase. He offered a million dollars in cash, proposed to spend another million to restore the monument, and expected to get his money out by charging admission. The journalists had a delightful time and several leading Italian dailies published fanciful illustrations depicting the Colosseum festooned with ads, graced by a movie marquee and with uniformed attendants hustling prospective patrons along toward a row of box offices. Startled spokesmen for both the city and national governments at first remained silent, then rather huffily declared that the Colosseum, along with Rome's other great ruins, was definitely not for sale. Mr. Merrick's emissary lingered in Rome for a few days, gave interviews from her hotel room in which she confessed she had been unable to get anyone in a position of power to take her seriously, and departed. "Too bad," commented one journalist to a friend of mine. "At least the American would have done something. Our people have done nothing."

In defense of the authorities, there is an incredible amount to be done and not only because the politicians have been ignoring their responsibilities for years. The country's artistic patrimony, according to figures released by the Ministry of Education, consists of some eighty million "important pieces," but no exact count has ever been made or is even possible. Doubling, tripling, even quadrupling personnel and appropriating additional billions of lire would only slightly alter the overall picture. Much has been written over the years about the state of the major monuments, but the situation is far worse in the smaller towns, the outskirts of the cities, and in the open countryside, where Greek, Etruscan, Roman, and medieval relics are being wiped out daily by simple neglect, as well as by theft, casual vandalism, and calculated dismemberment. In Rome itself, as in most Italian cities, it is impossible, for instance, to dig more than a few feet in the older quarters without unearthing a broken statue, a sarcophagus, an ancient pavement, a column, a frieze, an underground chamber or at least a few coins, pottery shards, tools, and weapons. Every time such a discovery is made, work is supposed to halt while experts from the Commissione delle Belle Arti come in to evaluate the find, confiscate it for the state or the city, and perhaps recommend further archeological excavation. A houseowner trying to dig himself a cellar, an architect in charge of a new apartment house, or an engineer overseeing a complicated public project is naturally reluctant to inconvenience himself or his employers for the sake of a few pieces of stone (especially when the find might look so well in his own living room) and he often keeps quiet. The result is that, in addition to the existing monuments quietly going to pieces everywhere, thousands of others disappear or never come to public light.

Soon after Thomas Merrick's purchase offer, the Colosseum, too, was closed, because quite sizable pieces of it had begun to split off and tumble into the arena as well as the surrounding area. Coming on top of the Palatine and Forum closings, the event shook the public consciousness more than any other, mostly because the Colosseum is not only the city's most famous landmark but also the subject of a celebrated Roman proverb dating back to the ninth century: "When the Colosseum falls, so will Rome and with her the world." Still, everyone agreed there was little else Professor

Gianfilippo Carettoni, the national government's Superintendent of the Antiquities of Rome, could do, since it was pointed out that legally he was responsible for any damage, injuries, or deaths suffered by visitors to the monuments entrusted to his care. In fact, he was being sued at the time by a South American tourist, who suffered a broken leg while attending a "Sound and Light" show in the Forum. Professor Carettoni, it was pointed out, could hardly have been expected, knowing the alarming condition of his trust, to wait calmly in his office for the police to show up one day with a warrant for his arrest on manslaughter charges.

The Colosseum, along with the Palatine and the Forum, was soon reopened to the public, but access to all sections of the monuments has been severely limited ever since. Visitors to the Palatine and the Forum, as well as to a number of other sites, now have to thread their way along narrow paths delineated through the less risky areas and entrance to a number of temples and other buildings is still being denied. The Colosseum itself is surrounded by five hundred yards of wooden barriers about thirty feet from the arches and access to the interior is limited to a narrow, fenced-in path leading into a corner of the arena; no one without a special permit is any longer allowed to roam the upper levels. Hardly anyone was cheered by the declaration of Elveno Pastorelli, the engineer who carried out the inspection and recommended the measure, to the effect that there was no danger of the Colosseum falling. His report also pointed out that parts of the structure, including large blocks of it, could and probably would come down, thanks to the damage caused by chemical erosion from polluted air, the vibrations of the heavy traffic in the adjacent avenues, and the many years' neglect of the upper walls, where plants and weeds have taken destructive root between the stones. "Two hundred and fifty to three hundred million lire are needed just to fix the Colosseum," declared Professor Carettoni. "But it's not only the amphitheatre that needs care. The entire archeological park needs urgent work that would cost three billion lire spread over a period of five years." Where the money is going to come from is the key question, since Italy has been undergoing serious economic crises for years now and the city of Rome's total accumulated indebtedness amounts to billions of dollars.

The sum estimated by Professor Carettoni is considered low now by most of the other experts who have recently commented on the situation and would, in any case, barely suffice to conserve in an adequate state of restoration the major monuments that are visited by half a million people a year. Much more money would be needed not only to take care of the thousands of other relics large and small scattered all over the city, but also to recruit, train, and pay the staff necessary to oversee them. The national government, for example, has only one chief and three assistant archeological inspectors to supervise the thousands of acres entrusted to its care. There are never more than five or six custodians on guard at any time in the vast reaches of the Imperial Forum and the Palatine, where for years people have wandered at will, chipping off and carting away bits and pieces of the monuments as souvenirs. The Trajan Forum and Markets, entrusted to the city, are watched over by three custodians, two of whom sit by the entrances. And the Museum of the Baths of Diocletian, which contains one of the world's most fascinating collections of antiquities, is so understaffed that two-thirds of it has had to be closed to the public.

The entire problem is also vastly complicated by the fact that the city's monuments and museums are administered by three separate entities, each entirely independent of the others, with their own staffs, funds, and methods of operation. Roughly speaking, the state has control over the most famous of Rome's antiquities, including the Colosseum, the Arch of Constantine, the Imperial Forum, the Palatine, the Domus Aurea, and the Baths of Caracalla; the city is responsible for the forums of Caesar, Augustus, and Trajan, the Ara Pacis, the Argentine, the Aurelian Wall, half a dozen museums, and a great host of minor sites; and the Vatican, which, of course, administers the city's thousands of churches and sacred relics, supervises the catacombs. This division of authority and responsibility has, like almost every other aspect of Italian daily life, its roots deeply embedded in history, but no one can any longer remember exactly why or by whom the original partitioning was made. For years critics have pointed out that city and state would do better to get together and jointly administer the common heritage, but, though everyone agrees matters would be simplified thereby, no one familiar with the ways of Italian bureaucracy seriously expects that any sweeping structural administrative reform will ever be carried out. "Do you know what we will do instead of carrying out any reforms, taking the necessary legislative steps and appropriating adequate funds?" I was once told by a Neapolitan archeologist. "We will form an organization under the patronage of several illustrious names and prominent politicians and we will try to raise the money from our friends abroad, just as we did for Florence and Venice. But this time for Rome, *urbe caput mundi.*"

Because I was anxious to see for myself exactly what sort of problems could come up from day to day and what the state of the monuments might be in one of the less frequented areas, I contacted the city administration's Division of Antiquities and Fine Arts one day and arranged to spend a working morning with one of its so-called *agenti archeologici,* who were described to me as sort of roving guards whose job it is to police assigned areas, report on their overall condition, and make specific recommendations based on their findings. The Division's headquarters is a charming, perfectly preserved medieval house on the Via Portico d'Ottavia, flanked by two magnificent Corinthian marble columns and hard by the awesome bulk of the Theatre of Marcellus. The setting, in the heart of one of Rome's most spectacular and best preserved archeological areas, is an entirely fitting one and seems calculated to inspire enthusiasm even among the undermanned, underpaid staff of public officials who work in a rabbit warren of crowded little offices inside the headquarters. The day I dropped in, at about eight o'clock in the morning, two of the Division's four archeological inspectors, Professors Giuseppina Sartorio and Eugenio La Rocca, both young and intensely serious, were already hard at work going through the reports handed in by the agents whose labors they supervise.

"My God, there is so much to be done, but so many difficulties to overcome," La Rocca said, confirming the overall situation as reported in the press. "But perhaps not enough has been written about the shortage of personnel and the kind of salaries even the most qualified people receive," he added, pointing out that he had obtained his own post by graduating from college with a degree in *Lettere antiche,* completing a three-year post-graduate course in archeology, and passing a very stiff series of written, visual, and oral exams. "For this I now earn a monthly salary equivalent to about two hundred and sixty-five of your dollars. Needless to say, though I am twenty-six, I live at home with my parents."

"Our colleague, Professor Lukos Cozza, refers to our pay as *stipendi stupendi,*" said Professor Sartorio, with a smile. "Of course the money we each receive matters less than the fact that there seems to be no money at all to make many of the repairs that are urgently

needed. Our Division cannot carry out this work. We can only
report and make recommendations based on what our agents in
the field find out, then we have to wait for the other communal
divisions to act. Sometimes we wait for months. Sometimes the
work is not done at all. It's very frustrating. You'll get some idea
of the problems during your walk with Consolini, the agent we've
assigned you to this morning. He's one of the best men in the
Division."

Luigi Consolini turned out to be a stocky, middle-aged Roman
with thick, black hair combed straight back, sharp features and
alert, shrewd dark-brown eyes. He and the other *agenti archeologici*
meet at about eight-thirty every morning in a ground-floor room
where they sign in and write down by hand in a large notebook
everything they've found or observed during the previous day's
inspection. To cover Rome adequately would require, I had been
told, a full complement of forty-five agents, but at present there
were only thirty. The city has been divided into thirteen main
zones and each agent has an assigned territory to oversee. Consolini supervised Zone 1A, an enormous pie-shaped slice beginning at the Piazza di Porta Capena, at one end of the Circus Maximus, and bounded on one side by the Viale Aventino, the Via
Piramide Cestia, and the Via Ostiense, on the other side by the
Baths of Caracalla, the Via di Porta San Sebastiano, and the Via
Appia Antica. It was a huge area for any one man to handle,
almost all of it teeming with relics from the past, and it took Consolini four or five days to cover it. "My main trouble spots," he
complained, tapping a large map of the city hanging on one wall,
"are the Appia Antica, where people carry away the paving stones
and vandalize the statues, the Aurelian Wall and the Porta San
Paolo, where we always have work going on." He informed me
that this particular morning he planned to visit the wall and the
Tor Marancio area, then walk to the Basilica of St. Paul Outside
the Walls. "We can take buses part of the way, but it's better to go
on foot in the zone itself," he said. "That way I see everything I
have to see and some things people don't want me to see."

From the Division to the section of the Aurelian Wall Consolini
was to inspect is about a twenty-minute bus ride and during it he
explained that he had been an agent since 1945, for the past
decade or so in charge of the same zone. His interest in archeology
was awakened during the Second World War, when he was serv-
ing with a motorized anti-aircraft battery in Greece in 1942. "We

were stationed on a hillside near the Acropolis and for a while we didn't have much to do," he explained. "Our captain, however, was a passionate amateur archeologist and one day he gave us all shovels and told us to dig. We turned up mountains of stuff, but then things began going very badly for us and we had to get out of there in a hurry. Anyway, after the war, I got this job through a friend and I've been here ever since." He then earned, after twenty-seven years of service, about three hundred dollars a month, but because he had no children, he said that he and his wife managed to live comfortably enough.

After our bus ride, we had to walk up a hill and past a cluster of private villas, then over an open field and along a dirt road running beside the Aurelian Wall. About half a mile south of the Porta San Paolo, we came upon a handful of workmen repairing and rebuilding a recently uncovered section. Consolini, accompanied by the foreman of the work party, walked along peering intently at what had been done since he had last seen it two days before. "It's not easy," he explained. "The new parts have to be set back and the bricks cemented evenly, to contrast with the rougher work of the original. That way it's possible to distinguish between the new sections and the old structure. The work is also complicated by the fact that parts of the original wall were torn down and built over several times since the Emperor Aurelius put it up, seventeen hundred years ago. Other later emperors and several popes added to or strengthened the wall in order to defend the city against invaders." He pointed to an obviously still untouched mass of crumbling ramparts and piled-up rubble just beyond where we were standing. "That bastion, for instance, was built in the Middle Ages and it was used to defend the city as late as the time of the Roman Republic. This wall is nineteen kilometers long. Professor Cozza, who's in charge of it, wants to rebuild it so that eventually it will be possible to make a complete tour of Old Rome by walking on top of it. That was his father's idea, too, and Professor Cozza has spent his whole life carrying the work out." Consolini gazed for a moment at the wall as if slightly dazed by the enormity of his superior's vision. "God help anybody who lays a finger on Professor Cozza's wall," he added softly.

As we stood there, a little Fiat 500 came bounding along the dirt road beside the wall and a heavyset young man with a large camera strapped around his neck got out and began to take pictures. He told Consolini he was a journalist and was going to write a story about the wall. He seemed angry about it. "You're not going to write anything bad, are you?" Consolini asked. "We have enough difficulties."

"I write the truth," the young man said. He waved toward a part of the wall beyond the ruined bastion where a large modern skylight jutted out. "You see that studio over there? There's a sculptor who's been living in it for twenty-five years and who pays no rent. I've been inside it. It's a fabulous place. There are apartments and studios in this wall where people can live for practically nothing. They're full of rich people who should be thrown out."

Consolini looked distressed. "But why? They behave themselves. They take good care of the wall."

"I'm married and my wife and I can't find a decent place to live that we can afford," the journalist said, grimly snapping pictures. "There are poor people with no houses at all. I say throw these rich people out and let the poor people in."

"What?" Consolini said. "They would tear the wall down."

"Too bad," the journalist said, getting back into his car. "People are more important than walls."

"He's just angry because *he's* not living in the wall," Consolini said, as the young man drove away. "What can we do? We can't evict the people who have been here for years and who will defend the wall. Come on, I'll show you what happens to a monument when there's no one to defend it."

Again by bus and on foot, we proceeded to the Tor Marancia, a medieval watchtower, built on the ruins of a Roman villa, that sits on a barren knoll surrounded by tacky-looking apartment houses. The area was a working-class district noted for its squalor and high crime rate, and Consolini told me that the bar on the corner of the street next to the monument had recently been the scene of a bloody gangland killing. The tower, a square brick building isolated on its little hilltop, looked dismal and forlorn. The ground around it was strewn with refuse and, on closer inspection, the structure itself revealed some savage scars. Someone had gouged a hole in one wall and built a fire in it, turning the masonry above it black. Other chunks had been torn out here and there and the walls had been scribbled on, chipped, and otherwise defaced. Consolini told me it had once been possible to enter the tower and climb a circular iron ladder to the top, but that he finally had had to order the entrance walled up. "They tore the door off," he said. "They stole two old cisterns that used to be inside and several of the original wooden beams. They even carted off sections of the iron ladder to sell for scrap. The monument this way, of course, is no good to anyone."

As he stood there, glumly staring at the tower, two small girls of about five came running up the slope toward him. "Remember when we used to go inside?" one of them said. "It was nice."

"You know what happens now, if you go inside?" Consolini said. "Bombs go off."

The children stared. "This was the house of a queen," the same little girl said.

"No, soldiers lived here," Consolini said. The child looked stricken. "But the queen used to come and visit them," he added.

As we left, Consolini shook his head and said, "Now, if that journalist wanted to move in here, I'd be happy to try and get him the tower rent-free."

We walked back to the corner and took another bus, then got out and began walking along the Via delle Sette Chiese toward St. Paul's. The street, one of the oldest in the city, stretches from the Appia Antica to the Via Ostiense and is named in honor of the seven great churches all pilgrims to Rome were once supposed to visit as a matter of course. It has become a main traffic artery and so is almost constantly under repair, which means digging. "Every year we find things in this quarter," Consolini said. "I never know where they're working, so I simply have to walk it as often as I can."

Miraculously, none of it was being actually worked on this particular day, but Consolini kept darting up side streets to check and peering intently at stretches of the road where he obviously suspected someone had recently done something or might be about to do something without having notified him. "Once, digging on this very road, they found the head of a statue and an engineer in charge of the work carted it off without telling me," he said. "One of the workmen tipped me off, but by the time I found the engineer he had already been warned and had turned the head over to the state. It really belonged to the city."

Toward the end of our walk, we crossed an open lot covered with weeds and rubbish. In the middle of it sat two small concrete huts with locked iron doors. These were the entrances to the Catacombs of Comodilla, Consolini explained, three levels of subterranean galleries, partly unexplored and not open to the public. They stretched for miles and probably linked up with the other catacombs, forming part of the great underground network of Christian burial grounds stretching under the city from the Appia Antica all the way to the Via Ostiense. "This was once a private vineyard," Consolini said. "For years now they've talked about making it into a park and opening the catacombs to tourists. This year gypsies were encamped here. They threw their garbage and defecated into the air vents above the tombs. After three months, I managed to get them evicted. But will they ever build the park? Who knows?"

He shrugged and we moved on, walking in silence. Consolini was sweating slightly and he seemed depressed. "You know, I could cover much more ground if I could use my car, but the city won't pay for the gasoline," he said. "I waste half my working day in buses." A few minutes later, as we topped the rise of a hill and began to descend toward the now visible bulk of the cathedral, Consolini stopped and took my arm. "You know, we Italians have been trying to ignore our past and think only of the future," he said. "But a country with no respect for its past must truly be a country with no future at all."

CHAPTER FIVE

HEROES OF
OUR AGE

I n the summer of 1972, Federico Fellini interviewed himself in an Italian magazine. "What is Rome?" he asked. "What do I think of when I hear the word 'Rome'? I've often asked myself. And I know, more or less. I think of a big, ruddy face that resembles Sordi's, Fabrizi's, Magnani's, its expression weighted and preoccupied by gastrosexual exigencies. I think of a muddy, brown terrain; of an ample, broken sky, like the backdrop of an opera, a sky painted in violets, blacks, silvers—funereal colors. But, all in all, it's a comforting face." In Fellini's film epic, a vastly ambitious quasi-documentary panorama of his adopted city entitled simply *Roma*, many of the faces had these same qualities, but I'm not sure the effect was especially comforting. So many of his characters—the priests, whores, officials, policemen, night owls, and street people who swarmed across his screen—had a more than slightly ruined, corrupted look about them, an air of something noble and once beautiful allowed to decay almost beyond hope of redemption.

But Fellini's people, I realized as I emerged from a screening of *Roma* into the late-afternoon hubbub of the Piazza Barberini, were incredibly alive. They shouted and cried and, above all, talked

incessantly. They were passionately and totally involved in themselves, as unthinkingly committed to the small pleasures of the
moment as Falstaff, and now that I had spent a couple of hours in
their company, the ominous words spoken to me by a middle-aged
Roman cousin of mine a few days earlier—words that I had taken
very seriously—suddenly seemed false. "We've survived two
thousand years of foreign invasion, pillage, disasters of all sorts,"
he had said over a sweet vermouth at Harry's Bar. "But I doubt if
we can survive ten more years like the last ten. Our lives here are
getting worse—even the way we see ourselves." Nonsense, I
thought. The Romans didn't see themselves at all; they simply
were. My cousin, a talent agent, had been working for and with
Americans for several years. Clearly, he had been far more deeply
corrupted than any of Fellini's people.

Still, there was plenty to worry about in what had been happening. In April, when the city had celebrated her two-thousand-
seven-hundred-and-twenty-fifth birthday (it was supposedly on
the twenty-first of April in 753 B.C. that Romulus, standing on the
Palatine, had founded the city of Rome by digging the blade of
his plow into the earth), the occasion had been a melancholy one.
For one thing, the wolf cage on the Capitoline Hill, where for
years the municipal government had housed one or two symbolic
mother wolves, was empty. One wolf had died, another had failed
to flourish and had been shipped off to a zoo, and no suitable
replacements had been found. The imperial Roman eagle was still
on hand, in its own cage, but some Romans claimed that it was not
the right bird but a smaller, darker one from the Apennines. In
any case, the empty wolf cage and the silent, scruffy little bird of
doubtful authenticity seemed to symbolize the current plight of
the city—broke, dishevelled, paralyzed by the automobile, and at
the mercy of real-estate speculators. "As always," a journalist
named Antonio Cederna had written of the birthday celebration
in Rome's largest independent daily, _Il Messaggero_, "the vacuity of
the official ceremonies and their accompanying rhetorical chatter
served only to throw into relief and to illuminate in a harsh light
the squalid conditions in which this poor city finds herself."

"Squalid" is hardly the word that any visitor to Rome would
use to describe the parts of the city most foreigners come to see—
the famous ruins, the squares, the monuments, the gardens, the
palaces, the museums, all linked to the luxury hotels of the Via
Veneto by fleets of air-conditioned tour buses—but it did accu-

rately describe the way a good many thoughtful Romans then felt about their city. Even the most casual visitor couldn't help being struck by the filth in the streets and the accumulation of trash in the parks. Against a tidal wave of debris being spewed forth by an industrialized society modelled closely upon that of the United States, the Roman street sweepers—underpaid, overworked, dressed in their familiar wrinkled blue smocks, and equipped only with their traditional long-handled brooms—battled hopelessly, apathetically. The city's budget deficit mounted by millions of dollars a month, and apparently there was no money to spend on keeping Rome clean.

It was easy to get the feeling, too, that Rome was swiftly being submerged in a stone sea. Apart from the so-called historic center, where the authorities had made an effort, however inadequate, to defend history from the present, the city—and especially what one commentator had referred to as "the infamous outskirts," built during the past two decades—had become an ugly sprawl of unrelieved concrete. The latest statistics showed that Rome's nearly three million inhabitants had at their disposal an average of something between two and three square metres of green, but the four-fifths of the city's residents who lived in the newer sections had access to no greenery at all. Developers had put up houses and office buildings without paying the slightest attention to the existing zoning laws, which, on paper, did provide for parks, gardens, and playgrounds. For example, in a new quarter built in the Monte Mario area, to the northwest, about eighty thousand people lived out of easy reach of any sort of park, or even open space. The same was true for tens of thousands of citizens in at least a dozen other parts of town. Though there was no way to make an absolutely accurate check, a reliable estimate was that in the past few years about three hundred thousand rooms had been illegally constructed. And the buildings in these parts of town were architecturally ugly—square, cold, and institutional-looking, packed together on top of each other, worn and slummy before their time. "What we are fighting here is a true ecological battle for survival," an official of the Unione Italiana per lo Sport Popolare had declared. "And this just when there's so much fashionable talk about ecology."

The plight of the humbler citizens of Rome was of little concern to those who lived in the historic center, in remodelled Renaissance *palazzi* along the banks of the Tiber or in the luxury residential areas of broad, tree-shaded avenues and verdant hillsides. Such people always have little trouble finding congenial places to live. Low-priced housing, however, was so scarce, even in the most depressing outskirts, that groups of angry citizens periodically invaded new buildings to establish squatters' rights. What concerned affluent Romans much more than the hardships of the poor was the aesthetic rape of the parts of the city they really loved. Two or three piazzas—the Farnese, the Navona, the Santa Maria in Trastevere—had been emptied of cars, and the more beautiful buildings remained unscarred by commercialism. Yet even the historic center had seen such a proliferation of advertising billboards and neon signs that I would not have been surprised to find some morning that the Castel Sant' Angelo and the Dome of St. Peter's had been put to use plugging somebody's airline or soft drink. When I first discussed my outraged feelings with an old Roman friend and suggested in the strongest terms that savagely restrictive laws ought to be passed to prevent such abuses, he said, smiling, "We have the laws—we've always had them. In Italy, we have laws to take care of everything. The problem is enforcing them. And that requires a will and a discipline we do not yet have."

The theme was a familiar one to Italians, who have always taken a perverse pride in the anarchic individualism and the genius for last-minute improvisation that supposedly go to make up the national character. It was sounded again that summer by Franco Zeffirelli—a man who has never shied away from saying in public exactly what he thinks about practically everything—when he paraphrased for the benefit of the Roman press a statement made earlier by the novelist Ennio Flaiano. "Yes, we are a rotten country, corrupt in our institutions, but free," Zeffirelli said. "We prefer this solution to that of a well-governed country in which all the social currents are respected but which is without freedom." That is the sort of remark any one of my Roman acquaintances could have made, accompanying it with much ironic smiling and eloquent shrugging, and in the past it would have terminated any further discussion of the multitudinous social, political, and economic ills afflicting the nation. At this time, however, there was a growing feeling—especially among the young, who in the past couple of years had taken, like their American counterparts, to agitating in the streets—that this sort of answer, however historically valid, simply wouldn't do. "We can't go on like this," I was told by a university student who had been suspended for battling the police in the cobblestoned streets just beyond the walls of his classrooms. "We can't go on waiting for these same old men of the government to do things they have promised to do but are never going to. Talking is useless. Everyone in Italy talks. We must force them to act."

These words turned out to be prophetic, because this was the year Italians became conscious of a new form of violence on the political scene. After many months of strikes, brawling in the streets, bomb-throwing, and police raids, the strange, lonely death of the left-wing publisher Giangiacomo Feltrinelli focussed public attention on the presence of terrorists in the land. Feltrinelli had gone underground and had apparently blown himself up in an attempt to destroy a power-line pylon outside Milan. It was a comic-opera beginning to what was soon to become a national nightmare. Meanwhile, of course, the shaky governing coalitions that succeeded each other year after year—the same faces, the same names, the same speeches, the same problems, always unsolved—seemed powerless to remedy the social disarray. To many outsiders Italy appeared ripe for a revolution or some sort of drastic political solution, but nothing happened. "Italy keeps going, as it always has," Luigi Barzini observed at the time, "because, tucked away here and there in various corners of the society, there are honest, hard-working men quietly doing their jobs well. They are the real heroes of our age."

That January, at the end of a damp, unpleasant day, two young Romans named Dante Ottaviani and Sabato Panico walked into the Colosseum and began to climb the rows of empty stone seats rising above the darkened arena. They were carrying a couple of blankets, some sandwiches, and a bottle of water. When they arrived at an iron grating separating the part of the edifice open to tourists from the upper arches, they climbed on over, and perched at the very top of the amphitheatre. A small group of friends and relatives who had watched their progress from below now announced to all who would listen that the young men were there to stay until someone did something about them; they were protesting their inability to make an honest living.

At first, no one except the police paid much attention. Less than two days after they had gone up, Panico got sick and came down. Ottaviani, however, refused to budge. Dressed in pants, a turtleneck sweater, and a windbreaker, his blanket around his shoulders, he peered down, increasingly haggard-eyed, at his indifferent city. He seemed like some great angry bird. Occasionally, he held up a crudely lettered sign that said, "Murderers, you've forgotten about me." To the policemen and other authorities who tried to persuade him to descend, he declared that he intended to stay in the Colosseum and, if necessary, die there rather than come back down to the same world that he felt had treated him shabbily. His sole concern, he said, was the care and feeding of his wife and baby girl. "We're not looking for luxuries—we only want to unmuck our lives," he told one of the first reporters to interview him. "It's an old story. Always hunger, from the day I was born."

By the time Ottaviani had been up there a week, he had become a minor celebrity, primarily because his adventure made good copy and occupied portions of the city's front pages, but also because his case and what he had to say about himself and his plight, bitingly elucidated in the language of the streets, stirred up the vast reservoir of discontent under the surface of ordinary citizens' lives. "I'm all smashed up, and I've got a cold and a cough," he said on the fifth day, after a fall. "But I'm not coming down. What for? I've got nothing, and I don't want to steal. So I'll stay up here, and before I croak I'll throw my clothes down. That way, I'll die as naked as I was born."

Ottaviani's story proved to be a simple and disturbingly familiar one. His father was a bricklayer, his mother a part-time nurse, and he and a brother and two sisters had grown up in the narrow streets of the Monti, one of the older quarters of the city. When his father became ill and could no longer work, Ottaviani began to steal. He spent three years in reformatories, and later, between the ages of eighteen and twenty-three, a total of three more years inside the medieval walls of Rome's Regina Coeli prison. After the birth of a daughter, in 1969, he told the press, he quit stealing. "I didn't want her to be ashamed of her father," he said. "I didn't want anyone pointing the finger at her." With a brother-in-law, he began operating a street-corner stand near the railroad station, selling transistor radios, clocks, and cigarette lighters. But he didn't have a license, so the police harassed him constantly and confiscated his merchandise. Finally, after considerable difficulty, he acquired the necessary license, but he was assigned an area that required a car to operate in successfully. Ottaviani could not afford a car, nor, as a convicted felon, could he even get a driver's license. His protests went unheeded, so he returned to his old corner, whereupon the cycle of arrests and confiscations resumed. All he wanted, he said now, from his refuge in the Colosseum, was a permit to sell his stuff where he could make a living, but, he added, "If I don't see something written, I'm not moving from here." When a city official trying to persuade him to come down promised that his situation would be resolved within a week, Ottaviani replied, "It's all a trick. I don't believe in anything anymore."

The presence of this solitary protester on one of the city's most famous monuments—especially one celebrated for spectacles involving the feeding of wretched Christians to lions—began to embarrass the authorities, delight tourists, and outrage the prostitutes, the hustlers, and the petty thieves who earn their own shabby living within the shadows of the ancient arena. The prostitutes, the hustlers, and the thieves, unhappy in the glare of publicity and unable to operate successfully in the presence of so many policemen, firemen, and sundry officials, took to calling angrily up to Ottaviani to jump. The reporters, by this time, were having a field day. They showed up in clusters to interview Ottaviani and the relatives and friends who rooted for him down below and sent him up an occasional sandwich. On the seventh day, Nino Longobardi, one of the most eminent journalists in Rome, took to the pages of Il Messaggero to comment. "We don't want to make a symbol of Dante Ottaviani, much less a hero," he wrote. "But a country that turns its back on a man alone can cause anguish in the hearts of men still truly free."

The anguish—for Dante Ottaviani and his people, at least—ended on the afternoon of the eighth day, when two city functionaries brought him a letter signed by a high official and guaranteeing him a license to operate his stand near the railroad station. Declaring himself satisfied, and complaining that his bones were aching, Ottaviani came down, and was whisked off to a hospital to recover. Within two days, he disappeared from the news, but his protest was not forgotten. In the weeks afterward, a couple of hundred equally desperate people, singly and in groups, scaled other famous heights—in one case, the Dome of St. Peter's itself—to roost in public and demand, almost always unsuccessfully, the happy ending granted Ottaviani. It was as if his gesture and his words had spoken for the Italy that no longer counted—the people unallied with any powerful interest group, who were struggling to make themselves and their needs heard. In a story hailing the happy ending of Dante Ottaviani's ordeal, Longobardi concluded, "Meanwhile, the empty eye sockets of the Colosseum stare unblinkingly at us. For too long, those old stones have stood there, and they know us—ah, how they know us." To many people in his city, the young Roman's seemingly foolhardy act had become a metaphor for much that had gone wrong in Italian society.

CHAPTER SIX

MAMMA ROMA

W hat many people seem to remember best about Anna Magnani in her films is the way she laughed. Her laugh was explosive, overwhelming, as if deep inside her a dam had burst, letting loose a torrent of mirth that came surging up from some ultimate awareness of the world's follies. She laughed most often with her head flung back and her hands planted on her hips, a visual confirmation of the rough, earthy, woman-of-the-streets parts she played in many of her movies. Her very closest friends, however, thought that her laugh, like much else about her, was a mask, a way of hiding sorrows and dissatisfactions. "Offscreen, I never saw her smile," a friend once said, adding that her eyes, no matter what the rest of her face was doing, remained "absorbed in their sadness."

Her importance as an actress has been hotly debated. Some have seen her as the greatest talent since Eleonora Duse, and maintain that, given the chance, she could have played the full range of great parts, from the classical tragediennes and the dual personalities of the Pirandellian era to the afflicted heroines of Tennessee Williams and the neurotic bitches of Edward Albee. (Williams is said to have written several of his plays with her in mind, and to have wanted her to star in *The Rose Tattoo* on Broadway, long before she played it in the movies; one of the bitterest regrets of her life was that she turned down a chance to appear in the first Italian stage production of *Who's Afraid of Virginia Woolf?*) Others have declared that she was less an actress than a personality, the sort of performer who overwhelms whatever part she is given and makes it her own. She had only to be herself, to trust her own deepest instincts, and the limits of what she could do with a role were defined by those of her own complex personality. "She's not an actress at all," a critic once complained. "She is a force of nature." This debate, like those over whether Maria Callas was a technically accomplished diva even in her prime or whether Judy Garland could sing on key, is really beside the point. The Italian journalist Indro Montanelli wrote in *Corriere della Sera*, "I know only that of all the women's faces that have paraded across the screen, Magnani's made the deepest impression, because it was by far the most truthfully human. Only of her can it be said that without her today's cinema could not be what it is."

Anna Magnani was an illegitimate child, who never knew more about her father than that he was a Calabrian, and she was brought up in Rome by her maternal grandmother. She was never a beauty, and frequently, all through her life, she complained of her looks. She was a heavy-shouldered, large-breasted woman with a thick waist and thin, slightly bowed legs. She once compared herself to a potato mounted on a pair of toothpicks. But no one ever forgot her face, with its dark eyes, strong Roman nose, and ferocious-looking teeth, all framed by tousled, long black hair. She looked, in her best pictures, like a trapped or wounded wild animal, still full of fight and desperately determined to remain free at all costs. She studied acting at the Accademia di Arte Drammatica in Rome, then went to work on the stage, where, after a series of small parts, she gravitated naturally to the looser, comic forms of the musical revue. She could play the guitar and sing so movingly that even late in life, if the mood seized her, she would entertain her friends until dawn with her songs—a spontaneous nocturnal recital of an intensely personal kind, which seemed to give her much satisfaction and delighted her impromptu audiences. She got her first movie part in 1934, and eventually appeared in forty-four feature films—an average of more than one a year. In 1941, in a picture directed by Vittorio De Sica called *Ter-*

esa Venerdì, she sang a little song called "Here in My Heart," which, in her rough, husky voice, seemed to capture exactly the cadences of her Roman streets and established her as a true *popolana*, a woman whose voice spoke most eloquently the humble emotions of local time and custom. This image became firmly and decisively rooted in *Open City*, the now classic Roberto Rossellini movie that, in 1945, launched the wave of so-called neo-realistic films and established Magnani and the director as its foremost exponents.

For a while, during the late fifties, she became a Hollywood star, playing opposite, and all but submerging, such leading men as Burt Lancaster, Anthony Quinn, and Marlon Brando. With the last she had a violent struggle over billing, which she won, and she later said of Brando that he had talent but worried too much about his face. She was not impressed by Hollywood personalities (the only one she genuinely admired was Bette Davis), and eventually she tired of the whole so-called art of moviemaking. "I don't like the movies much anymore," she told an interviewer some years ago. "The time has passed in which I could delude myself that making a movie means making art. I don't dream anymore." In her last years, she appeared in very few films, most of them failures, and achieved her greatest late success as an actress by returning, nine years ago, to the stage in the title role of Verga's *The She-Wolf*, directed by Franco Zeffirelli. In a clumsily written but tragic, potentially melodramatic role, she gave an intelligent, disciplined performance that proved, if anything could, that as an actress she was far more than a personality.

To some extent, of course, her personal life strongly influenced the public's emotional response to her and led to confusion between the identity of the actress and the astonishing phenomenon of the Magnani personality. Her love affairs were tempestuous and became periodic clamorous events on the front pages of the country's popular press. "I'm not a weak woman," she once said. "I'm a woman who knows what she wants, and I've always known it." But she never found any man she wanted who was strong enough to weather the storms she broke daily over his head. Rossellini, probably the great love of her life, confessed that in two hours with her one ran the gamut of human emotions, and that in doing so one leaped from one crisis to another. From everyone close to her, including friends and relatives as well as lovers, she demanded complete submission, and perhaps for this reason, her happiest, longest-lasting domestic relationships were with small animals.

As she grew older, she was alone a great deal of the time and relied on fewer and fewer people—Luca, her son by her only marriage (to Goffredo Alessandrini, a director), and a few of her oldest, dearest, and most patient cronies. A compulsive night owl, she no longer toured the city's clubs and restaurants but lurked wakefully at home, sometimes not going out for weeks, and using the telephone to maintain her increasingly eccentric and tenuous ties with an outside world she had come to distrust. To some extent, she felt she had been discarded as an actress and forgotten by the people who had once loved her. "In this country, only the monuments survive," she told a friend.

On September 26, 1973, after a brief illness and an unsuccessful operation, Anna Magnani died. She was sixty-five years old and had often talked about death, regarding the whole process as an unjust and badly managed business. "Why shouldn't we die as easily as we're born?" she once asked. Apparently, she herself almost did so. The news, abrupt and unexpected, shook the nation and especially her city. Ironically, as she lay suddenly lifeless on her hospital bed, the public she thought had forgotten her was watching her final acting performance on its television screens, in a drama entitled *1870*.

Her funeral service, held in the Church of Santa Maria Sopra Minerva, in the heart of the old city, where she had spent her entire life, was attended by an enormous weeping crowd. The people of Rome came en masse to say goodbye, and so dense was the crush that some of her old friends could get no closer to the ceremony than the packed piazza outside the church. Inside, the proceedings were interrupted by occasional shouts of grief, and when the service was over and her coffin was raised up to be carried out there was a spontaneous, startling burst of applause. It was as if the community were mourning for and applauding itself, because she had been, without willing it or realizing it, the living expression of its spirit. She, too, had at last become a monument.

CHAPTER SEVEN

SEE NAPLES
AND LIVE!

W hen cholera broke out in Naples during the summer of 1973, the event was regarded by a number of people who know and love the city as a judgment on, and a predictable consequence of, its ancient way of life. Though the highly infectious disease is most commonly transmitted through polluted food and water, its spread can be controlled by not only antibiotics and vaccination but also such everyday means as boiling food and water or the judicious use of vinegar, wine, and even lemon juice. It can only thrive and spread in a slum area where large groups of people live too close together without light, fresh air, and adequate sanitation. It has sometimes been defined as "the disease of the poor." Cholera was one of the plagues that decimated the cities of the Middle Ages, but in recent times it has sprung up and flourished only in poverty-ridden parts of Asia. Between 1823 and 1923, there were six major outbreaks of the disease in Europe, the last one in Naples occurring in 1884, when several thousand people died. "The point is that nothing has changed here since 1884," a Neapolitan friend of mine told me at the time. "The same frightening cor.ditions of extreme misery still exist, just as they always have and perhaps always will."

In its roughly twenty-five hundred years of existence, Naples has unquestionably suffered more than its share of disasters, from wars, revolutions, earthquakes, floods, volcanic eruptions, and bombardments to slightly less drastic calamities of all sorts, but throughout its tragic history plague reappears as a leitmotiv. The great bubonic epidemic of 1656, for instance, wiped out well over half of the city's approximately four hundred thousand people and flourished, naturally, in the poorer and more crowded quarters. "Such statistics can seem unreal in our time," a Neapolitan author named Alfredo d'Ambrosio has commented, "but we have to keep in mind the epoch in which these events took place, a period characterized by extreme overcrowding, with a consequent absence of hygiene; the nonexistence of preventive medicines . . . the scarcity of doctors; and the overall backwardness of public sanitation." The irony is that, according to most observers of the cholera outbreak of 1973, these are almost exactly the conditions that existed then, and to them could be added the astonishing inertia and unawareness displayed by local authorities during the early phases of the epidemic.

The first cholera cases were officially acknowledged on August 28, in a cautious communiqué from the Ministry of Health in Rome, which stated merely that a number of people suffering from what had originally been described as "acute gastroenteritis with cholera-like symptoms" were actually "under suspicion" of having cholera. By then, at least six people had already died and about thirty others had been hospitalized. The disease, which had broken out in Ercolano and Torre del Greco, squalid waterfront suburbs at the foot of Vesuvius, had quickly spread to Naples itself, but, according to the Ministry's bulletin, "there is every reason to believe that the hotbed is limited to the above-mentioned cases" and the authorities were very much on top of the situation.

Actually, as the Italian journalists who immediately rushed into Naples while the tourists were rushing out quickly discovered, the official terminology was merely, in the words of one correspondent, part of "a continuous succession of manifestations of irresponsibility at various levels." The first suspected cases, it turned out, had been reported locally at least a week earlier, but not until the afternoon of August 27 had anyone in authority ordered the necessary laboratory tests to identify the cause of the infection.

Two of the city's leading medical officials happened to be out of town—one at a doctors' congress in Bavaria, the other on vacation—and no one else, it seems, was in a position to give the necessary orders. No one thought to inform the Ministry of Health in Rome, whose officials learned of the outbreak through a radio news bulletin on the morning of the twenty-eighth. This did not, however, prevent one of Naples' highest medical functionaries from blaming Rome anyway. "The fault is the Ministry of Health's, which gave us no forewarning," he said. "In 1972, we were stormed with circulars. This year, nothing." No one on the spot, apparently, would accept responsibility for anything, though, as a reporter acidly pointed out in the weekly *Epoca*, "Cholera, before spreading, doesn't wait for the circulars to arrive."

The initial efforts to cope with the epidemic were chaotic. There was, to begin with, very little cholera vaccine on hand, though most of the city's notables, including Mayor Gerardo De Michele, were among the first to be vaccinated. Even after big shipments began to arrive from Rome in the early days of September, the authorities remained seemingly incapable of organizing an effective way to administer the serum. In the Traiano quarter, for instance, where about sixty thousand people lived in a hive of decrepit buildings and narrow streets, a single vaccination center was opened in a ground-floor office of a public building in Piazza Giovanni XXIII. The only access was through a narrow glass door, and the office could not hold more than five patients at a time. By eight o'clock on the morning of September 1, the piazza was packed with ten thousand worried people jostling each other to reach the door, and by ten o'clock, when a hot sun began to beat down on them, they had become restive. There were only three policemen present to cope with the situation, which threatened several times to get out of hand, since there was obviously no effort to hurry up the snail's pace of the vaccinations. A possible riot was averted when the cooler heads in the crowd spontaneously took charge, hurriedly found some ramshackle wooden barriers, and set them up to create an orderly flow of patients toward the vaccination center, with preference given to small children. The incident was regarded by one observer as a typical example of the Neapolitans, betrayed as usual by their leaders, desperately improvising their own salvation.

By early November the epidemic was over, even though the

soul-searching and economic aftereffects were not. The statistics in cold black-and-white were hardly devastating, but they cheered up no one, despite the determined optimism of the official announcements. Twenty-four people had died, and two hundred and seventy-four cases had been authenticated, most of them in Naples and Bari, with a few reported in several other population centers, including Rome. It was never established exactly how the disease broke out, though the most comforting theory seemed to be that some travellers from North Africa had brought it into the city. Also under suspicion were the various kinds of shellfish illegally cultivated in the polluted waters of the bay and sold openly in the streets and markets. In fact, forty-nine persons, including a dozen public officials, were eventually indicted, mostly for the growing and selling of mussels, but it was never proved that the shellfish carried cholera. The mussel beds were destroyed by teams of divers, thus effectively putting several hundred people out of work and causing a good deal of public indignation. The general attitude seemed to be that Naples had suffered enough without adding to the unemployment rolls—a point of view heartily shared by everyone connected with the tourist industry. "Last year was catastrophic," Luigi Torino, president of the Ente Provinciale per il Turismo, declared. "Many small hotels were forced to close and to fire their employees. In August, five hundred thousand tourists fled in terror. Fear and its exploitation by our competitors brought us to the edge of a precipice. Today things are going better because we've made it our business to make known the limited nature of the evil."

Signor Torino's attitude, though widely shared by other bureaucrats, was not endorsed by at least one of the city's leading medical authorities, who pointed out that anyone can carry the cholera bacteria and that not much had been done since the epidemic to correct the conditions in which it thrives. During the following winter it was announced, for instance, that twelve hundred men were being hired to swell the ranks of the city's overworked and underpaid street-cleaning force, then consisting of about two thousand employees, half of them inactive for one reason of another on any given day, the rest equipped mostly with long-handled brooms and pushcarts. No one seriously imagined that "this little army of street sweepers," as it was described in one deadpan newspaper story, would make much headway against the roughly twelve hundred tons of refuse dumped daily in the streets. A much more prevalent attitude was the cynically fatalistic one I encountered over a series of *espressi* with some local journalists at a coffee bar in the Gallery. None of them thought anything significant had been or would be done to improve matters. "Naples has always had cholera," one of them commented cheerfully. "In other years, we called it colic or gastroenteritis or stomach flu. The real trouble is that, before all these wonder drugs, hundreds of thousands of people died whenever the plague broke out. The city was emptied and we could start over. Today hardly anyone dies, and so the city itself is being suffocated by the weight of all these hot, living Neapolitan bodies."

The hot, living bodies of Naples are its greatest, and perhaps its only, remaining major resource. Not even Venice has suffered so much from the attendant evils and totally predictable consequences of Italy's disorganized, practically uncontrolled post-war industrial boom and the economic depression that succeeded it. Today great stone clusters of terraced apartment buildings are massed along the heights of the Vomero, which used to be crowned by parks and the gardens of small villas, and the once verdant district of Posillipo, along the northern arm of the bay of Naples, has almost completely disappeared under heaps of what look like shoeboxes. It is almost impossible today to find a stretch of relatively uncluttered open space, and even along the lower slopes of Vesuvius a long belt of cement gives the impression of cutting off the dormant volcano from its natural sloping descent to the sea. "We had a city once that nestled between the hills and the water," a local architect explained some time ago, "but we had no effective control over the construction boom of the past ten years—at least until 1971, when new zoning laws were passed, much too late to do any good. The only concern was the most profitable way to make use of the space available, which meant the quick and careless throwing up of buildings whose only reason for being was to make money."

Between 1951 and 1970, dwelling units containing about six hundred thousand rooms were "thrown up" in this way, only a small percentage of them legally sanctioned even by the badly outdated so-called Regulatory Plan, or city zoning law, of May 29, 1939. This did not prevent most of these projects from being approved by the local authorities, from the mayor's offices on down. Both public and private sectors of the housing industry built pretty much wherever they felt like it, even in zones reserved for farming, set aside for public parks, or supposedly protected by the national Commissione delle Belle Arti, which attempts to defend historically and aesthetically important areas from despoliation. A report submitted in 1972 to the Ministry of Public Works in Rome eloquently documented the facts and fearlessly named names, including those of the city's highest officials, but it was clearly too late to do much more than simply punish the people responsible, some of whom had already been indicted, though few were ever actually brought to trial and convicted. A typical case involved a state housing authority acting in collusion with private interests and revealed, among other astonishing facts, how a land investment of a hundred and twenty-six million lire (then about a hundred and eighty thousand dollars) grew nearly eightfold in a period of nine days.

The physical consequences of all this illegal construction continue. For years now Naples has been subjected to frequent cave-ins. Holes suddenly open up here and there, and even entire hillsides slide away. Underneath the city is a huge catacomb of caves, abandoned wells, canals, and subterranean passages, some of which were carved out of the soft clay and rock by the ancient Greeks and Romans. During history's worst sieges and sackings, the Neapolitans have traditionally taken refuge in the larger of these underground caverns, and immediately after the liberation of the city during the Second World War hundreds of homeless families were found to be living in them. Now abandoned and often carelessly sealed over, their roofs periodically give way beneath the enormous added weight of all the new construction, and houses, cars, and people are sucked down into them. During one three-year period, eleven people died and sixty-two were injured in slides and cave-ins of one kind or another. The Neapolitans, who can't seem to get too worked up over the by now familiar corruption of their politicians and their most prominent private citizens, have complained loudly about the peril and inconvenience of living with the prospect of a possible sudden descent into the void, but not much can now be done about this aspect of the construction boom either. What everyone in Naples has had to learn to live with is the destruction of the city's most precious visible asset, the beauty and uniqueness of its once incomparable setting.

The Naples that still survives intact and unchanged is to be found in the dense latticework of tortuous streets and alleys, the famous *vicoli*, that crisscross each other up the Vomero to one side of the Via Roma and extend like a huge, incredibly tangled cobweb over the heart of the old city, split in two by a rectilinear succession of narrow avenues known generically as Spaccanapoli, or Splitnaples. From the hilltop of San Martino one can still look down along the entire length of Spaccanapoli and see a large part of Naples much as it was in Bourbon times. To walk the full length of it is to be in close touch with history, because a stretch of it, between Piazza del Gesù and Via del Duomo, is flanked by numerous decaying monuments, crumbling statues, and the great baroque *palazzi*, now in an advanced state of ruin, of the city's vanished Spanish nobility.

It is off these main avenues that the real day-to-day life of old Naples goes on, by no means entirely bereft of its traditionally picturesque and folkloristic qualities (the public maintenance of which is an economic necessity to most Neapolitans), but still amidst an increasingly desperate struggle with the terrible poverty the city has borne like a curse for centuries. The reality and consequences of that poverty can, to some extent, be grasped by simply walking through these teeming *vicoli*, where a quarter of the city's million three hundred thousand people live. The worst off are the dwellers in the so-called *bassi*, which are windowless single rooms opening directly onto the street, often inhabited by entire families, sometimes as many as a dozen people or more. Here, "in this fetid labyrinth of lanes buried between tall and monstrous-looking buildings," observed an Italian traveller passing through in 1896, "the numberless *plebe* of Naples, which is to say two-thirds of the inhabitants, lead a miserable life, deprived of air and light." So little has changed since long before these words were written that the poor of Naples are still referred to in Italian as *plebe*, a term with its roots in ancient Roman history.

No statistics can quite convey what life for these people is like, but the statistics are astonishing just the same. More than twenty-five percent of the population is unemployed. The city has the highest infant mortality rate in the country; six out of a hundred babies die during their first year of life. Only about a quarter of the children in the poorer sections even complete elementary school, though supposedly obliged by law to do so. Among other unenviable "firsts," Naples has the most polluted waterfront and air in Italy; the greatest population density in Europe—about fifteen thousand persons per square mile; the heaviest and noisiest traffic in the nation, circulating at the lowest average speed of about two miles per hour; the largest and worst slums, including vast areas, like the Traiano, constructed since the war; the most yearly cases of typhoid and viral hepatitis, as many as in all of West Germany; and a rat population estimated at eight million. "I get up in the morning and I ask myself what's happened, what *could* happen today," a local union leader once commented. "There's only one main problem here that is at the base of all the others—the question of work. We are sitting on a powder keg."

The impression one gets, however, is not one of incipient mass violence, of some possible spontaneous uprising against the unbearable conditions of life, such as have occurred from time to time in a number of less afflicted Italian towns. Traditionally, Naples has always been a conservative city, nourished by nostalgic memories of the monarchy and Fascism. It has occasionally risen in revolt, but usually for purely political reasons or against some particularly noisome foreign occupation. Poverty, to the average Neapolitan, seems to be merely a normal state of affairs, unfair and difficult to deal with, perhaps, but a situation to be confronted with expediency, not moral indignation. The noisy, confused, crowded, incredibly active comings and goings of the people swarming through the rubbish-strewn *vicoli* from dawn till late at night testify to nothing more than the ingenuity and vitality of a population living largely by its wits.

"What haven't the Neapolitans done to survive?" a Milanese journalist observed admiringly in the *Corriere della Sera* some time ago. "During the war they caused ships and soldiers to disappear. Today they traffic in contraband cigarettes and pornographic photographs, sell themselves as witnesses at the law courts, shine shoes, set themselves up as tourist guides, offer to mediate disputes, sell lottery tips, hire out as mourners at funerals, guard parked cars, beg, seize whatever tiny opportunity comes along to make it through the day." Such people are known in Naples as *millemestieri*, or thousandjobs, and no one can be in the city very long without having to cope with them. One of their other occupations is "painting" fish on market stands to make them look fresher and more salable. Although some *millemestieri* traffic in real crime and will deal in anything, from fake Swiss watches and phony Parker fountain pens to drugs and prostitutes, most are merely desperate citizens improvising a way to stay alive.

The profession of *millemestieri* doesn't really fit comfortably into the state's figures on unemployment and underemployment, just as the gangs of ragged children, the famous *scugnizzi*, hustling whatever they can find to sell through the streets, don't either. The problems of the city are so vast and chaotic that they simply cannot be illuminated by statistics or cured by the considerable sums of money the government and private industries occasionally pump into the moribund economy. Every attempt at such economic amelioration, no matter how well-intentioned, seems to be defeated. Some years ago, for example, the state-supported Alfa Romeo auto works opened an assembly plant in Naples, under the promising title of Alfasud, which was to provide eighty-five hundred new jobs and help to stimulate the local economy. During Alfasud's first year of activity, the unemployment rolls went up ten percent and more small businesses failed than ever before. What happened in part was that the new plant recruited workers almost exclusively from the city's tiny pool of skilled workers and technicians, thus causing a number of shaky minor manufacturing enterprises to fold. "The government and the northern industrialists make grandiose plans and dispense their princely favors," an engineer explained. "To starving people needing bread and cheese they promise lobster."

All such ventures are, in any case, regarded as utopian, particularly if set up by government representatives in Rome or a company with its home base in Turin or Milan. The reality in Naples is that nothing survives and nothing can be done without local political connections and the protection of some big shot in a position to dispense credit and personal favors. *Clientelismo* (an untranslatable term meaning, roughly, patronage) is the only technique by which the Neapolitan economy manages to survive at all, and nothing is more valuable to a struggling citizen than to come under the benevolent wing of someone with direct access to political power and public money. Without it, literally nothing can function, and the intrigues and maneuverings involved in some celebrated cases of enrichment by *clientelismo* have achieved a complexity well beyond the merely Byzantine. At the heart of every enterprise, of course, is an acceptance of things as they are that outsiders usually interpret as cynicism. Although most business ventures in Naples never come to anything, they always somehow manage to cost a great deal of money without providing jobs, and they vanish, leaving trails of promissory notes in their wake. In a city in which small companies have been known to fail because they could not meet payments of a few thousand lire, and the only credit readily available was at the usurer's, the air of resignation and cynicism is all too understandable. *Clientelismo* offers the only safety, and the one sin Naples inevitably punishes is ambition. Some years ago, a *millemestieri* nicknamed Giovanni the Immortal made a good economic thing out of stepping in front of moving automobiles. He survived twenty-six accidents and was regarded as something of a local hero in his *vicolo* because he not only supported his family by sticking the insurance companies but also provided an income for the neighborhood cronies who inevitably testified in court on his behalf. The day inevitably came when he misjudged a car's speed and was fatally run over on the Via del Duomo. At his funeral, a reporter for a local television program asked one of the mourners, an old man who had been a frequent witness at Giovanni's court appearances, how he felt about his benefactor's demise. The old man shrugged and said, "This time he exaggerated."

In this sea of resignation and indifference, only the young seem to have attempted any cohesive protest. In the sixties, when high-school and college students all over Italy began to agitate in the streets for better living and working conditions, young Neapolitans also began holding demonstrations, and since then various major rallies, periodically organized either by students or labor leaders, have brought out as many as fifty thousand people, most of them under thirty. But in concrete terms they have accomplished little, and the protesters are still very much a minority in a city with the largest and most virulent neo-Fascist movement in the country. Nor do these young people express anything like the same optimism and hope that have characterized some workers' and students' movements in the past. I once watched a demonstration, a parade of banner-carrying students, coming through the Piazza Municipio, and I was struck by the indifference on the faces of both the demonstrators and the older people watching them from the sidewalks. "But don't you understand," wrote a Neapolitan named Pasquale Villari to a Piedmontese minister in

1860, "that to destroy the abuses (of the system) means to destroy the city? In fact, all the professions, the trades, the arts of life, and life itself are founded on and fed by these abuses. Once you eliminate them, I can assure you that there will be quite literally no way to live."

It is not surprising, under the circumstances, that during the past thirty years many of the city's leading cultural and artistic figures have gone elsewhere, usually Rome or Milan. They rarely come back, even to visit. "We've remained a handful of old cats who don't even know where to meet," the writer Domenico Rea said a few years ago. The popular-song industry, once a Neapolitan specialty, has also practically disappeared. It once employed about three thousand persons—composers, lyricists, singers, arrangers, editors, typographers, and record producers—and dominated the Italian pop-music scene, but its yearly festival, the Piedigrotta, now ranks behind several others in importance. "Naples sings less and less," a retired impresario explained to me in the lobby of the San Carlo Opera House. "The young people look to London or America for musical inspiration. Who can blame them? That is where success is to be found."

A magnificent exception to the flight from Naples of its artists is Eduardo De Filippo, the most complete and universally admired man of the theatre the country has ever produced. The author of over sixty plays, at least a dozen of which are considered masterpieces, Eduardo, as he is usually referred to, has also written verse, a book of essays, and numerous movie and television scripts. He produces, directs, and stars in his own productions, and his gaunt, hollow-cheeked, deep-eyed, sensitive-looking face is as familiar to Italians as that of the Pope. Despite the success a few years ago of one of his plays in London, De Filippo's work is almost unknown abroad, mainly because it is written entirely in Neapolitan dialect and depends upon an absolute rapport between word and gesture to make its full effect. A critic once said, "De Filippo is one of those artists who can interpret the spirit of an entire people in a shrug, convey deep suffering in the raising of an eyebrow." "I want to say that everything begins, always, from an emotional stimulus," De Filippo himself has explained in one of his essays, "a reaction to an injustice, contempt for my own and others' hypocrisy, a feeling of solidarity and human sympathy for a person or a group of people, a revolt against laws that are outdated and anachronistic in today's world, dismay when confronted by events that, like wars, disrupt the lives of populations, and so on."

Eduardo was born in Naples in 1900 and made his debut in the theatre at the age of six in a play by Eduardo Scarpetta, his most prolific and best-known Neapolitan predecessor. Whenever he wasn't in school—which was often—he continued to work for Scarpetta, then later for Scarpetta's son, Vincenzo. By the age of fourteen, he was playing important parts in a repertory company that rehearsed every morning from ten till noon and put on three performances a day. With his brother and sister, Peppino and Titina, he began during the early nineteen-twenties to play in revue sketches he wrote and directed himself. By 1929, he was writing one-act comedies, and that same year, with Peppino and Titina, he formed his own company, which put on performances several times a day between showings of movies. In 1932, his first full-length play, *Who's Happier than Me?*, became such a hit that it established him on the national scene. After twelve years of continuous success, only briefly interrupted by the war, he reorganized his company under its present title, Il Teatro di Eduardo, and opened triumphantly at the San Carlo with "Napoli milionaria!," a typically bittersweet portrayal of Naples making the most of its dubious opportunities during the Allied occupation. In 1954, he took over, reconstructed at his own expense, and reopened the Teatro San Fernando, an old and celebrated theatre gutted by wartime air raids. Since then he has divided his time between Naples and the rest of Italy, while continuing to turn out his extraordinary plays. He has by now become such a national institution that when he had to interrupt the Rome run of a new play to undergo surgery for the installation of a heart pacemaker, the successful outcome of his operation, his convalescence, and his return to the stage just twenty-five days later were the subject of front-page news stories, editorials, and public rejoicing all over the country.

The secret of the enormous appeal of De Filippo's theatre is to be found in its absolutely truthful depiction, at every level, of Neapolitan life and the compassion it expresses for the suffering humanity of his city. As a young man, De Filippo used to frequent the law courts, where, he says, "Little by little, I assembled a crowd of the disinherited, the ignorant, the victims and the jailers, thieves, prostitutes, swindlers, heroic creatures and brutal beings, angels thought to be devils and devils thought to be angels." It is with these people, he explains, that he goes on "talking and reasoning, listening to their cases, their aspirations, too often followed by disillusionments and inevitable protests." He speaks, in other words, unsentimentally but with passion and irresistible humor for the great glory and wealth of Naples—its people.

An Englishman I met in Naples some years ago told me that he felt there was something basically wrong with anyone who didn't like Naples. "You can't explain it to them, either," he said. "It's like trying to describe the B-Minor Mass to someone who's tone deaf." To him, as to many others, the social indifference and flaunted cynicism of so many Neapolitans are merely the mask they've adopted to cope with history's betrayals; it's their form of protest. In his *Storia di Napoli*, a history of the city up to its "takeover" by the Piedmontese when Italy was unified in 1860, the historian Antonio Ghirelli depicts the *plebe* as a great tribe that, instead of living in a desert or jungle, finds itself isolated in its city, where it has chosen to retreat into itself as the only defense against the oppression, injustice, neglect, and exploitation it has undergone for so long, and which today still finds an ultimate chance to express itself in an impersonal modern state blindly committed to industrial progress.

Meanwhile, the dried blood of the city's patron saint, San Gennaro (or San Gennà, as he is affectionately called), continues to liquefy on schedule three times a year. The blood is kept, between ceremonies, in a couple of ornate vials in a side chapel of the Duomo, and the symbolic miracle of its liquefaction never fails to cheer the Neapolitans, if only because no one has yet satisfactorily explained or debunked the phenomenon. Even after Vatican II, when the Holy See revised its calendar of saints and reduced San Gennaro to the rank of a "local" personage, whose actual existence could not even be proved, the Neapolitans reacted, as always, with surface indifference. On the great main door of the cathedral, however, an anonymous hand expressed the city's real feelings. "San Gennà," it wrote, "futtetenne," which can only be inadequately translated as "San Gennà, don't you give a fuck."

CHAPTER EIGHT

UNCOUPLING, ITALIAN-STYLE

U ntil 1970, Italy had no divorce law. Marriage "until death do you part" meant exactly what it said. People separated, of course, but they remained married and, separated or not, it was dangerous to fool around, especially for the woman. An Italian wife incautious enough to be caught in bed with anyone but her husband could be sentenced to a year in jail. If she happened to be living with the man, it could cost her two years. Adultery, in other words, was—and still is—a crime, but usually only for the woman. Law or no law, men were expected to be adulterous; it increased their standing in male society as bone fide Latin lovers. Almost the only men who ever got into trouble in this area were the few misguided and reckless souls who brought their mistresses home to live with them. If their wives happened to object, they could summon the police and have their husbands arrested.

The one foolproof way to unload an unwanted spouse was murder, but here again the system favored only the male. Section 585 of the Italian penal code still provides that a man who kills on the spur of the moment in defense of his honor goes to jail for no more than seven years and usually no more than three. There is no death penalty in Italy, but a cold-blooded, premeditated slaying can put an offender away for life, so it becomes crucial, in a case of wife-killing, for a man to prove that his loved one provoked him beyond reason. Almost any Italian husband with murderous inclinations can usually do this. The ideal situation is to catch one's wife in the act with her lover, thus permitting the husband to kill them both. It's important to have an efficient weapon handy, and it also helps the husband's case if the wife happens to heap inprecations and insults on his head, thus goading him into a "wholly justifiable homicidal frenzy." This will enable him in court to claim extreme provocation and temporary insanity and be swept off to serve his brief jail sentence on a tidal wave of public sympathy and adulation.

Still the best place to practice this form of instant bond-severing is Sicily, where questions of honor underlie all social obligations and can also lead to the justifiable slaughter of mothers, daughters, nieces, aunts, even grandmothers, and cousins. Sicilians and most other southern Italians believe that woman's role is to be docile and submissive; a woman who kills her husband for the same reason he would kill her is considered a freak of nature. Things have changed a good deal in southern Italy since the Second World War, with the advent of an increasingly industrialized society and decadent modern concepts concerning the rights of individuals—even women—but murder in defense of one's honor remains the classic way for a Sicilian to unload an unwanted bride. The chief virtue of this technique, immortalized in a hilarious movie called *Divorce, Italian Style*, is its finality and admirable simplicity.

Madness used to be another solution to an unhappy marriage and the one favored by most northern Italians, who tend to be more practical than southerners and less concerned with questions of honor. Italian law had long provided for the civil annulment of a marriage, regardless of what the Church might decree, if one of the partners were to be declared legally insane. During the late nineteen-forties, the State also recognized rulings on such matters by courts in other countries with which Italy had concluded bilateral treaties. The only way to exploit this loophole was to find an accommodating Italian judge to validate the foreign decision—no easy matter in a country where the magistracy seemed to consist solely of ferociously conservative septuagenarians. Miraculously, one such jurist did pop up, in the person of Domenico Peretti-Griva, an amiable ancient in Turin. Between the end of the Second

World War and 1950, literally thousands of unhappy middle-class couples fled abroad and established residence, after which one member of the union would be declared legally mad, usually by enlisting the services of an expensive psychiatrist, and have the marriage annulled in a foreign country. The couple would then return to Turin, where they would maneuver to get the decision validated by Judge Peretti-Griva, who almost never failed to come through. Unfortunately, the helpful old jurist eventually went to his grave and the practice stopped.

For a while, it became fashionable for Italians to go abroad to get divorced. The only trouble was that Italy simply didn't recognize such divorces nor the subsequent unions of either partner, and offenders could be denounced to the authorities upon their return home. Celebrities were especially vulnerable, as they were constantly exposed to the public gaze. Carol Ponti, Sophia Loren's movie-producer husband, was frequently featured on the front pages because his foreign divorce from the first Mrs. Ponti was not recognized in Italy. He was forced to flee abroad, divorce Sophia, and simply settle down with her in a "state of sin" in order to be able to go on living in his own country.

Under such a system, most unhappy Italian couples didn't even bother to separate legally but simply split and moved in with new partners. This situation worked well enough as long as it was at least tolerable to everyone involved, but it could and often did become nasty if one of the old partners objected. Large sums of money could sometimes buy off an angry discarded mate, but a truly vindictive one could summon the police, with ugly results for everyone involved, including any children. The latter, in fact, often suffered most, because in Italy offspring born to an illegal union are officially designated bastards and cannot be legally recognized by their fathers.

Prior to the passing of the divorce law, the only absolutely ethical way of dissolving a marriage was to get it annulled or dissolved by an apostolic tribunal of the Holy See called the Sacra Rota, or "sacred wheel." This special court is still around and has been for about eight hundred years, but no one is quite sure how it got its name or what the "wheel" in the designation stands for. An Italian writer I know thinks that it alludes to the rotation of the judges, who vary in number from twelve to twenty and can only be removed if picked for some higher ecclesiastical post or when they reach the retirement age of seventy-four. The court sits in an enormous, appropriately gloomy medieval *palazzo* called the Cancelleria, which, like apparently every other building owned by the Vatican in Old Rome, seems to be unequipped with electricity, for it never shows a light burning. Inside the Cancelleria, the Rota judges weigh the merits of the petitions presented by lawyers especially accredited to the ecclesiastical court, and which have already been scrutinized and passed on by one of the Church's eighteen lower regional courts. Although Pope Paul attempted to reform the process somewhat, historically it has always been glacially slow (a matter of years), costly (as high as twenty thousand dollars), and never less than humiliating to the petitioning parties, even when the proceedings, as often happens, dip refreshingly into areas of low comedy and farce.

The Sacra Rota hands down basically two kinds of sentences: a dissolution and an annulment. A dissolution recognizes the fact that a marriage once existed, whereas an annulment, the much more common ruling, simply wipes the marriage out of history. The Rota will dissolve a marriage if it has never been consummated, or if one of the two partners in a non-Catholic marriage becomes a convert to Catholicism and the other, as a consequence, no longer wants to live with him or her. Annulments, on the other hand, are granted for a wide variety of reasons, such as impotence, religious differences, rape, blood relationship, vows of chastity pronounced prior to wedlock, and so on. The broadest and best qualification for annulment, however—the one favored by most petitioners—is called, vaguely, "the vice of consent," which can mean just about anything. Unfortunately, this category is not so much a loophole as a treacherous swamp through which the miserably married must wallow looking for a way out and at a stiff cost in time, money, and simple human dignity. Here are a few typical cases, somewhat disguised, that the Sacra Rota has handled.

Gino and Anna have been married for four years, and now Anna wants out. She avers that Gino promised her before they got married that he would become an accountant. "I told him I'd only marry a lawyer, a doctor, or an accountant," Anna claims. "He told me he was studying to become an accountant. I agreed to marry him, but only on the condition that he'd succeed in becoming one.

My father was a lawyer, and I couldn't lower myself to marry someone not in the professions." Anna's parents and friends all back her up. "She really set great store on marrying a man who would become someone," her best friend testifies. "Anna told me many times she wouldn't even think of marrying a nobody."

After four years of marriage, Gino has confessed to Anna that he is not now nor has he ever intended to become an accountant. He is merely a clerk in an accountant's office. "I immediately packed up and moved out," Anna tells the court. "I couldn't stay married to a man who wasn't what he said he was." The judges of the Sacra Rota sustain her argument and annul the marriage, convinced not so much by the oral testimony as by the evidence of the postcards the couple exchanged while they were courting, in all of which Anna laid down her conditions and Gino affirmed that he was meeting them. It never seems to occur to the judges that the postcards Anna and Gino mailed to each other years before could have been blank, stored away and filled in later. This practice is a sort of insurance many Italians took as a matter of course before tripping lightly to the altar.

Antonio agreed to marry Ludina only if she promised to remain absolutely faithful to him. In one of the many postcards the lovers supposedly exchanged before their wedding, the theme was struck over and over again. "I will marry you only if you promise to remain faithful and obedient," reads a typical card from Antonio. "Otherwise I'll divorce you and go far away, to Australia or America." Fair enough, even if a little one-sided; Ludina presumably never asked Antonio for the same guarantees, but then such a demand might have offended his Latin sense of sexual grandeur. Ludina accepted Antonio's conditions, which he also, according to subsequent testimony, prudently communicated *a voce* to a couple of dozen acquaintances. Alas, nine years after their marriage, Ludina confesses to her husband that she has, indeed, betrayed him. Antonio demands an annulment and gets one, again on the strength of the postcards.

Umberto and Maria ask for a dissolution of their marriage on the grounds that the fourteen-year union has never been consummated, despite the disquieting fact that they are the parents of a teenaged son. "I attempted the conjugal act on the very first night," Umberto testifies, "but she wouldn't let me near her." The unfortunate Umberto kept trying, but with no success. "Every night, during the first months of our marriage," says Maria, "Umberto would ask and I'd always refuse." Why did Maria always refuse? Could she not have sacrificed herself every now and then, no matter how great her revulsion? "I was terrified of having children," she explains.

How is it then that Umberto and Maria did actually manage to have a child? It happened one hot summer night, during a vacation on the French Riviera, say the long-married couple. The moon, the stars, soft breezes from the sea, swaying palms. And a great deal of liquor. "I got her drunk," confesses Umberto. "Even then she resisted, turning every which way. I wasn't really quite able to consummate the act." "I made him withdraw almost immediately," says Maria. "It was more of an external contact than a true consummation." The near-miss, however, did produce a son, born nine months later. This happened during the first year of their marriage. After that, Umberto waited thirteen years before giving up hope. The Sacra Rota carefully sifts the testimony—and dissolves the union on the grounds that it has never been consummated.

The memorable aspect of these case histories, considered to be among the more brilliant of the Sacra Rota's more recent decisions, is that in each instance the petitioners were successful in obtaining an annulment or a dissolution of the marriage. The unsuccessful cases, however, can be equally bizarre. My favorite one concerns Carlo, Rosa, and her friend Claudia. Carlo, a wealthy young businessman, meets and falls in love with Rosa, a struggling young actress. He proposes and she turns him down, because, unknown to him, she is a homosexual and in love with Claudia, an older woman who owns a small antique store. Claudia, however, is hard up for cash, so she urges Rosa to marry Carlo; the two women will be able to go on seeing each other and Carlo will never know. Rosa accepts Carlo's proposal and they get married. The union is not a happy one, but Carlo convinces himself that things will get better in time. He suggests to Rosa that she see a psychiatrist who might be able to help her overcome her sexual coldness and obvious distaste for love-making. She refuses. She also refuses to give up her career and move to a small provincial town where Carlo, after two years of marriage, has been offered a lucrative partnership. A few months later, Carlo and Rosa separate; he moves to his new job in the provinces, she stays in Rome and goes on seeing Claudia. She also writes to Carlo and at last tells him the truth about herself.

Carlo presents his case to the Sacra Rota and waits confidently for the verdict. The venerable ecclesiastics weigh the known facts very carefully. Has the sacramental nature of the marriage vow been violated? Has the wife refused to perform the conjugal act or expressed a strong reluctance to bear children? No. The annulment is denied. Carlo, a good Catholic, is stuck forever with his lesbian bride.

What is one to make of all this? The very best that can be said, really, for the decisions handed down by the Sacra Rota is that quite often, usually by accident, justice is done. People who have been living unhappily with each other for years or who have separated but been unable to build new lives with other partners are at last freed. The freedom, however, especially in the case of annulment, benefits the man far more than the woman. The most important thing to remember about an annulment, as opposed to dissolution or divorce, is that it imposes no financial obligation on either partner; as far as the Sacra Rota is concerned, such marriages, once annulled, never existed. In a country like Italy, where women are still largely educated to become wives and mothers and the professions are so dominated by male chauvinism that independent-minded career girls are viewed as peculiar, at best, a woman thrown onto her own resources can find herself in serious economic difficulties. What she usually does is immediately look for another husband, if she doesn't have one already lurking in the wings.

The examining procedure of the Sacra Rota is also weighted against women; it is usually the wife who is asked to shoulder most of the blame, and she is subjected not only to a lengthy, excruciatingly detailed cross-examination but occasionally to a physical one as well. An Australian woman married to a Roman obtained a dissolution by claiming that her three-year marriage had never been fully consummated because her hymen was unusually strong and the sex act caused her much pain. She had to submit to a physical examination during which artificial phalluses of various sizes were inserted into her vagina. A cousin of mine succeeded in shedding her first husband by confessing, falsely, to having participated in orgies and to a preference for the sort of love-making considered perverted by the ecclesiastical authorities (whose knowledge of sex would presumably have to be secondhand). Is it any wonder that most educated Italians consider the workings of the Sacra Rota a grotesque and a highly unsatisfactory way to undo the marriage knot?

When Italy finally got around to passing its divorce law in 1970, it was only after eleven previous attempts in ninety-two years. The first few were never seriously considered. Even when King Victor Emmanuel III threw the prestige of the crown behind one try, in 1902, the divorce bill still failed to pass. The Church has always been ferociously unyielding on the subject and campaigned actively against all attempts to adopt a divorce law. In 1929, the Fascist Government of Benito Mussolini made its peace with the Vatican by concluding an accord known as the Lateran Treaty, Article 34 of which gave the Holy See absolute say over the whole question of Italian marriage and divorce, even if the parties involved happened not to be Roman Catholics. After the Second World War and the installation of a parliamentary democracy, the question of civil divorce was reopened and became ever more insistently debated. "The proponents of civil divorce," wrote Luigi Barzini in the *New York Times* some years ago, "point out that the measure would in no way weaken the bonds of conscience that keep good Roman Catholics married even in places where divorce is as cheap and easy as it is in Reno, Nevada." But the Church, seeing itself threatened nonetheless, quite naturally continued to oppose any change in the status quo. The Vatican was able successfully to do so—and for so long—by exerting pressure on the Christian Democrats, the country's largest political party, which has traditionally depended on the support of the Church for its very survival.

Some kind of divorce law became inevitable, however, if only because so many unhappily married citizens wanted one; eventually, their combined voting power proved effective enough to persuade the minority-party legislators to coalesce and force such a measure upon the reluctant government. The bill that was finally passed by the Italian Parliament in 1970, under the guidance of its author, a Socialist deputy named Loris Fortuna, was supported by all the smaller democratic parties as well as the Communists, and opposed by the Christian Democrats and the neo-Fascists of the Movimento Sociale Italiano. It would, said its most ferocious critics, destroy the social fabric of Italian life, dignify unbridled licentiousness, and cause untold suffering to millions of helpless women and children.

What was this law that supposedly threatened the country with chaos? It provided the possibility of divorce to people whose partners had been condemned to a minimum of five years' imprisonment for any sort of crime or for such sexual offenses as incest, rape, or compelling one's wife and/or daughters to prostitute themselves; to those whose partners had been confined to insane asylums for a minimum of five years; to citizens still considered married to foreigners even though the foreigners had divorced them under the laws of their own lands; and, most important, to all people who had already been separated for a minimum of two years prior to the adoption of the law or who would in future separate officially for at least five years for any reason whatsoever. The law could hardly be considered radically permissive, but the outcry against it was loud and shrill. Its opponents estimated that some three million Italian "matrimonial outlaws" would storm the courts demanding instant divorces and that such an event would topple society.

Nothing of the sort happened. During the first six months of the law's application, only forty thousand three hundred and eighty-two persons petitioned for a divorce and less than five thousand received final decrees. Today, only a few thousand divorces continue to be granted yearly, this in a nation of sixty million people. One deterrent is the cost, about two thousand dollars; another is the opposition to divorce from conservative judges in whose courts many cases have to be tried. Most important, however, is the simple fact that many childless Italian couples who have been living with each other for years simply don't wish to legitimize their status.

Most of those who have divorced—an estimated four out of five—have done so in order to remarry and thereby to legitimize any children born out of wedlock. The structure of family life in Italy has not been toppled but actually reaffirmed; only customs have been altered. "At last! I'm happy to announce my divorce from Maria T. and my marriage to Severina G.," proclaimed an announcement put up on a Milanese wall. "Our Daddy and Mommy can now live happily with us," said another bulletin, this one including a snapshot of two beaming tots. "After forty-three years of waiting, I'm a bachelor at last, but not for long," began a third. Such proclamations of felicity are limited pretty much to the north; in the south, the old forms are still respected. "I'm handling the case of a Sicilian who's been living for many years with a woman who is not his wife," a lawyer told me. "Whenever he refers to her, it's always, very respectfully, as 'my fiancée.'"

For the past ten years the Church has continued to oppose the law and backed a referendum to repeal it, which was defeated. The section of the law that the Church finds most unacceptable is the one specifying a divorce for any reason whatsoever after a legal separation of five years, but how long should couples be made to wait? "To maintain that after five solid years of a separation a marriage is not dead," one Italian expert has observed, "is to say that a corpse can't be interred until two weeks after death, and then only after a medical exam establishes beyond doubt that the carcass isn't breathing." Such arguments have so far failed to impress the Vatican, which, in an effort to further undermine the law and to prove that divorce is not a necessity, has been liberalizing its own procedures. It now costs less to petition the Sacra Rota than it used to, the preliminary hearings and investigations have been simplified, and the whole business, if handled properly, can sometimes be wrapped up in a few months instead of years. So-called "irregular families" (man and woman, either or both married but not to each other, living together with or without children) deserve, according to one papal proclamation, the respect and understanding of their fellow man. Some priests will even grant absolution to remarried divorcées, on the condition, however, that they refrain from sex with their new partners. And if they don't? "Certainly it can happen," said one priest in an interview. "The flesh is weak. Well, then, the couple will come to confession, like all relapsed sinners."

CHAPTER NINE

THE STONES
OF SELVOLE

T he cemetery at Selvole, a hilltop village in the Chianti region of Tuscany, is enclosed by a stone wall, which stands high in back, against a hillside, and lower in front to afford a magnificent view, through surrounding tall cypresses, of a narrow valley below and heavily wooded slopes beyond. The burial ground is very small, containing about sixty graves, which are laid out in even rows on either side of a dirt path leading from a rusty iron gate, usually left unlocked, to a tiny abandoned chapel, which now holds tools, a broken ladder, chunks of plaster, and discarded objects of one sort or another. Most of the graves have simple rectangular headstones no more than two or three inches thick, the older ones usually of gray stone, standing on low burial mounds; some of the newer ones are fancier, made of white marble, and the dead are covered by small tombs of the same gleaming rock. They all proclaim not only the names and ages of those buried but almost always something about the circumstances of their deaths and the feelings of the survivors:

IN MEMORY

OF

ZELINDA BUCCIARELLI

BORN LOSI

24-5-1888

PASSED ON TO A BETTER LIFE

AT 70 YEARS OF AGE

AFTER A LONG ILLNESS

CHRISTIANLY BORNE

HER HUSBAND AND DESCENDANTS

And

HERE RESTS THE BELOVED BODY

OF GAGLIARDI GIOCONDO

EXEMPLARY HUSBAND AND FATHER

WHO PASSED SERENELY AWAY

IN THE KISS OF OUR LORD

25 JUNE 1954

AT THE AGE OF 82 YEARS

HIS WIFE, HIS CHILDREN, AND HIS

RELATIVES

REMEMBER HIM FONDLY

Upon a number of the newer headstones are small, glass-enclosed framed photographs of the dead—pictures undoubtedly snapped years before at some formal ceremony or family celebration. Signora Bucciarelli, one might guess from her plump cheeks and soft features, must have loved to mother people and to eat well, while Signor Gagliardi, with his brush mustache, close-cropped white hair, deep-set eyes, and stern expression, looks as if he very much enjoyed his role as head of a large clan. The typically Tuscan names in the cemetery, such as Pagni, Gagliardi, Soldani, and Cresti, repeat themselves, but the Gagliardis outnumber all the others. In the photographs of the dead, the common denominator is a look of straightforward, uncomplicated rectitude, on features weathered and hardened by life on the soil. Selvole is in the heart of the Chianti, famous for its grapes and the dark-red wines made from them.

Most of those who lie in this graveyard died either very young or very old; hardly any adult less than seventy or any child more

than five. There were a few exceptions. Among these was Marco
Gagliardi, who died at eighteen. The picture on his tombstone is
that of a big-boned, innocent-looking boy with a shock of
untamed curly hair. His death was apparently both unnecessary
and unjust, and most of the older people in Selvole remember it
well. During the summer of 1944, when the German forces in
these hills were fighting a delaying action against the Allied
advance up the boot, young Marco was asked one afternoon to
carry some baskets of food to one of the partisan bands operating
in the area. Although much has subsequently been made of the
Italian partisan resistance, the activities of these guerilla groups
were too often disorganized and irresponsible, and accomplished
nothing but the deaths of a good many innocent people. On the
day Marco Gagliardi set out from Selvole with his baskets, two
German couriers riding a motorcycle and sidecar had been shot,
and presumably left for dead, at a crossroads a couple of miles out
of town. The partisans had not examined their victims, however,
and one of them survived to report back to German headquarters
at Vistarenni, a large nearby estate. Troops were immediately sent
into the area, where they burned and destroyed local farms. Even
today, a few blackened, hollowed, roofless buildings are scattered
through the countryside to testify to this act of reprisal. On their
way back to Vistarenni, the soldiers found Marco Gagliardi sitting
by the edge of the road with his food. They took him to Vistarenni, questioned him, tried him summarily, and sentenced him to
death. He was returned to the place where the attack on the couriers had occurred, and hanged. The spot is marked by a small commemorative stone, partly buried now in tall grass.

There are two other commemorative plaques in Selvole itself—
on either side of the main entrance to the community's only
church. Each records the deaths of three men in each of this century's two World Wars, with young Gagliardi properly listed. It
seems an unduly heavy loss, because the village of Selvole, standing on the steep ridge adjoining the cemetery, with a commanding
view of the surrounding country, now houses only a couple of
dozen people, and at its peak probably had only three or four
times that many permanent residents. Like almost every other Italian hilltop town, the place was once fortified with its own *castello.*
It played a not insignificant role in the seemingly interminable
wars between Florence and her great and hated rival, Siena. In

1229, for instance, Selvole crops up in history as a Sienese strong-hold that repulsed an attack by the Florentines. Three years later, again under siege, it was betrayed, taken, and destroyed. As late as 1479, once again in Sienese hands, it was referred to in a contemporary Florentine account as a *"forte castello,"* and was considered an important prize, because it dominated a main road to several neighboring towns and to Siena itself. Though it was constantly fought over, it remained mostly in Sienese hands until 1555, the date that marks what a local historian, Antonio Casabianca, has defined as "the tragic and fatal fall of the Sienese Republic," after which Selvole and the rest of the Chianti district came under Florentine domination.

Little is left today in Selvole to testify to such ancient glories. The *castello* is gone; only its outline can be traced in the way the town's few houses—the walls of some of them incorporating those of the old fortress—now huddle about a tiny main square dominated entirely by the church. The buildings are gray and brown, of stone and brick cemented together, with rust-colored tile roofs, and windows framed by green shutters. Behind and around the houses are small gardens, growing flowers as well as tomatoes, other vegetables, and the omnipresent bunches of fat grapes. The old main road, over which so many battles were fought, is now merely a footpath that winds out of the square under an archway and trails off into the woods below. (A dirt road connects the other end of the square with a nearby highway.) Above the piazza, the bell tower of the church dominates the scene, but now the bells ring only on Sundays and a few major religious holidays, because there is no longer a parish priest and the building is kept locked between the Sunday visits of a pastor from a large town twenty miles away.

Selvole, like thousands of such villages all over Italy, is dying. In another year or two, more people will have left, and most of those who remain will be, like the dead in the cemetery, either very old or very young. This vast internal emigration, of course, began—here, as elsewhere—with the Industrial Revolution. In 1833, Selvole had a population of a hundred and thirty-five. It has declined steadily since, and the process—here as everywhere—has been vastly accelerated by the country's post-war total commitment to the creation of an American-style consumer-goods society. Indeed, beginning in the late fifties, factory buildings began to sprout all over the countryside as the government encouraged all sorts of ventures designed to slow down the rush to overcrowded manufacturing centers such as Rome, Turin, and, most notably, Milan. Inevitably, too many of these enterprises, hastily conceived and underfinanced, failed, and the empty buildings, broken-windowed and rubbish-strewn, remain as hideously eloquent testimonials to human folly, like the burned-out husks of the ravaged farms left by the retreating German armies.

"If it is true that Italy is the most beautiful country in the world, if it is true that Tuscany is the garden of Italy, then it is equally undeniable that the heart of this gentle Tuscany of ours is the Chianti," writes Casabianca in his *Guida Storica del Chianti*. Oddly, however, the exact boundaries of the Chianti area have never been determined; the secret, as in the case of so many other historical regions of Italy, has doubtless been buried for centuries in some public or private archive. Everyone seems to agree, though, that the Chianti is a small, roughly oval area of rolling, wooded hills and deep gorges, about thirty miles long, lying directly between Siena and Florence. The three traditional population centers of the ancient League of Chianti were the towns of Castellina, Radda, and Gaiole, each now inhabited by only a few thousand people. In 1932, the legal boundaries of the region were extended to include a number of more populous towns, which gained the right to call their wines Chianti Classico. But in much of the area only the land once encompassed by the League is felt to be truly the Chianti. And even now the entire region retains the distinction of being one of the very few relatively underpopulated parts of the peninsula.

Nor is there any general agreement among historians and geographers as to how the area got its name. The most plausible theory seems to be that it derives from an old Etruscan name, but Casabianca, for one, maintains that the designation evolved from the Latin verb *"clango,"* which in the Middle Ages was used to refer to the clamorous horns used by the hunting parties of the nobility as they swept through the woods in pursuit of game. From the beginning, the area has been in the hands of powerful aristrocratic families, who hunted, sported, and fought over it while the *contadini,* who depended on them for shelter and protection, quietly continued as best they could to grow their vegetables, harvest their olives, and make their wine.

The relatively few peasants who still remain on the land are almost all tenant farmers, who work for absentee landlords in Siena, Florence, Rome, and Milan. During the nineteen-fifties and the early nineteen-sixties, as the exodus to the manufacturing centers accelerated, foreigners, and especially the English (who have always favored this part of Italy), began to buy abandoned farmhouses and land, quite literally for a pittance. Then, as property values began to soar, the older houses and other buildings, including abandoned *castelli* and monasteries, were snapped up by rich Italian businessmen for country retreats. Lately, winemaking-and-exporting combines, with headquarters in the larger cities, have bought up large tracts of land to manufacture wine on a truly sizable scale.

This latest attempt to make a paying proposition of the Chianti region seems to have a much better chance of success than the government's misguided attempt to encourage small-scale manufacturing and industry. In any case, it has altered the landscape far more definitively. The natural terrain of the Chianti is wooded— thick forests of oak, poplar, elm, chestnut, and willow, with a dense, briary undergrowth of wild plum and olive and all sorts of berry-laden greenery. The earth is stony, suitable mainly for olives and grapes, otherwise adaptable merely to small vegetable gardens and small stands of grain. The part of the land put to cultivation was conquered foot by foot over the centuries, carefully terraced, buttressed by handmade stone walls, and planted in a way that made use of every inch of space. The traditional look of the Chianti is that of forested hillsides dotted with small farms, each surrounded by terraced land under silver-leaved olive trees and emerald-green rows of vines.

The peaceful, breathtaking beauty of this landscape, of course, is what first lured foreigners and wealthy Italians from Milan and Rome into the area. These newcomers, uninterested in making money from the land, tend to regard any commercializing of the region with horror. Like most expatriates, they derive their incomes elsewhere, and they tend to cluster together and socialize mostly with each other—a habit that makes them largely indifferent to or unaware of local realities. (At a cocktail party given by some members of the Anglo-Saxon colony around Gaiole, the wife of a retired British brigadier, newly settled in the vicinity, was heard to inquire of an old resident, "By the bye, are there many other Europeans living in the area?") They do provide a flow of capital into the country, and they furiously defend their picture-postcard views of the scenes before them, so they can be said—in that sense, at least—to exert a strong positive influence.

It is clear, however, that, no matter how many outsiders choose to stay on in the Chianti, the old, traditional peasant life here is doomed and the look of the countryside will be altered permanently; it has, in fact, already changed. And the flight of the young to the towns and cities will continue. An Italian friend of mine who now lives most of the time in Milan but who grew up in these hills and still spends his holidays at a family estate very near Selvole recently explained why. "Why shouldn't the people leave?" he said. "The old houses are cold and damp and uncomfortable, and there is no way to make a living. The only crop that pays is wine, and only the largest properties can make money. Why shouldn't the young people go to the cities? What is to keep them here, on land they don't even own?"

Until fairly recently, the *contadino* was able to survive on the land he farmed because he was largely self-sufficient and his needs were minimal. Between his vines and his olive trees, he grew some grain, fruit, and vegetables. On the ground floor of his stone house he kept his tools and livestock, and did his own slaughtering. But the consumer society that developed large-scale, mechanized ways of growing food also created needs that people didn't have before. "The peasant's son wants a TV set, a car, and a hi-fi," my friend explained. "Not only have we told him he should have them but we have shown him another way of living entirely. The old methods of doing things are not for him."

Nor are the old methods competitive. Traditional farming was forced here to follow and respect the contours of the land and make use of basic tools familiar to men of the Stone Age. New machines, powered by huge, noisy engines, can reshape the land to suit their own purposes. It's almost impossible to go anywhere in the Chianti these days without hearing the roar of a bulldozer at work somewhere or coming upon a great stretch of newly smoothed land where centuries-old terraces and groves of trees have simply vanished, as if they had been scraped away by a giant trowel. In their place the winegrowers plant long, straight rows of vines supported by perforated concrete pillars instead of the traditional wooden stakes. Nor is there any longer a need to grow anything between and around the vines, so during the winter months the land thus used acquires the somewhat desolate look of a prairie. The people who tend these new vineyards drive to them from the larger towns in cars of their own and go back to the towns at night. Land worked on such a large, impersonal scale inevitably ceases to reflect the smaller, purely personal needs of people living on it.

Still, whatever the penalties of the new farming methods may be, nearly everyone who knows and loves this part of Tuscany feels they are probably preferable to any other economic solution for the area. "Let's put in as many vineyards as possible," a local baron with a small but growing wine business of his own remarked not long ago. "The alternatives are unthinkable—more factories, the sort of thing that has happened in northern Italy, which has become an unholy, chaotic mixture of agriculture and industry. In the Chianti we still have our forests, which are protected now by new and stronger laws. They cannot be burned down with impunity, as they could even a few years ago, when land speculators were setting fires everywhere. And then, you know, I like to walk among my vines. There is something archetypal about a thick cluster of fat grapes hanging in the autumn light. It makes you think that a few things are still right with the world."

CHAPTER TEN

THE FRENZIES
OF THE MOMENT

At about eight o'clock on the evening of September 30, 1977, a young man named Walter Rossi was shot to death in the streets of Rome. One of a gang of about forty youthful militant radicals belonging to a Communist splinter group called Lotta Continua, Rossi had been distributing propaganda leaflets with his friends since the early afternoon in the Balduina, a zone of the city known for its right-wing political sympathies. According to some early newspaper accounts of the affair, mainly those of the left-wing press, that is all Rossi had been doing, but as the full story began to emerge, and was eventually pieced together from eyewitness accounts, it became clear that he and others had spent at least some of their time provoking—by threats, insults, and hurled missiles of one sort or another—a group of toughs hanging around the local headquarters of the neo-Fascist Movimento Sociale Italiano. At first, the toughs, apparently restrained by the presence of a police van in the area, reacted only in kind, but then, as the situation grew more tense, they suddenly launched a savage attack. Some-body in the crowd fired a pistol several times. One of the bullets grazed an elderly gas station attendant. Rossi, shot through the head while retreating, died on his way to the hospital, even as carloads of policemen who were rushed to the scene separated the combatants and began arresting suspects. Fifteen men were taken into custody. Most have since been released, and no one has yet been charged with the killing.

Rossi was twenty years old. The son of a small businessman, he was an unemployed university dropout who had had at least one brush with the police and the courts, for having allegedly assaulted two persons in a political argument. His death immediately made him a martyr and touched off several days of rioting in a dozen Italian cities. In Rome, beginning on the night of the shooting, gangs of angry, masked left-wing *ultras*, or extremists, appeared in the streets armed with pistols, clubs, and homemade incendiary bombs. They smashed and looted M.S.I. offices, set fire to cafés, bars, and shops thought to be Fascist meeting places, attacked buses and streetcars full of terrified passengers, overturned and wrecked cars, and, in general, did whatever damage they could to anyone and anything suspected of being connected, however tangentially, with the M.S.I. or, in some cases, merely with the current political power structure.

For nearly a week, squadrons of police and carabinieri moved through the streets to quell the more serious disturbances, occasionally by the use of tear gas, and in time restored some sort of order, though in the process a few outlying areas of the city, where acts of political and criminal violence had long been daily occurrences, took on the aspect of wartime occupied territory. In the Balduina itself, a middle-class residential section behind the impregnable-looking bulk of the Cavalieri Hilton Hotel, which overlooks the center of Rome from the heights of Monte Mario, the local population stayed out of sight behind locked doors and shuttered windows while police and left-wing demonstrators faced one another uneasily for several days. Dozens of protesters, seeping into the area from all over, staged traffic-stopping sit-downs in the streets, laid wreaths on the sidewalk where Rossi fell, scrawled anti-Fascist slogans on nearby walls, and lashed red flags to lampposts and traffic signs. The Balduina, it was pointed out in a number of newspaper articles, had long been a site of Fascist-inspired acts of provocation, including, only the day before the Rossi killing, an apparently random attempt on the life of a nineteen-year-old woman student, wounded by two shots fired from a passing car as she was chatting in the street with a friend.

Murder was the logical outcome of a campaign of terror that had afflicted the neighborhood for many months.

The trouble in the Balduina and elsewhere was not a recent phenomenon. For many months, each day had brought its quota of politically inspired violence. Students of all ages battled one another in the hallways and classrooms of their schools; sharpshooters sniped at passersby from cruising automobiles; platoons of masked youths hurled Molotov cocktails through the windows and doorways of private and public buildings or roamed the streets and piazzas casually overturning parked vehicles and setting fire to them. Now and then, for days at a time the violence would seem to die down, to be limited to a few relatively minor incidents, but the least provocation would set it off again, as if the society tolerating it were a diseased, twitching body afflicted sporadically by frightening convulsions.

The worst disorders always seemed to take place in the wake of demonstrations protesting previous acts of hooliganism, often Fascist-inspired. After Rossi's public funeral, on October 3, attended by thousands of mourners, groups of young men broke away from the procession in the late afternoon and fanned out through the streets around the Piazza San Giovanni in Laterano, a working-class district that votes Communist in every election. They fired at police and carabiniere units and attacked several M.S.I. offices. They also indiscriminately burned cars, wrecked shops, and hurt several innocent passersby—one seriously. "They threw Molotovs and rocks," the owner of a bar in the vicinity told a reporter. "We and the waiters were inside. We heard the explosions. Then a fire started up, and we put it out ourselves. They destroyed all five of the glass counters, completely destroyed them. It's the second time. Three years ago, they also smashed the inside of the bar. I don't know why. We're only working people."

On October 14, after a rally that was sponsored by most of the major political parties and presided over by Rome's Communist mayor, Giulio Carlo Argan, and that attracted fifty thousand people to the Piazza San Giovanni, what amounted to a civil insurrection broke out in several other parts of Rome. A second demonstration, staged by left-wing splinter groups in the Piazza Esedra, a huge square in the commercial heart of the city, between the main railroad station and the luxury hotels and travel offices of the Via Veneto area, quickly degenerated under cover of darkness into guerrilla warfare. Shots, explosions, the sound of windows being smashed and furniture broken, shouts, screams, and sirens filled the night. One group broke into the main headquarters of the Christian Democratic Party, brandished pistols in the faces of the staff people on duty, and set the offices on fire. About thirty youths burst into a bar on the Corso Vittorio, almost directly in front of the residence of Premier Giulio Andreotti, and, with drawn guns, herded those inside into a corner, after which they looted and devastated the premises, appropriating bottles of liquor, boxes of candy, and about three hundred thousand lire in cash. In front of the Castel Sant' Angelo, a squad car of police officers was surrounded by and under fire from a crowd of seemingly well-organized street fighters. By some miracle, even after several hours of these and similar disturbances, no one was killed or seriously wounded.

On October 20, an assembly of ten thousand students at the University of Rome debating the recent deaths of three German terrorists in Stammheim prison became still another excuse for violence. Forbidden by the authorities to hold a public protest meeting, about five hundred young people, their faces hidden by kerchiefs, hoods, or ski masks, forced their way into the adjacent streets and fought a two-hour running battle with police and carabinieri through the quarter of San Lorenzo, another working-class district. For a while, the local police station itself was under siege, with the officers inside returning, from their windows, the fire of the youths spraying bullets at them from behind parked cars and some nearby trees. In another section, about twenty passengers found themselves trapped on a bus between a platoon of police firing tear-gas shells and students shooting handguns and lobbing Molotov cocktails. Once again, by a miracle, no one was killed, though nineteen persons were hurt seriously enough to require medical attention.

Perhaps even more frightening than such outbreaks of mass violence, which could be attributed to the frenzies of the moment, were the skillfully planned, cold-blooded attacks on individuals that began to occur every four or five days. The technique was simple. The victim, whose daily routine and movements had been observed in advance, was ambushed by perhaps three or four people in a stolen car, which was later abandoned far from the scene. The attackers fired at the legs of the victim and fled, usually leaving him bleeding on the sidewalk. In 1976, about a dozen such attacks were carried out against journalists, but more recently the targets had been businessmen and officials of the Christian Democratic Party.

On the morning of November 2, a young politician named Publio Fiori was cut down in the street near his home by three terrorists—two men and a woman—firing from a stolen Fiat sedan. When Fiori, who had recently obtained a gun permit, produced a pistol of his own and returned their fire, the terrorists came back, took his gun away, and shot him twice more. Apparently, they could easily have killed him but chose not to. Two of the bullets struck him in the chest and ribs, and he is lucky to be alive. The terrorists escaped, as usual.

Not until quite recently had either the moderate press or the government itself been willing to face up to the fact that nearly all the recent mass violence and organized individual acts of terrorism had been perpetrated by left-wing bands of extremists, most of whom operated independently of one another. For a long time, only such conservative newspapers as the Corriere della Sera, Il Tempo, and Il Giornale Nuovo—Indro Montanelli, the editor-in-chief of Il Giornale Nuovo, was himself shot in the legs—had consistently pointed out that even the worst Fascist acts of provocation could not justify the growing disorder in the streets. The columnist Lietta Tornabuoni acidly wrote in the Corriere that Minister of the Interior Francesco Cossiga, a Christian Democrat, who had been in office since February, 1976, had made at least ten major public declarations to the effect that violence would not be tolerated, that order would be maintained and democracy defended. Her statement was soon echoed in an unsigned editorial in the moderate weekly Il Settimanale: "Francesco Cossiga continues to assure us that 'we will not allow ourselves to be intimidated.' Meanwhile, the revolution spreads, public opinion is dismayed, everyone's personal security is in danger, one lives in a climate of civil war and reprisal. The Minister must go."

Now that the politicians themselves were becoming daily terrorist targets, a few cynics were quick to assure the public that at last something would be done, since, as an apolitical Roman friend of mine told me, "These fat-bellies aren't going to let themselves be killed while the eating is still good." An effort was made to ban, or at least, control, all demonstrations, parades, and rallies that could foment violence—the tactic had already backfired, though, and caused at least as much violence as it has prevented—and there were loud calls from all sides, including spokesmen for the Communist Party, for stricter enforcement of the laws and for new, more repressive ones primarily aimed at closing not only all M.S.I headquarters but the so-called *covi*, or nests, frequented by left-wing groups who were known to favor the use of violence. Also under consideration were much stiffer penalties for persons arrested carrying weapons of any kind or persons arrested for having taken part in any sort of rowdyism. The government was reported to be training special anti-terrorist police squads on the German model, although, as most observers were quick to point out, events seemed to have no connection with the Palestinian question or other general questions but to be motivated solely by the local social and political situation.

The increased violence throughout the country was due at least partly to the unofficial yet actively supportive role the Communist Party, Italy's second-largest political entity, had played in the nation's affairs during the previous year. Andreotti, a Christian Democrat, presided over a coalition government of a handful of parties, including his own, which could not count on a day-to-day working majority in the Chamber of Deputies, Italy's main legislative body. Without the cooperation of the Communists, who controlled more than a third of the votes, on major questions in Parliament, and without their behind-the-scenes support of such important social legislation as tax reform and emergency measures to combat unemployment, no government could survive for long. Before the Communists decided to, in effect, back the coalition, with the idea, perhaps, of eventually assuming a formal role in the government—a possible development always referred to as "the historic compromise"—governments in Italy fell every few months, brought down by the disenchanted, often capricious maneuvers of the smaller parties and of dissident factions within the majority Christian Democratic Party itself.

Under Enrico Berlinguer, an ascetic-looking Sardinian intellectual, who had emerged in recent months as the leading spokesman for "Eurocommunism" (basically a program ostensibly committing the Western Communist parties to the achievement of Marxist aims by democratic means rather than by adherence to the traditional dogma of the class struggle and the dictatorship of the proletariat, as it was still preached in Moscow), Italy's Communists had made it possible for Andreotti to stay in power. A highly articulate, cagey administrator and compromiser, Andreotti, who was considered by many to be the cleverest and most able politician the nation had had since the late Alcide De Gasperi, whose protégé he was, had provided the most enduring and stable political atmosphere the country had had in years. Ironically, it had been paid for by the violence in the streets, which was largely an expression of disenchantment with Berlinguer's policy by militant leftists, who considered the tactic a clear betrayal of principle.

These militants were young, largely middle-class, and divided into various groups, often confused and as angry with one another as with the established power structure. The largest entity was Lotta Continua, which published its own newspaper, had branches everywhere, and promoted unarmed, purportedly non-violent public demonstrations aimed at lowering prices by the tactic of invading stores and theatres and refusing to pay for goods and services, and of occupying unused land and empty buildings. It considered the Communist Party unsalvageable, even if Berlinguer and his policies were to be cast out, and it cooperated with most of the other smaller, more aggressive splinter groups.

These independent groups had been pretty much lumped together by the press under the term *autonomi,* and they included all sorts of movements, ranging from Lotta Continua and Autonomia Operaia to tiny cells and collectives scattered nationwide in factories, schools, and neighborhoods. The *autonomi* espoused all sorts of doctrines, from basic collectivism to pure anarchy, but most of them advocated violent action in one form or another to achieve their goals. (The slogan of Autonomia Operaia, for instance, was "Armed Struggle Against the State.") Also considered *autonomi* were the half dozen most radical women's-rights groups; FUORI (Outside), a homosexual organization; and the Indiani Metropolitani, mostly students who had organized themselves very loosely into "tribes" and considered themselves adherents of the ecological doctrines espoused by the flower children of the sixties.

The most violent of all the *autonomi* were the Brigate Rosse, or Red Brigades, which were originally organized in the factories of the industrial north, and which openly proclaimed responsibility for a number of kidnappings, bombings, and acts of arson, and the well-planned shootings of journalists, businessmen, and politicians. Also considered extremely dangerous were *i nappisti,* or the partisans of NAP (Nuclei Armati Proletari), a terrorist group organized several years ago in the prisons, whose members carried out acts of brigandage, such as armed holdups and bank robberies, that were essentially indistinguishable from run-of-the-mill felonies.

Late in September, the Communist Party made an attempt to lure at least some of the *autonomi* back into the fold by sponsoring a three-day rally for them in Bologna, which had been Communist-ruled for thirty-two years and still has the reputation of being the most efficiently and honestly administered city in Italy. Forty thousand young people showed up, to find most of the shops and restaurants prudently shuttered and the streets and *piazzas* swarming with policemen and soldiers. After much public debate and heated wrangling, the *autonomi* peacefully dispersed, unreconciled either to the Party or to one another. "Terrorism is the normal answer to a Communist Party that carries on a dialogue with bankers" is the way one *ultra* summed up the attitude of many, explaining, "Because either the Communist Party wanted to make the revolution, in which case it's made every mistake, or it didn't, it doesn't want to, in which case it will have to pay this price."

Meanwhile, the violence continued, and people—participants and innocents alike—went on being hurt and occasionally killed. During the disorders following the fatal shooting of Walter Rossi, a twenty-two-year-old man named Roberto Crescenzio was burned to death in Turin. A member of no political party and, according to his acquaintances, "an honest person," he had been standing in a bar drinking an aperitif with a friend when a gang of *ultras*, who had evidently mistaken the bar for a Fascist hangout, attacked. One of them lobbed a Molotov cocktail into the men's room, where Crescenzio had taken refuge, and the flaming gasoline immediately turned him into a human torch. He died two days later of his burns. Perhaps because he had no claim to martyrdom, his death at first passed almost unnoticed and was mentioned only briefly on the inside pages of most Roman newspapers. His burial, however, was attended by twenty thousand silent mourners, who seemed in that moment, by their sober restraint, to represent the conscience of an entire, deeply troubled nation.

CHAPTER ELEVEN

DEATH OF
A POLITICIAN

I f the main purpose of the Red Brigades and Italy's other terrorist groups was to bring the country to a standstill, then it can be argued that by the kidnapping and murder of Aldo Moro, the leader of the Christian Democratic Party, this purpose was at least temporarily accomplished. Between March 16, 1978, the day Signor Moro was seized in Rome, and May 9, when his lifeless body was found abandoned in the rear compartment of a Renault sedan, the political life of the nation ceased. With the sole exception of a long-awaited abortion law being debated in the Senate, the upper house of the parliament, no major piece of legislation was under consideration—or was even submitted for consideration—in either the Senate or the Chamber of Deputies during that anxious period of fifty-four days. The attention of the nation was focussed exclusively on the personal drama and tragedy of Aldo Moro and his family.

The crime astonished most Italians, not so much for its violence as for the extraordinary efficiency with which it was carried out. Shortly after nine o'clock on the morning of March 16, a blue Fiat sedan in which Moro was riding with a driver and a bodyguard and a white Alfa Romeo carrying three more armed bodyguards were stopped by a group of perhaps as many as a dozen terrorists armed with automatic pistols and submachine guns. Not one of the bodyguards even had time to draw his own weapon. Within a minute, some eighty shots were fired, wiping out Moro's escort, and Moro himself was quickly loaded into a waiting car and spirited away. The bodies of the guards—three policemen and two carabinieri—were abandoned where they died, in their cars and on the pavement.

Newspaper and magazine photographs of these corpses, together with extensive news coverage of the event on television, shocked the public. During the past few years, Italy had become used to acts of political violence. The previous year, there had been two thousand one hundred and twenty-eight reported cases of one sort or another, and by mid-May of 1978 fourteen persons had died and twenty-three had been wounded so far that year. But nothing quite like the Moro kidnapping had ever before occurred. Moro himself was by far the most eminent personage to have been attacked, and to many citizens it was almost inconceivable that such an act could have been so easily and successfully carried out in the very heart of an elegant residential section of Rome. Via Mario Fani, where the event took place, is one of a network of new streets flanked by expensive, terraced apartment houses that have been built since the war on the low-lying hills to the north of the hub, in an area inhabited mainly by well-to-do, middle-class families fleeing the noisy confusion of the *centro storico* and its proliferation of petty crime. "I left the Campo de' Fiori to get away from the thieves," a woman who lives in the area told me, "and now look—I'm in with the terrorists."

The Moro kidnapping convinced most Italians that no one could any longer consider himself safe from the guerrilla warfare being waged by the Red Brigades and other organized armed bands in the streets of nearly all the nation's major cities. Until then, it had been possible to go on living from day to day with little fear of being caught up in any sort of political violence. Large demonstrations and protest rallies of one kind or another could be safely avoided, and it was well known that only politicians, prominent businessmen, magistrates, high-ranking police officers, and conservative journalists risked being shot in attacks of the sort that have come to be known as "kneecappings." It was also well known that the intent of such attacks was always to maim, never to kill. If people died, it was usually by accident or in confrontations between groups of armed demonstrators of the right and the left. The horrifying bloody photographs of Moro's slaughtered young guards changed all that. These men, although they were on active police duty and were assigned as armed escorts to a political figure, were nevertheless regarded as innocent victims, and this opinion was confirmed by the sight of their grieving relatives and friends strewing flowers on the spot where they died and by a joint public funeral that for several days monopolized the attention of the whole country.

The most immediate effect of the Moro kidnapping was, inevitably, a display of unity by all the major political parties in confronting what was at once defined as an act of blackmail. The Red Brigades quickly put Moro on trial before a so-called people's tribunal and, predictably, condemned him to death as an enemy of the proletariat, then demanded the release of thirteen jailed terrorists as the price of his life. It was generally agreed that the government could neither legally nor morally accede to any such demand—a response that was widely praised abroad and was understood by most local commentators and editorial writers, regardless of their political affiliation.

Under the country's system of proportional representation, with a dozen or more political parties and splinter groups competing for the attention of the often bewildered voter, no Italian government in recent years had been strong enough to govern without at least the tacit support of the Communists or to provide the atmosphere of stability and accord necessary to rescue the nation from impending chaos. The escalating violence in the streets, culminating in the Moro affair, was a direct outcome of this collaboration with the Communists, because left-wing extremists regarded the collaboration as a betrayal of revolutionary doctrine. In mid-April, when a terrorist hideout was raided and some incriminating documents were seized, no one was surprised to discover that Berlinguer himself was apparently the first choice of the kidnappers. He turned out to be too well protected to attack, though, and Aldo Moro, the most respected of the Christian Democrats and the man regarded as the most responsible for working out the current governing formula (which he liked to define, with exquisite pedantic subtlety, as the outcome of his political doctrine of "converging parallels"), was the logical second choice. When he was taken, the kidnapping was correctly regarded by the nation's rulers as an act aimed at compelling the state to negotiate with and ultimately give in to a group whose political legitimacy it could not recognize without hopelessly compromising itself.

The official stand was generally approved, even by spokesmen of strongly opposing political views. The Christian Democrats, according to one independent writer, had known "how to react to the blow without ever deviating from the constitutional line assumed in the immediacy of the tragedy," while the Communists were also to be praised. "If the biggest party of the left," the writer continued, "were not today unequivocally committed to the defense of democracy and the independence of the judiciary, and if the labor unions did not fully share the same courageous attitude in defense of the constitution, we could find ourselves in conditions far worse, and perhaps catastrophic for the future of the Republic." The writer added that the only ray of light in the surrounding darkness was "this climate of national unity which has been formed."

It soon became evident, however, that the climate was an unstable one, not because of any weakness on the government's part but simply because of the nature of the developing tragedy and the enormous toll it had begun to take on Moro and his family. Two weeks after the kidnapping, the Red Brigades began to supplement their own communiqués with open letters written by Moro himself to various public figures—mostly members of the government or other Christian Democrats—and with more private ones to his wife and children. Between March 29, when the first of these letters surfaced—it was addressed to Francesco Cossiga, then the Minister of the Interior—and the day Moro's body was found, a total of sixteen became matters of public knowledge. Subsequently, it was learned that there were others, perhaps as many as forty or fifty in all, but an exact count will probably never be possible, because not all of the letters received by his wife and children were made public. What was certain was that Moro's letters made a very strong impression on all who read them, primarily because they tapped into Italian social attitudes that are centuries old and are deeply ingrained in the national character.

Moro's letters, most analysts agreed, were neither those of a man broken in body and spirit by incarceration and, possibly, torture nor those of a heroic public figure preparing himself for martyrdom. They were the frightened, realistic, loving outcries of an ordinary human being fully aware of his impending fate and more than ready to plead, bargain, even demand political compromises in order to obtain his release. In the first message to Cossiga, Moro hinted that an exchange of prisoners might possibly be worked out to gain him his freedom. He wrote lucidly, intelligently, in a style that was regarded as a model one for exactly the sort of political rationalizations that had characterized his entire career. The tone of the letters varied, depending upon whether a letter was written to a purely professional colleague, an admirer or disciple, a religious figure, an old friend, or a member of Moro's family. He even proposed the convocation of an emergency session of the parliament and the passing of a special law that would enable the government to negotiate on his behalf without compromising its principles. "These letters that are raining down," commented an unsigned editorial in the *Corriere della Sera*, "are morally unreliable and not ascribable, either intellectually or spiritually, to a statesman who for thirty years has been at the top of our national and political life." It was thought that Moro's pleas did not represent the real man but merely the only way he felt he could beg for his life that would prove acceptable to his captors.

Considerably more sympathy was expressed for Moro the man—as distinguished from the politician—in casual street interviews with ordinary citizens that most Roman newspapers began to publish daily as a sort of running commentary on official developments. "Well, I hope they send him home soon," was a recurrent theme. "They should have thought about Moro earlier," a homeward-bound municipal employee observed on the eve of a long holiday in late April. "We wouldn't have reached such a point if we'd had a good police force and a well-equipped secret service. Now what can we do? At three o'clock, I'll go say a prayer for that poor man."

"There are two ways of looking at the world, a political one and a non-political one," Natalia Ginzburg, a novelist and playwright, declared in Turin's *La Stampa* in early May. "I don't think one is better than the other; I think that they are both legitimate, assuming they are honest. The politicals see in every public event the origins, the reasons, and the ends; the non-politicals see nothing—they simply have feelings and follow them." Moro's letters inspired only a great pity, Signorina Ginzburg wrote, a sentiment aroused by the sense of loss most citizens profess to feel when they contemplate what has happened to the quality of life in our time. "Although Moro asks us not to weep for him, we cannot read his words without tears and without feeling that the entire scenario of our present has been suddenly swept away."

On the morning of May 7, after the Red Brigade announced that they were about to carry out the sentence of execution, the arrival of a last letter from Moro to his wife was reported in a Roman daily, *Il Tempo*. "Dear Norina," it began. "They have told me that in a little while they will kill me. I kiss you for the last time." His only political reference was to the effect that the government and members of his own party "could have done something, if they had wanted to" to save his life.

The actual discovery, two days later, of Moro's body, riddled with bullets, in a car abandoned in the middle of the city, at a point almost equidistant from the party headquarters of the Communists and the Christian Democrats, was an event that horrified the nation. Despite all the public declarations to the effect that Moro's death had made him a martyr to the cause of democracy and the survival of its institutions, most Italians were appalled and angered not by the political implications of the act but by the merely human tragedy. Signora Moro and her children remained silent and did not attend any of the official ceremonies; not even the state memorial service held in the Basilica of St. John Lateran on Saturday, May 13, where Pope Paul put in an appearance—the only time since the unification of Italy that any Pope had taken part in such an event.

Much was made of the family's dignified comportment and its insistence that Moro's last wishes be respected. In one of his letters, Moro had asked to be buried in the cemetery of Torrita Tiberina, a tiny medieval town about twenty miles north of Rome, where he had a villa, and which he regarded as home. He had also specified that he wanted no state funeral and wanted no one connected with the government or his party to be present. He was buried under a cold, rainy sky three days before the official state ceremony and in the presence only of his wife, his children, some other relatives, and a handful of local friends.

Although no one admitted it openly, this event struck many observers as a typical expression of where the nation's real sympathies lay. It was clear to many that Moro had believed himself betrayed by his Party colleagues, and had felt that his life was being sacrificed to a public principle which—to him, his family, and most citizens—did not seem worth dying for. The loyalties of most Italians are not to the state or to abstract principles but to far more mundane realities. "No Italian who has a family is ever alone," wrote Luigi Barzini in *The Italians*. "He finds in it a refuge in which to lick his wounds after a defeat, or an arsenal and a staff for his victorious drives. Scholars have always recognized the Italian family as the only fundamental institution in the country, a spontaneous creation of the national genius, adapted through the centuries to changing conditions, the real foundation of whichever social order prevails. In fact, the law, the State, and society function only if they do not directly interfere with the family's supreme interests." In this sense, Aldo Moro and his family believed his death to have been unnecessary. They were not alone. The outrage expressed by many citizens arose out of a conviction that the tragedy was an offense against the traditional loyalties of most Italians as well as against common humanity.

The coldhearted killers of the Red Brigades thus forfeited whatever shred of public sympathy they had formerly laid claim to, and, in so doing, had permanently sealed themselves off from possible connection with any but the most embittered, disenfranchised social elements, on whose continued tacit support their very survival undoubtedly depended. The day after Moro's body was found, a Roman friend of mine remarked, "What could these animals do now that would be any worse? Kidnap and murder the Pope?"

CHAPTER TWELVE

PEOPLE LIKE US

On February 19, 1980, near the merry-go-round of a small amusement park in Turin, two carabinieri arrested a twenty-six-year-old man named Patrizio Peci, who was suspected of being a terrorist and had been under surveillance for several weeks. Peci was carrying a gun. He was imprisoned, immediately tried on this charge, and sentenced to three years and four months, while an investigation continued into his background and his possible involvement in dozens of the bombings, killings, maimings, and kidnappings that various terrorist groups had been carrying out in Rome, Milan, Turin, Genoa, and other major Italian cities for the past few years. Peci, isolated in a maximum-security cell after his arrest and trial, reportedly broke down and asked for a meeting with General Carlo Alberto Dalla Chiesa, the carabiniere officer in charge of anti-terrorist operations. Peci indicated that he was willing to talk, but he wanted certain guarantees.

The two men met for the first time in a small, bare room in the carabiniere barracks in the village of Cambiano, about twelve miles outside Turin. Peci—slight, mustached, hair combed down over his forehead à la Julius Caesar—looked in pictures even younger than his years. He was described as very nervous and unable to sit still throughout the meeting. General Dalla Chiesa—middle-aged, portly, armored by his uniform, gold braid, and rank—peered stolidly at the prisoner through thick horn-rimmed glasses. He promised nothing, but he indicated that if Peci was willing to make a complete confession and tell everything he knew about terrorist activities past and present, he might do what he could to obtain a reduction in sentence—and eventually, perhaps, even a full pardon.

As proof of good will, Peci then admitted that he was indeed a member of the Red Brigades, the most efficient and most feared of the country's half-dozen militant underground organizations, and revealed the address of a terrorist hideout in Genoa. A week later, on March 28, the carabinieri raided the lair and in the ensuing gunfight killed four terrorists, including two men—Riccardo Dura and Lorenzo Betassa—who were known to be leading *brigatisti*.

Peci continued to talk and his confessions dominated the headlines for months. He named names and revealed details of thirty-four specific terrorist attacks over a period of four years, and he admitted to taking part himself in sixteen of them, during which he fired a gun half a dozen times—but without, he said, hitting anyone. Among his most sensational statements was the claim that Marco Donat Cattin, whose father Carlo was a prominent Christian Democratic politician, and who had been away from home since 1977, was also a terrorist, with a group called Prima Linea (Front Line); he was supposed to have taken part a year before in the killing of a Milanese judge.

This disclosure led the elder Donat Cattin to offer his resignation as deputy secretary of his party. The resignation was instantly declined, but the matter refused to cool down. Peci's revelation was soon seconded by another presumably penitent terrorist, named Roberto Sandalo, who testified that he had met several times with Signor Donat Cattin and his wife, and that the politician had told him he had been in touch with Premier Cossiga himself concerning possible criminal charges against his son. Public accusations of favoritism and collusion were quick to follow, and the ensuing uproar in the press eventually led to a parliamentary inquiry into how much Signor Donat Cattin knew about his son's activities and whether he and/or other members of the government, including Cossiga, got word to young Marco that he was being hunted by the police and urged him to get out of the country. Although this inquiry was resolved in the government's favor, Signor Donat Cattin was forced to resign again, and this time his resignation was accepted. He continued angrily to deny most of Sandalo's accusations.

The saddest of Peci's revelations concerned the kidnapping and assassination in Rome two years earlier of Aldo Moro, then the leader of the Christian Democrats. The operation, according to Peci, had been carried out by nine *brigatisti*, including a woman, and was masterminded by Mario Moretti, one of two suspects named by Peci who were still at large. Peci claimed to have taken no part in the operation himself, but to have heard about it in detail from several of those involved. The picture he provided of Moro in captivity (he was held in an empty store on the outskirts of Rome) was that of a "courageous and, in fact, dignified" man who refused to barter state secrets for his life, spoke only in general terms to his captors of political matters, and, though bitter at a number of his colleagues for not trying harder to save him, resigned himself to his death when it became clear that neither the government nor his own party would negotiate with the Red Brigades on terms that might have spared him. Peci also claimed that Moro had written a number of letters as a sort of last testament, leaving various personal belongings to specific members of his family, but for some reason, according to Peci, these letters were destroyed by the kidnappers.

Although Peci's version of the Moro affair was occasionally vague, and conflicted in some details with accounts by eyewitnesses of the actual attack in Via Fani, during which Moro's driver and bodyguards were gunned down and he himself was kidnapped, Peci's testimony seemed chillingly authentic. It was offered, Peci declared to the investigating magistrates in Rome on April 4, because he had been undergoing a "profound moral crisis and had been reflecting on the events of the last few years." He considered it his "duty as a man and a Communist" to tell all he knew, directly or at second hand, about the Red Brigades and other "subversive organizations."

Whatever his motives, Peci's confessions proved to be extraordinarily useful to General Dalla Chiesa and his unit, as well as to local police. Peci was the first of the captured terrorists to talk, and his often fascinating narrative illuminated past events, explained the internal structure of the organization, provided clues to dozens of unsolved crimes, and also made it possible for the state to begin to defend itself, by dealing not only with the terrorists but with sympathizers and contacts in the society at large, including a number of radical lawyers, without whose support such organizations could not flourish. If Peci was to be believed, there were no more than five hundred active members of the Red Brigades, but during the months following Peci's arrest there were hundreds of other arrests, and many people were jailed—almost a hundred of them known to be *brigatisti.*

Despite Peci's collaboration, the increased number of arrests, and indications that quite a few other suspects had begun to talk, terrorist violence continued. Every few days, the newspapers reported attacks on politicians, functionaries, policemen, magistrates, and journalists—members of the groups that were the gunmen's favorite targets. On May 12, Alfredo Albanese, the thirty-three-year-old head of the Venice police's anti-terrorist unit, was shot to death near his house by a Red Brigades team waiting in ambush, and a few days later a Christian Democratic politician was killed in his car at midday in the crowded streets of Naples. In the latter case, the four *brigatisti* (three men and a woman) were caught, but most of the time the terrorists managed to get away.

At about 11 A.M. on May 28, in Milan, a respected young journalist named Walter Tobagi was shot and killed by Red Brigades assassins in front of a popular trattoria only a few hundred yards from his home. Tobagi had specialized in investigative and analytical articles on Italian terrorism, and his name had already cropped up on a Prima Linea hit list found in an abandoned suitcase in Milan about a year or so earlier. That same morning, another terrorist unit attacked a police car parked in front of a high school in a residential section of Rome, killing one officer and wounding two others, while hundreds of horrified students looked on. Three different terrorist groups, one of them Fascist, immediately claimed responsibility.

On August 2, an explosive device equivalent to ninety tons of TNT devastated the Bologna railroad station, killing seventy-nine people and injuring about two hundred others. In terms of casualties, it was the worst act of political violence in the nation's history, and eventually proved to be the work of right-wing terrorists, who have always been less discriminating in their choice of victims than their spiritual colleagues on the left.

Though badly mauled, the terrorist organizations continued to operate effectively and no one could predict if they could ever finally be eliminated. It had become clear over the previous months that the ability of these clandestine entities to survive at all was due in large part to continued support, even if largely passive, from society's outcasts, the subproletariat of the nation's biggest slums. Though the terrorists themselves often turned out to be the disenchanted, introverted offspring of the middle class (Peci was the son of a factory foreman, and was remembered by a high-school friend as a shy, quiet, emotional young man), most of the underground movements' fiercest partisans were really what a journalist for the weekly *Panorama* defined as "nobody's children." They were drawn mainly from the thousands of unemployed, restless, ignorant young people, whose inability to make a place for themselves in an industrial society and a political order that seemed indifferent to their aspirations led them naturally to violence. Some of those who had actively joined the terrorist bands were petty criminals whose first contact with violent political activism came while in jail. Suddenly supplied with organizational support, money, and a political philosophy, it was easy for them to make the transition from a life of personal crime to one devoted to the higher cause of bringing down by force the social order they despised. What continued to surprise everyone, however, was how very ordinary even the most renowned of the fugitives were, once apprehended and exposed to public view. "We thought they were different," a magistrate observed shortly after Peci's arrest, "but they're people like us, with their own fears—normal people, not heroes at all. Perhaps for some of them this is the end of a nightmare."

For the political and legal organs of the state, however, the nightmare was far from over. One long-range effect of the continuing terrorist activity turned out to be an immediate political swing to the right, accompanied by the promulgation of some stiff legal measures designed essentially to facilitate all sorts of police operations. The publication in two issues of *Il Messaggero* in early May of excerpts from Peci's testimony before the examining magistrates in Rome led to the arrest of a reporter, Fabio Isman, and the deputy chief of Italian counterintelligence, a veteran officer named Silvano Russomanno. After being held in jail for two weeks, both men were brought to trial and convicted of collaborating to violate an official-secrets act regarding pre-trial testimony. Isman was sentenced to eighteen months' imprisonment, Russomanno to two years and eight months. The ferocity of the sentences, even though they were quickly appealed, alarmed the press, which saw its freedom threatened. The gist of Peci's testimony, observers pointed out, had already been widely disseminated in other publications, but the authorities chose to strike at a newspaper known for its left-wing sympathies. "In reality, this is, in part, a trial of the press, of information as a whole," *Il Messaggero* commented in a front-page editorial. Another reporter said privately, "How sad and how ironic if, even as the terrorists are being hunted down, we Italians destroy our own freedoms. Then these delinquents will indeed be able to claim the final victory."

CHAPTER THIRTEEN

THE LONGEST STREET IN THE WORLD

"It was good to know that you are very much alive and aware of the fact that letters should be written occasionally to us," my father wrote to me during the winter of 1949. "Of course we did read the 'Black Panther' article, never realizing that you were responsible for it. It's a damn good job. I know you will keep me informed of any future developments."

This was the next to last letter my father wrote to me before his death in New York, a few weeks later, of a heart attack. By then I had been living in Italy for over a year and had begun to work as a stringer for the Rome bureau of an American news magazine. In the beginning, I had been used mainly as an interpreter and translator, but the bureau chief, an optimistic soul who saw hidden talents in me that I certainly never imagined I possessed, had decided, after my first few weeks on the job, that I was destined to be a journalist.

I was reminded of all this while I was going through some old files some time ago and came across my father's letter. He had never approved of my attempts to become an opera singer and had been dismayed by my sudden departure for Italy to pursue my career. He and my mother had been separated for many years by then and we had never been close. Nevertheless, I had wanted and needed his approval, especially in my late teens. The few sentences he wrote to me about my first reportorial effort were the first words of praise I had ever received from him and, as it turned out, the last.

The so-called Black Panther was a young Roman woman named Celeste Di Porto, who had lived with her family in the old Jewish quarter of the city. Originally nicknamed Stella (Star) for her exceptional physical beauty, she had slipped through the Nazi roundup of Jews in the area on October 16, 1943, by running out of her house in the early morning and survived to become infamous as Pantera Nera, the Black Panther. She had reportedly become the mistress of a Fascist officer and, despite being Jewish herself, escaped deportation to a German concentration camp by selling out some fifty of her fellow citizens. Most of them perished either in the camps or in the massacre of the Ardeatine caves on the outskirts of the city, where the Germans shot three hundred and thirty-five people, seventy-three of them Jews, in retaliation for a Partisan attack that had killed thirty-three of their soldiers. One of Pantera Nera's victims was a professional boxer named Lazzaro Anticoli, better-known to his fans as Bucefalo, who had been fingered as a Jew by Celeste Di Porto and arrested in her presence. He scrawled a note on the wall of his jail cell testifying to this effect and his last written words were "Avenge me." What made the Black Panther's behavior even more heinous was that she had reportedly been paid five thousand lire, then about fifty dollars, for every person she turned in.

Arrested by the Allied authorities after the liberation of Italy, the Black Panther had spent several years in prison but had recently been released. She was supposedly coming back to her old haunts and the quarter was up in arms. Some of those who had survived the German occupation had sworn to kill her if she showed up and I had been sent into the area to find out what was going to happen and to interview anyone I could find who had ever known her.

The Di Portos were an old established Jewish family in Rome. A woman named Giuditta Di Porto owned a dress shop in the quarter, and other Di Portos sold clothing and housewares in the daily open-air market in the nearby Campo de' Fiori, where they had long had the right to a *banco fisso,* a permanent stall licensed by the municipal government. None of the Di Portos, even those not directly related to the Black Panther, wanted to be interviewed, but I was told by others who knew the family that Celeste had been disowned by her parents and that, if she did return, she would certainly be assaulted, perhaps killed.

As it turned out, the Black Panther never did show up. I was told later that she had gone into hiding under an assumed name in some other city, reportedly somewhere in the north, and has apparently stayed out of sight ever since. What I remember best from my first time in this part of Rome was the incredulity and outrage expressed by everyone I talked to that she should have received such mild treatment for her wartime activities and that she could even have considered coming back home after what had happened. One middle-aged man, who had spent most of the later war years hiding out and fighting with a Partisan band in the hills south of Rome, cried with rage and frustration. "Eight members of my family were killed," he said, "and I come home to find this slut still alive." He sat drinking wine in the dark front room of a trattoria called Gigetto and banging his glass on the plain wooden table to emphasize the depth of his feelings on the matter.

I had long known, in a vague sort of way, that Italy had a Jewish population. During the late thirties and the war years in New York, my mother and grandmother had introduced me to Italians, some of them old friends, who had fled Italy to escape persecution. I also remember my mother's surprise at discovering that several of her schoolmates, people she had known most of her life, were Jewish. Questions of faith and racial origin had simply never come up during her childhood. Italy's Jews had never been considered anything but Italians. Most of them, I gathered, came from very old families who could trace their origins back hundreds of years, in some cases even to ancient Roman times.

In 161 B.C., a Jewish leader named Judah the Maccabee, then leading a revolt in Palestine against the Seleucid dynasty in Asia Minor, dispatched an embassy to Rome seeking friendship and protection. It was the first recorded contact between Jews and Italians. Rome, with ambitions of her own in the area, supported Judah, and traffic between Palestine and Rome increased. A small number of Jews, mostly traders and merchants, apparently settled in the city during these relatively tranquil years.

By the time Pompey the Great conquered Palestine in 69 B.C.

and incorporated the region into the Roman province of Syria, there were several thousand Jews living in Rome. Their numbers swelled with the arrival of prisoners sent back to the city as slaves, most of whom were eventually ransomed and/or freed. Many stayed on and the Jewish population, with added immigration from the Levant and Egypt, grew until the colony numbered between thirty and forty thousand people.

Protected at first by favorable imperial dispensations, the Jews apparently flourished in Rome, until a revolt broke out in Palestine in 67 A.D. After three years of bloody fighting, a large Roman army under the Emperor Vespasian's son Titus finally crushed the rebellion and sacked Jerusalem, burning the temple. The dead were said to number in the hundreds of thousands, while tens of thousands of others were sold into slavery. Seven hundred prisoners were paraded behind Titus's triumphal chariot in Rome, including the captured leaders of the resistance. Among the booty displayed in the procession were the spoils of the temple—a seven-branched candelabra, silver trumpets, and the golden tablets of the shrewbread. These objects are all still plainly visible in the elaborate relief decorating the Arch of Titus, erected at the foot of the Palatine in 81 A.D. to commemorate the event. A Roman coin bearing the inscription *Judaea capta* also celebrates the victory. "One consequence of the defeat," according to the Italian Jewish historian Attilio Milano, "was that the Jews of all countries ceased to be considered by the Romans as a privileged nation, but became merely followers of a permitted religion."

The Jewish population of Italy never again achieved such numbers nor the security it had enjoyed in the century before the razing of Jerusalem. "The Roman Jews continued to be numerous," writes Milano, "thanks also to the recent advent of ex-slaves. But their social status remained low, because that is what was desired by the ruling class, and because, on their part, they tried not to make themselves too conspicuous, especially after having been forced into a somewhat ambivalent position." In fact, after 70 A.D., the first of history's by now familiar restrictive measures against Jewish communities everywhere were imposed by the Emperor Vespasian himself, beginning with a census and the imposition of a tax, the so-called *fiscus judaicus,* amounting then to two small silver coins annually per person. "The unitary value of the tribute was small," comments Milano, "but the implications great." The technique of a head count followed by a tax has almost always been the first restrictive measure a totalitarian government imposes on a minority. It was the one first used by the Nazis to force German Jews out of the country soon after Hitler came to power.

Misconceptions and prejudices concerning Jewish religious practices abounded, even under Augustus, that most lenient of Roman despots, and were effectively propagated by the empire's intellectuals and historians. Seneca, for instance, declared himself opposed to observance of the Sabbath because it meant committing one-seventh of one's life to idleness. Tacitus declared that the Jews worshipped the image of an ass, abstained from pork because of scabies (a disease then apparently endemic to the animal), and ate unleavened bread to commemorate their flight out of Egypt. Cicero considered the religion as a whole barbarous and Juvenal was convinced that the Jews worshipped clouds. In such an intellectual atmosphere, it is not hard to imagine what the social status of the colony must have been and impossible to believe that it could have improved very much with the rise of Christianity, even though it is known that Pope Gregory I, between 590 and 604 A.D., was a magnanimous and humane overseer. His bull *Sicut Judaeis* placed the Jews directly under papal protection, forbade violence against them or persecution for their beliefs, and established a workable basis for the relationship between the papacy and the Jewish community that was to evolve, with many startling ups and downs, over a period of thirteen hundred years.

Although the Jews, after Pope Gregory, proceeded to drop out of recorded history for nearly four centuries, it is reasonable to assume that at no time has Rome been without its Jewish community, even during the Dark Ages, when the entire population of the city had been reduced by repeated barbarian invasions to an estimated forty thousand people. We do know that in 1007, for instance, Rome had at least three rabbis, and that in 1020 a mob attacked and killed some Jews, after it had convinced itself that the Jews as a whole were to blame for an earthquake. The little bits and pieces of factual knowledge that surface through the murk of history too often glitter with a familiar light, as if not even the most recent and awful of tragedies can lay claim to originality.

I had never realized, until I set out to track down the story of the Black Panther, that Rome's Jews had ever occupied any specific section of the city, much less an actual ghetto. The area I first visited that winter of 1948–49 consisted of no more than a few city blocks of ancient, picturesquely dilapidated houses lining a broad street called the Via del Portico d'Ottavia, named after the ruined columns and cornice of the portico originally erected in 149 B.C., later rebuilt and dedicated by the Emperor Augustus to his sister Octavia in 23 B.C. In addition to this handsome ruin, the street was anchored at the south end by the vast dramatic-looking bulk of the Theatre of Marcellus, also completed by Augustus and later converted into a Renaissance palace. The street extended for a few hundred yards to the Piazza Costaguti and the adjacent Via Arenula, a busy main avenue clogged even then by traffic. The few streets leading off the Via Portico d'Ottavia were narrow alleys that meandered away between the dark-stone walls of still other *palazzi*, some of them, like the Mattei and the Cenci, with long, gloomily romantic histories. I was immediately charmed by the whole district, which lay directly across the river from the medieval clutter of Trastevere, the Tiber Island, and the Bridge of the Four Heads, all famous Roman landmarks.

I had not been in the quarter very long, however, before I gained an inkling of its brutal history. It was into this tiny section that the Jews, who had until then been free to live anywhere in the city, were herded by Pope Paul IV with his bull *Cum nimis absurdum* of July 12, 1555. "Since it is exceedingly absurd and unbecoming that the Jews, who have been condemned by their own fault to eternal slavery, should—with the excuse of being protected by Christian love and allowed to live among Christians—show such ingratitude toward the latter so as to do them injury for the mercy received . . ." it began and went on from there in the same vindictive tone. The Jews were from then on to live along a single main street and a few surrounding blocks, shut off from their fellow citizens by a wall and prohibited from practicing most normal human pursuits, except the selling of old clothes and junk. Even though the best doctors in the city were Jewish, for example, they were forbidden to treat any but their own people. The Jews were also to be physically distinguished from everyone else by having the men wear a yellow cap and the women a shawl or a veil of the same color.

At the time of this proclamation, most of the city's several thousand Jews lived in Trastevere. They were dispatched to the opposite bank, where the houses crowded together in a maze of dark alleys and so close to the water's edge that the whole quarter was frequently inundated by the dirty waters of the Tiber. They remained there, even under the more lenient and merciful of the popes who succeeded Paul IV, for over three hundred years. (The ghetto as such was a Venetian invention and took its name from the Venetian word for foundry, since it was into this section, *il ghetto nuovo*, of the Serenissima that Jews were first shut up, in 1516. Rome's is thus the world's second-oldest ghetto, though its Jewish community is older than Venice's.)

In 1870, after the unification of Italy and the installment of a national government, the walls of the ghetto were at last torn down, as were most of the houses between the Via Portico d'Ottavia and the water. The Tiber was contained between high embankments and new buildings were erected, including in 1904 the *tempio maggiore*, the main synagogue, built in Assyro-Babylonian style, that still squats majestically above the river, its reassuring bulk and gleaming aluminum dome seeming as eternal today as the faith it enshrines.

It was not surprising to me to discover, given the area's long history, that so many Jews still lived in it. At the beginning of the Second World War, about twelve thousand of the country's roughly forty-five thousand Jews lived in Rome, more than half of them in and around the ghetto. By the time I first visited it, those numbers had diminished, but I had been told that several thousand members of the community still lived either in the district or no more than a few blocks from it.

It seemed entirely appropriate to me, since by their very survival and continued presence over so many dark and bloody centuries Rome's Jews gave added meaning to the adjective most often applied to the city; the Jews were as eternal as Rome itself. "If one wanders through Rome and its splendors and leaves aside the sights of antiquity, everywhere the spirit and form of Hebraism strike the eye, even in the pinnacles of Christian art," wrote the German historian Ferdinand Gregorovius in 1853. "In sculpture we have Michelangelo's *Moses* on the tomb of Pope Julius II, the noblest production in marble of the Christian genius. In painting Raphael's *Stanze* and loggias, the Sistine Chapel, and countless other examples are filled with representations from the Bible of the Jews. In music the noblest and profoundest chants of Holy Week, the *Lamentations* and the *Miserere*, are the Lamentations of Jeremiah and the Psalms of the Jews. And of this people, to which fate has entrusted the charters of mankind and which Christianity has so to speak displaced from its heritage, there dwell here in the ghetto one of the oldest and historically most remarkable remnants, upon which history has exacted its great and tragic irony."

I have been in the old ghetto often over the years since my first visit, partly because the area contains several good restaurants and partly because it is one of the most interesting and pleasant to stroll in. One afternoon in the spring of 1980, after an absence of nearly a year, I walked across the bridge from Trastevere, where I had been visiting some friends, and into the Via Portico d'Ottavia for a coffee. The street angles into the quarter from the embankment for about a hundred yards, then turns left at the portico itself toward Piazza Costaguti and the Via Arenula. It had rained hard all morning and the old stones and ruined columns gleamed under the sun. I stopped to admire the view, as I had so often before, and for some reason I happened to notice for the first time a marble tablet with an inscription in both Latin and Hebrew over the entrance to the small Church of San Gregorio on the corner of the street. "I have stretched out my hands every day to an unbelieving people," the first part of it read, "who have walked in a way that is not good, after their own thoughts."

I wrote the words down and proceeded up the street, which was, as usual, crowded with shoppers, playing children, and small groups of mostly middle-aged men chatting and joking with each other. Along the side of the Via Portico d'Ottavia nearest the Tiber the buildings have all been put up since 1900 and consist of several large rectangular apartment houses and a couple of public schools, none of them distinguished architecturally. On the other side of the street, however, are the ancient houses of the ghetto, still crowded together in disarray, as if assembled hastily by chance and making use of the tumbled fragments of Roman ruins that must have once littered the area. More than a few of these *palazzi* have bits of marble columns and cornices embedded into their walls and framing their windows. Behind them the narrow alleys of the quarter can still be seen, dark even at midday and occasionally with drying laundry stretched across them from window to window. It looked exactly as I had first seen it over thirty years before, but then one of the great pleasures of Rome is to be able to come back year after year to find one's favorite parts of the so-called *centro storico* unchanged.

Toward the end of the street, I went into a small bar called Totò, which is directly across from the public schools and sandwiched between a one-room restaurant, Da Remo *"Specialità Romane,"* and a clothing store. Totò is almost always crowded with people from the quarter buying coffee, drinks, or cigarettes, and functions as an informal social center for the community. Its two public phones seem to be constantly in use and a section of wall space between the cashier's booth and the zinc bar counter carries announcements of forthcoming group activities: picnics, excursions to nearby beaches and resorts, free lectures, political meetings, soccer games and other sporting events, as well as group rates for trips to Israel. Outside the entrance, several men were arguing and jokingly insulting each other. As I drank my *espresso,* I stood in the doorway and listened to them.

It was difficult to follow their conversation, because they spoke very rapidly in their version of the Roman dialect, which includes many Hebrew words and phrases that over the centuries have been Italianized and worked into local usage. I could tell, however, that the banter, most of it rough but harmless, was directed at one of the group, a stocky, black-eyed man in his fifties, who seemed well able to take care of himself and had the loudest voice in the street. He shifted his ground and bobbed his head as he talked, much like a fighter sparring for an opening, and jabbed back at his tormentors in a husky, dark baritone that could have filled an opera house. Though I couldn't understand everything that was being said, the scene made me smile and I stood there until, after about ten minutes, the group began to disperse.

I introduced myself to the man in Italian and offered to buy him a drink or a coffee. "Here they call me Mouth," he said, shaking my hand. "But it is not my name. You are American. I'll buy." Inside, over two more *espressi,* he told me that his real name was Giacomo and also gave me his last name, which I knew to be one of the most common Jewish surnames in the quarter. His nickname of Bocca, the Italian word for mouth, was simply what he was called by his friends, undoubtedly in tribute to his formidable speaking voice and his mastery of often obscene street language. "Many of us have other names here," he explained and indicated two of the other men who had been bantering with him. "The young one there is Chocolate," he said, "and the tall one is Drin-Drin. Most of the time he is all right, but some days he hears the sound of bells in his head—*drin-drin."*

I told Giacomo that I had long been interested in the area and he immediately offered to walk me through it. Outside in the street, he put his arm through mine, as if he had known me for years, and guided me along. While we strolled past the narrow doorways of the *palazzi* and the small shops—mostly food and clothing stores—lining not only the Via Portico d'Ottavia but the two cobblestoned streets branching off it, the Via della Reginella and the Via di S. Ambrogio, he indicated that he knew very little about the ancient history of the ghetto. His own family, he told me, had lived in this part of Rome for centuries and they had always considered themselves Italians who happened also to be Jewish. As a boy growing up in the streets of the district, he had not even thought about it, until in 1937 the Fascist government of Benito Mussolini, yielding to pressure from its German ally, passed the so-called racial laws.

Giacomo could not recall his life changing as a result of these laws, which, among other restrictions imposed on their activities, required all Jews to register as such and banned them from all offical government posts. The legislation stipulated numerous exemptions—war veterans, citizens with official titles and/or holding high decorations, anyone who had ever been a member of the Fascist Party or who had a relation, however distant, who had ever been a member. This last stipulation, in fact, made it almost impossible to apply the racial laws to any Jew in Rome, a city of civil servants in which nearly everyone was connected by blood or marriage to somebody in the governing bureaucracy. "We did not suffer until the Germans came," Giacomo said, "but I remember asking my father then if I was a Roman or a Jew. 'You are a Roman *and* a Jew,' he told me. I have never forgotten that and I always tell my children not to forget. Since that time, after all that has happened, I have become more and more Jewish, always more and more Jewish, until now I am an extremist."

Giacomo said that he and his family had for many generations been iron-workers and that he had a small factory of his own outside the city. He and his wife and the two younger of their three children still lived in the quarter, however, in a quiet side street just outside the old ghetto itself. It was clear to me that he had never considered living in any other part of town and I asked him how many of his friends felt as he did. "Mostly the older ones," he answered. "There are perhaps a thousand of us now. The young people move away and foreigners are buying up apartments in the old buildings and fixing them up. Soon there will be only a few of us and the memories we have. Also, the temple is here. There will always be Jews because of the temple."

As we walked about the quarter, stopping here and there to admire the architectural eccentricities of the old buildings and to speculate on the past, Giacomo became increasingly excited by the experience. I realized that, like many people who have lived all of their lives in one place, he had grown up taking the area for granted, without really informing himself concerning its history and the specific events that had kept him and his people rooted in the district for so many generations. "Incapable of confronting their enemies by bold offense," Gregorovius had written, "they fortified themselves behind the strongest and saddest weapon of misery—habit and the tenacity of Jewish family life."

Although Giacomo had only a dim sense of much of the ghetto's recorded history, he was familiar, like everyone else in the area, with some of the local legends. At number thirteen on the Via Portico d'Ottavia, we stood in a small, dark courtyard, under a pillared gallery and hemmed in by two apartment buildings festooned with drying laundry. There had been a well here and several old Roman columns, Giacomo had been told as a boy, but suddenly one day they had all simply dropped out of sight. Below the whole quarter were the ruins, supposedly, of the ancient Roman Circus Flaminius and catacombs that stretched in all directions as far as the Vatican, some even all the way to the Alban Hills south of the city. No one knew whether there was any truth to such stories, Giacomo informed me, but he had grown up believing in them.

When we reached the columns and cornice of the Portico of Octavia, I asked Giacomo if he had ever been inside the tiny Church of S. Angelo in Pescheria, which is built behind the portico and incorporates a portion of the ruin into the façade of the church itself. It is open for only a few hours at midday on Saturdays, but its austerely barren interior contains nothing of interest to the casual tourist. Giacomo admitted that he had never set foot inside the building and knew no one who had. There was a marked antipathy in the quarter to this particular church, but he had never known exactly why.

I told him it was here that intermittently on Sundays, between 1572 and the early eighteen-hundreds, depending on the whim of the ruling pope, some of the Jews of the quarter, whoever could be rounded up by the police, would be compelled to attend conversionist sermons delivered by Dominican priests. "It does not surprise me," Giacomo said, taking my arm again as we proceeded up the street. "Come, I will show you now something I do know about."

High above the street, on the rear wall of a small, perfectly preserved Renaissance house that now functions as a local headquarters for the Department of Antiquities and Fine Arts, hangs a large white-marble tablet. It was placed there on October 25, 1964, by the National Committee to Celebrate the Twentieth Anniversary of the Resistance and it recalls the wartime German roundup of the Jews as follows:

> On October 16, 1943,
> here began
> The merciless hunt of the Jews
> and two thousand ninety-one Roman citizens
> were dispatched to a ferocious death
> in the Nazi extermination camps
> where they were joined
> by another six thousand Italians,
> victims of infamous
> racial hatred.
>
> The few who escaped the slaughter,
> the many local sympathizers
> invoke from men
> love and peace,
> invoke from God
> pardon and hope.

German troops had sealed off the streets in the early morning, Giacomo told me, and conducted a house by house hunt through the quarter, taking everyone they found. "Some of us saw it coming," Giacomo said. "A month before, I told my father, 'Let's go, let's go,' but he said, 'No, the Germans have a war to fight. They haven't time to worry about the Jews.' My father did not know the Germans. Ninety percent of the people who were taken were caught because they didn't believe the Germans could do such a thing or that the Fascists would turn Jews in. Many people in the community had been Fascists themselves, including some very big bigshots."

Giacomo had finally persuaded his own family to disperse and go into hiding, moving from one place to another all over the city till the liberation. "Half the people of Rome were hiding the other half," he explained, "and not just the Jews either." He himself left the city to live in the mountains of the Abruzzi for five months, until he rejoined his relatives. "All of us who survived that period have stories, so many stories, to tell. We could all write books," he observed. "I came back because nine of my wife's people were caught. I wanted to be with her, if we were all going to be taken sooner or later."

Of the eleven hundred and twenty-seven people seized during that first roundup in the ghetto, eight hundred of them women and children, most were sent in boxcars to Auschwitz. A year and a half later, the only survivors, fourteen men and one woman, returned to the quarter. "They are all still here, I think," Giacomo said. "But then we, too, are all still here."

We walked in silence up to the end of the street, where I pointed out to Giacomo the bilingual inscription above the entrance to the Church of San Gregorio. He smiled. "It can be read two ways," he said. "Perhaps it is the Jews who are stretching out their hands to an unbelieving people that does not know what to think. Who is to say?"

Only a few days after my informal tour of the quarter with Giacomo, I again found myself in the ghetto. The occasion this time was a summer street festival called Rendezvous at the Portico of Octavia, sponsored by the Cultural Center of the Jewish Community and various city agencies. First launched in 1977, the Rendezvous, held on a Sunday in mid-June, was designed to create in the area a traditional celebration of the kind put on in various other old districts of the city, such as the week-long Festa di Noiantri in Trastevere, an annual carnival that overwhelms that part of Rome every September. The ghetto, with its grim and sorrowful past, has rarely had occasion to celebrate anything. The intention of the Rendezvous was to change all that. In addition to a central exhibit designed to illustrate a particular historical theme (this year's was "The history, customs and traditions of Roman Jewry from 1500 to the present day"), the one-day *festa* includes music, dancing, lectures, sporting events, and open-air booths selling artifacts, books, and comestibles.

Some weeks earlier, I had dropped in at the Cultural Center and had been told by Signorina Bice Migliau, the young woman who directed the institution and helped to launch the festival, that the event now stood a good chance of catching on, despite a good deal of initial resistance from some of the residents in the area. Signorina Migliau's small, unpretentious office was located in one of the newer buildings on the Via Portico d'Ottavia and looked down over the street. Her walls were decorated with blow-ups of old maps and photographs of the quarter, mostly of the parts torn down and filled in after 1870. When I asked her why she had encountered resistance to what seemed such a worthy project, she smiled a little sadly and waved toward the people in the street below. "They are full of doubts and they do not trust easily," she said. "They are always expecting the worst. The first year no one was prepared for the crowds that came and everyone ran out of food and other things to sell. It has taken us nearly two years now to organize this second manifestation. We hope it will be different and become permanent."

I arrived at the Via Portico d'Ottavia on the day of the *festa* in mid-afternoon to find the whole area blocked to traffic and a cheerful-looking crowd milling about dozens of booths set up along both sides of the street under awnings and umbrellas. Next to the Department of Antiquities and Fine Arts, almost directly beneath the tablet commemorating the German raid, a large blue pavilion had been set up, open to the street. Inside, a loud recorded lecture illustrated by colored slides explained the origin and practices of the Jewish faith and how they had evolved in Rome over the centuries. Beginning at the corner of the Church of S. Angelo in Pescheria were stands selling pottery, linens, household goods, books, handicrafts, and food, while in front of the church itself a large table exhibited a meticulously complete reproduction in painted cardboard of the street itself; it had been built by elementary-school children of the district.

I walked down the street, then turned into the Via del Tempio, a broad, short avenue leading to the synagogue and the embankment. A pick-up soccer game involving a couple of dozen boys of all ages was in full, raucous cry. I watched it for a while, then went inside the temple where I spent an hour or so looking at an exhibit, mounted in the basement of the building, recreating in maps and photographs the vanished Piazza delle Cinque Scole, demolished after 1870. Tiny, cobblestoned, its houses jammed together in the familiar ghetto style, it had clearly been, with its five synagogues, the very heart of the community.

Upstairs, while strolling through a small but well-stocked museum that features texts, building fragments, prints, drawings, ceremonial textiles, and silver objects belonging to the community, I suddenly came across a large, framed black-and-white portrait of Pope Paul IV, the creator of the Roman ghetto. That "founder of the torture chamber" and "pitiless reformer of iron determination," as Gregorovius had described him, had a long, lean, unsmiling face, with a drooping mustache and heavy-browed eyes. He looked, indeed, exactly as I had imagined he must—a wolfish, inquisitorial face out of an early Verdi opera.

By the time I emerged into the street again, it had begun to rain, but not hard enough to stall the festival. The soccer game was still in progress and people huddled together around the booths, still buying, eating, and chatting. Among the more frequented exhibits, I noted, were those advertising the plight of today's Jewish refugees. Rome now had a permanent community of about twelve hundred Jews from Lybia, who had been expelled from that country in 1967, and several hundred Russian *yordim*, who had settled around the beach area of Ostia. At any given time there were an estimated several thousand refugees, most of them from the Soviet Union, passing through Rome on their way mainly to the United States, Canada, Australia, and Israel. "These new refugees have very little in common with Italian Jews," Signorina Migliau had informed me, "but they are here and they remind our people, if they should need reminding, that the Diaspora is not just ancient history."

Later, outside Totò, I again bumped into Giacomo, who was carrying a large black umbrella. "Look at this," he exclaimed, waving a hand at the sky, "weather for dogs!" Nevertheless, he immediately took my arm in his proprietary way and again steered me back up the street past the exhibits. "Listen," he said, after a few minutes, "I have been thinking about you. How is it that you speak Italian so well?"

I told Giacomo something about my background and he asked me if my family came from Rome. I explained that one branch, the Traversari, had come originally from Ravenna. The other, more numerous branch, the Danesi, had been in Rome for many generations. There had even been a Danesi *palazzo*, outside the Porta Flaminia, but it had been torn down to make way for an office building. "Danesi, Danesi," Giacomo said, "that means 'the Danes.' Is it possible you are part Jewish?"

I knew immediately what he meant. The surnames of many Italian Jews—Milano, Anticoli, Fiumara, many others—are derived from points of origin and place. I had been asked quite often before, by Italian friends of mine, whether the Danesi had indeed once been Jewish, but I had long ago found out differently. This branch of my family had come into Italy from some northern country, probably Denmark, burdened by the weight of an unpronounceable (to Italians, at least) last name. They had settled first in Naples, where the residents of the quarter had undoubtedly begun to refer to the newcomers as *i danesi*, "the Danes." It had obviously been easier for my ancestors, immigrants in a new land, to accept their new appellation rather than struggle along trying to impose on their adopted culture such a tongue-twister as Johanssen, say. It had been an easy transition, after a generation or two, simply to accept a name any other Italian could easily pronounce.

I explained all this to Giacomo, who listened thoughtfully to my account and nodded. "Too bad," he said, when I had finished. "You could have been a true Roman, like me. Because you know something? We Jews are the true Romans today. We have been here longer than anyone else. The stink of Rome is in our bones."

When we completed our second tour of the quarter together, we headed back toward Totò for a coffee. It was still drizzling, but very few people had left and some of the booths were doing a fairly brisk business. The tall man nicknamed Drin-Drin was lounging in a doorway and staring sourly out at the crowded street. I greeted him and commented that, despite the uncertain weather, the festival seemed to be a success. Drin-Drin did not seem pleased by my remark. "Why don't they get out of here?" he said, indicating the crowd milling around the booths. "Once they used to lock us in here. Now I'd lock them all out."

Giacomo led me away. "You mustn't pay attention to him," he said. "Today he hears the bells in his head. He has lived here all his life and to him this is the longest street in the world."

CHAPTER FOURTEEN

OUTCASTS

M uch has been written during the past few years about Italy's many, perhaps insoluble, problems, but the one great, paradoxical truth about the country is that, regardless of what happens, no matter what goes wrong, life for a great many people somehow remains extraordinarily pleasant. Anyone who hasn't recently spent at least a few days in Rome, for instance, and has derived an idea of daily life in the city simply from a perusal of news stories and TV programs could not conceivably imagine that such a thing was possible. Nevertheless, the fact is that for those who live in or near the *centro storico*, with its elegant old *palazzi*, expensive shops, and hotels, the pace of living is much as it has always been. The theatres and movie houses are full, the sidewalks and alleys swarm with shoppers, the cafés and bars are crammed with contented-looking citizens sipping *espressi* or spooning elaborate *gelati*. Despite strict new parking laws, and regulations banning the use of private automobiles in various zones of the *centro* during daylight hours, the streets seem to be nearly as full of cars as ever, and mopeds and motor scooters, apparently exempted from all rules, zip about with that reckless abandon characteristic of any vehicle driven by the average Italian. To anyone who has spent time in the city, Rome can come to resemble a huge open-air bazaar patronized almost exclusively by the well-to-do.

This appearance may be deceptive, but it is not altogether without foundation. It's an accurate portrait—on the surface, at least—of one aspect of the society. Rome, like most other large Italian municipalities, has become two cities, harboring separate and quite unequal urban civilizations, as isolated from each other as if they were the products of entirely different cultures. This curious phenomenon has evolved, almost unnoticed, over the past twenty-five years, for by the early nineteen-fifties the nation's political leaders and industrial managers had established economic policies for the country that were committed to the achievement of an American-style material well-being.

With the flowering in the mid-fifties of what was called *il* boom and the runaway commitment to an economy founded solely on the supremacy of heavy industry, arrayed behind its banner of the automobile rampant over all mere ecological and social considerations, came inflation, followed by the economic crisis that has gripped Italy ever since and that has been greatly aggravated in the past few years by the energy crisis. "We are paying now for a generation of insanity," a Milanese journalist told me one day. "We've ignored our cultural patrimony, which could be our major source of wealth. We've allowed our agriculture to deteriorate to the point where we now have to import artichokes, oranges, and tomatoes from Israel. We've shunted our artisans aside, so that all sorts of crafts, from basketmaking to ceramics, are dying out. By concentrating everything on industries that we have to maintain through imports—Italy has almost no basic raw materials, like coal, petroleum, and iron—we've put the nation permanently in debt, and our cities have become great, festering slums, choked by people hoping to get jobs in the factories. Obviously, this policy is suicidal—a self-destructive madness, if you like, for which we are paying now."

What survives from *il* boom is the social structure that the average visitor glimpses as he tours the sights of the *centro* in his hermetically sealed, air-conditioned bus. It's the face of the city I now think of as Upper Rome, which reflects the class of people that the boom enriched: luxury-shop owners, real-estate speculators, builders, bankers, industrialists, the professional white-collar class. This is not a small group of corrupt profiteers but includes a large segment of the working population—that portion which by superior education and geographical circumstance had a head start and knew how to make the most of it. These are the Romans most foreigners meet. Some of them, especially among the intellectuals, are Communist party members, quite vocally anti-American, who deplore the same things that my Milanese acquaintance complains about. But they are also very well off: they live in splendid apartments in the best residential areas, drive fast cars, own summer retreats, and eat in the finest restaurants, and, as a conservative Roman crony of mine once remarked, "they would gladly go to China, but only on a first-class round-trip ticket."

The sole contact that Upper Rome has with Lower Rome—the "other" civilization that has grown up here, mainly in the outlying so-called *borgate*—comes in the form of daily inconveniences, mostly strikes. The *borgate* are veritable subcities rather than neighborhoods—huge, ugly housing developments that have been thrown up hurriedly and haphazardly since the war by public and private capital to accommodate the enormous numbers of people attracted to the cities by the prospect of finding work. It is there that most of Rome's working-class people and unemployed live, and it is from the *borgate*, and in the name of what they represent, that the agitation in the streets arises. The irritating work stoppages at airports, railroad stations, and public offices that continue to be a feature of daily life in Italy, and over which the Communist Party has little control, are not, as Upper Romans would like to believe, just senseless manifestations of arrogance by lazy unionized workers but, most often, genuine expressions of dissatisfaction with overall conditions and the economic hardships enormously aggravated by a yearly inflation rate of about twenty percent.

In any case, Upper Rome never seems to be seriously inconvenienced—not even by the worst disturbances and strikes. These can usually be anticipated by a careful reading of the morning newspaper, and one learns to plot one's daily life around them. People planning trips or visits to government offices do so on days when the unions have neglected to schedule stoppages—events that are usually announced well in advance and last no more than a few hours. The larger demonstrations take place in any one of several main squares, such as the Piazza San Giovanni, the Piazza Navona, or the Piazza del Popolo, and one simply avoids those parts of town where rallies and parades have been scheduled.

Individual acts of terrorism cannot, of course, be anticipated, but one learns to cope with them. An American friend of mine was caught one afternoon by a spontaneous armed confrontation between marchers and police in the Piazza Cavour, not far from where he lives, and he calmly lay down in the hallway of an apartment building until the shooting stopped, then walked home. "It was all over in a few minutes," he said. "And anyway nobody was hurt." During the worst outbreaks of violence, in October and early November of 1977, life went on exactly as usual in most of the *centro*, even while the guns were going off and bombs were being thrown no more than two or three miles away.

Of far greater concern to most Upper Romans and resident foreigners are such continuing irritations as the increasingly inefficient bureaucracy, the filth in the streets, and the collapse of the postal and other public services. Such drawbacks can seem trifling to anyone who doesn't have to cope with them constantly, and it's a comment of sorts on how most foreigners feel about Italy that the tourists keep coming every year. The money they spend pays over half the nation's yearly oil bills.

Such considerations and statistics are of no comfort to the Rome of the *borgate*, which most foreigners and tourists never see and are largely unaware of. Even some of my oldest Roman friends can't quite believe that the situation is as bad in them as many commentators say it is. They will, for the sake of argument, usually grant that Italy's single largest problem is providing hope and jobs for the more than a million young people under the age of twenty-five—about two-thirds of the unemployed—who can't find work. Many of these young people live in the *borgate*. Another major problem, and a complementary one, is the overcrowded, chaotic schools, since, as social observers continue to point out, these will produce the citizens of the future, educated, presumably, to qualify for the jobs available and to become integrated into the society as productive, law-abiding citizens.

I was once given an unofficial tour of a school in one of the *borgate* by a young assistant dean who had been teaching there for five years and whom I'll call Aldo Criveri. A dedicated, idealistic Roman in his mid-thirties, Criveri had told me when I met him that the situation in his school was desperate, but, even so, not quite as bad as in some others. "At least, our students are trying to study," he said. "In some schools, they spend much of their time protesting, holding rallies, and so on. Even in the better ones, students have occupied the buildings, gone on strike, marched—everything—but here they work. These are the children of the poor. They need to learn, and they have no time for agitations."

The school at which Criveri taught is an Istituto Tecnico Industriale, one of about thirty such schools in the city, and the equivalent of a trade or technical high school in the United States. The humanities are also taught, but the emphasis is on the learning of a specific industrial skill. In this particular Istituto, about eighty percent of the fifteen hundred students—almost all male—were enrolled in electronics, which, according to Criveri, was another example of how things can go wrong. "It's the fashion now to be in electronics," he said. "I don't know why—perhaps because it seems glamorous. But there are no jobs today in electronics; the category is glutted. We tell this to the students, but most of them don't believe us. They get no guidance from the Ministry of Education, and there is no program of student counselling. There are openings for mechanics, and we tell them so, but few of them listen to us."

The Istituto, like so many others in the *borgate*, has been improvised on the premises of three buildings originally constructed as apartment houses. The speculators who created this particular quarter, on the outskirts of the city toward the east, built only units they thought they could sell or lease, and neglected, as other speculators have done elsewhere, to provide what the zoning laws require: open spaces, parks, paved streets, market areas, schools. The result, here as elsewhere, has been the creation of an area crowded with large, slablike stone tenements jumbled together like huge pink-and-brown dominoes on a dusty expanse empty of grass and trees. The municipal authorities seem never to have the inclination to force the builders to adhere to the law, or to prosecute those who don't. What usually happens is that once a new *borgata* appears, schools are organized in whatever buildings happen to be available, and staff and students adapt to the circumstances as best they can.

The circumstances can be grim. The first thing I noticed as Professor Criveri showed me around was the noise. The buildings were made of concrete, steel, and stone; they echoed and magnified every sound. In the basement of one structure, a teacher who was trying to conduct a class was forced to shout in order to make himself heard above the din of a laboratory with a lot of machines going full blast across the way. Every time students changed classrooms, they clattered up and down a single flight of stairs and made so much noise that all work elsewhere came to a halt. The classrooms themselves were damp and cold, and were each equipped with a single small blackboard and a couple of dozen battered desks. In many, the windows were broken, and most of the rooms were dark, lit only by a single line of fluorescent or a few naked bulbs suspended from the ceiling. The recreational facilities consisted of three basement areas, the largest about a third the size of a normal basketball court, which were equipped with iron hoops and a volleyball net or two. None had windows, all were damp, and there were no washroom or locker-room facilities of any kind.

"The absence of space is our number-one problem," Criveri told me. "We have double, sometimes triple sessions here, and our classes overlap. Our students have no room—no space they can call their own. When things break or have to be replaced, everything must go through the Ministry, which tells us it has no money. We can fix or replace almost nothing . The machines in the laboratory, at least, work and are sufficient. But I think you would agree that it is a sad school."

I did agree. It was the saddest school I had ever been in, Dickensian in its squalor, and I could only ask myself what sort of students, what kind of citizens such an institution could produce. After I had thanked Criveri and left him, I walked out, past a group of youths lounging around the front entrance, and stopped to read graffiti spray-painted in red all over the outside walls. Above one window, a bit to one side, somebody had written in bold, clear letters, "We are not drugged, we are not hoodlums—we are outcasts."

CHAPTER FIFTEEN

A ROMAN FROM ROME

I n 1976, a then thirty-five-year-old Roman actor
named Luigi Proietti decided he was tired of
appearing in other people's productions. He had
been working hard in the theatre, television, and
movies for ten years, having given up law school to try his hand
at performing, and had made a considerable name for himself in
both classical and contemporary roles of all sorts—especially with
the Teatro Stabile of L'Aquila, one of the finest of eleven state-
supported regional repertory companies. (He is probably best
known to American audiences for his brief but hilarious appearance in Robert Altman's movie *A Wedding*, in which he played Vittorio Gassman's scapegrace younger brother.) "I wanted to do
something for myself," he later told an interviewer. He had some
ideas, he had written some sketches, he had jotted down some
songs, and he had a group of talented friends, all amateur actors
and musicians, who wanted to work with him. He also enlisted
the collaboration of a well-known young scriptwriter named
Roberto Lerici, who for some years had worked closely with Car-
melo Bene, an actor whose odd, highly individualistic, often satir-
ical interpretations and "re-creations" of classical texts have made

him a celebrity in Italy. "My idea was a sort of one-man show, an expression of myself as an actor, a musician, a man," Proietti explained. "I wanted to play it for a week in L'Aquila, then perhaps tour it in the provinces." He had no plans at the time to bring it to Rome.

A few months later, in the fall of 1976, Proietti was engaged to appear in a new play at the Teatro Tenda, a huge tent theatre set up in Rome's Piazza Mancini, in a working-class district. When the new play proved to be unproduceable, Proietti decided to risk a ten-day run of his one-man show, which he had entitled *A Me gli Occhi, Please (Your Eyes on Me, Please)*. He was prepared for a possible flop, since the show had already been seen, at Proietti's request, by Luigi Squarzina, a leading playwright and director, who had not been especially enthusiastic about the project. *A Me gli Occhi, Please* opened without much advance notice or publicity, but by curtain time two thousand people had crowded into the theatre, and hundreds of others had been turned away. When Proietti first appeared onstage alone and saw the size of the audience, he began to shake, and stammered, "But how many are you?" He was greeted by a roar of approval. "It was an explosion," an eyewitness recalled. "An incredible outpouring of affection and recognition, as if we had all been waiting for him." Despite mixed reviews from the critics, the show was an immediate hit and ran for three months to sold-out houses. Afterward, it toured all over Italy, appeared a number of times in excerpted form on television, and has been periodically revived in Rome, for runs of a few months at a time—usually sandwiched between and around the actor's other commitments in movies and TV. For two years, it played exclusively, off and on, at the Teatro Brancaccio, a drafty old ex-music hall and movie palace that Proietti took over in late 1978. There he began not only to play in and produce his own shows but also to run a full-time workshop for a couple of dozen aspiring young performers selected by him and a small staff of professionals. By the fall of 1980, more than three hundred thousand Romans had seen *A Me gli Occhi, Please*—a figure that established it as the most successful and popular theatrical presentation of any kind in the history of the city; at least since the Colosseum shut down.

Proietti's appeal to Roman audiences is difficult to account for simply by explaining what he does in this show. He's a tall, strongly built, dark man with a thick shock of black hair, dark-brown eyes, and a heavy jaw. He appears onstage dressed in black slacks and a loose white shirt, open-necked, with sleeves rolled up to just below the elbows. He walks on carrying a large, scuffed gray box on his downstage shoulder, then slowly turns so that the audience can finally see his face, and, backed by a six-piece band onstage behind him, sings a typical old Roman song in a light, husky, pleasant tenor, after which he sets the box down center stage, sits on it, and begins to talk. The conversation is casual, unforced. At first, it seems to be merely about the actor's craft— especially its often peculiar relationship to real life. Then the talk leads Proietti imperceptibly into examples of different kinds of acting, of different sorts of entertainment, of changing styles, criteria, modes of performing, modes of being. Props begin to appear out of the box—hats, scarves, masks, a cane, gloves, more hats, eventually a whole puppet theatre. The box itself turns out to be a usable object: it becomes a chair, a table, a podium, a weapon. The conversation dissolves into a sketch or, occasionally, a song, a dance, a lecture. Different people materialize—three Neapolitans performing Kabuki, a madman babbling Hamlet's soliloquies while a critic dogmatically dissects them, a Method actor belaboring Brecht, a barely literate Calabrian professor drunkenly lecturing children on sex, a Pulcinella brokenheartedly serenading a lost love, a manic American folksinger gibbering in pig English about the beauties of "cowntry" music. Each of these characters, it turns out, can also sing very well, in one of five or six different voices, ranging from basso profundo to high tenor. They can play various instruments. They can not only make the audience laugh but sometimes move it to tears. They look very different, too. Some are ugly, some handsome, some merely strange, but all of them are profoundly human. The evening appears to have no shape, and no real point to make. It seems to flash by in half an hour or so, but it runs nearly three hours, not including a fifteen-minute intermission. And it is enchanting.

Proietti's father is a retired civil servant, and his mother is a housewife. He grew up with his younger sister in the streets and piazzas of Rome, went to school there, and began his career in a small "Off Tiber" basement theatre in Prati, a middle-class residential district. He became a polished performer not so much through study as by observation and experience. According to a colleague who has known him for many years, he has an extraordinary capacity for responding instantly to an emotion or an idea and improvising brilliantly on it until he has safely embodied it within the context of a public performance. Though he rarely strays outside the framework of a sketch or a number, every night during the run of his show he would find some part of the evening to improvise on, especially verbally, and occasionally some new personality would appear—or, at least, a hint of a voice or a glimpse of some other face in the crowd of extraordinary characters he brought to life onstage every night.

Not since the death of Anna Magnani—then Rome's finest living monument—a few years ago had any performer so captured the hearts of his fellow-citizens. Watching Proietti onstage reminded me of Roberto Rossellini's remark about Magnani—that in two hours she could run the entire gamut of human emotions. Perhaps that was Proietti's secret, too. All those voices, those faces he conjures up are as familiar to his audience as were Magnani's celebrated feelings. In every one of both these performers' creations one perceives the strong, black, haunted eyes of the true "Roman from Rome," who has seen everything, assimilated everything, condemned nothing, and blamed no one. (Proietti's satire, for example, is never cruel, never savage, and is unfailingly compassionate, even at its funniest.) Like the city he was born in, he knows better than to hope for much in the way of change. He speaks to his people and for them about what he knows, shows them what he has absorbed and observed, and he makes them laugh. That talent is history's greatest gift to this ancient city.

FINALE

s I write these words, on a Sunday morning in mid-May, 1981, I am once again back in Rome. It is as if I have never left. I sit on the terrace of my aunt's apartment on the Via Cassia and stare dreamily out over the green hills, now peppered by the gaudy apartment houses of the new bourgeoisie. The sky above is a deep, limpid blue, and everywhere foliage blooms. Through the ancient stones in the heart of the *centro storico* knots of tourists wander, gaping at the marvels discarded so carelessly by the past, and from the cupolas of a hundred churches the bells summon the faithful to Mass. At midday, the city will eat and then sleep, immobilized under the weight of sun and pasta. By mid-afternoon, it will once again become a beehive of social activity, as the Romans emerge to flock to a movie, a café, or merely to swarm contentedly, in chattering groups of friends and relatives, through their streets and piazzas.

To even the most skeptical eye, nothing will seem amiss, because on a beautiful Sunday in spring no political demonstration or strike or protest rally or ugly act of violence will be permitted to interfere with the simple act of faith implicit in the quiet enjoyment of time. "Everything passes" should be the motto of this city, perhaps of this whole country, which has seen too much, experienced too much, and survived everything. I am reminded once again of the words spoken by a Milanese friend of mine a few years ago, after I had expressed some alarm concerning the inability of Italy's governments to deal effectively with any of the nation's most pressing social problems. "Italy has been going downhill for five hundred years," he said cheerfully. "I see no reason why it can't go on doing the same thing for five hundred more."

He may be wrong, of course, and his attitude, so prevalent among the older generations, may be precisely what is amiss with the country's governing institutions. Still, on such a morning as this one, it's impossible to worry and difficult to think seriously about anything except the savoring of the moment. Compared to it, the public wranglings of politicians, the raised protesting voices of contending factions in the streets, even the ever-present miseries of the poor and the exploited seem unreal, another confirmation of the fatality of the gift Byron celebrated in his verses.

Curiously enough, I know that not even this gift of beauty will hold me here permanently now. Today, I am totally contented, but in a few months I will be ready to leave again. Like many people with roots in more than one country, I am tortured periodically by nostalgia for the place where I am not, and this has since become one of the permanent emotional hazards of my life. I know that my children will probably never experience this, but I'm not so sure I envy them. They will be forever cut off from certain sources of rapture.

Like Nathaniel Hawthorne, more than a century ago, I will leave Italy and Rome with relief, eager to get on with my American life, glad at last to get back to my own less ancient and complicated country. Soon, however, I will begin to feel restless there, too, as if something vital has gone out of my life. I will remind myself of all the things I didn't like this time about Italy while I was here, but I will yearn more and more to come back again. There is no explaining it, really, except to say that the fatal gift is addictive. "When we have left Rome in such a mood as this," Hawthorne wrote in *The Marble Faun*, in 1860, "we are astonished by the discovery, by and by, that our heartstrings have mysteriously attached themselves to the Eternal City, and are drawing us thitherward again, as if it were more familiar, more intimately our home, than even the spot where we were born."